GRETEL'S STORY

Gretel Wachtel was born in Germany in 1915 and was twenty-four years old when the Second World War broke out. After the war, she moved to England, where she remained until her death in 2006.

Claudia Strachan was born in Germany and moved to England in 1993. After meeting Gretel, who shared with her stories about her time in Hamburg during the Second World War, she spent the next nine years researching the historical background of Gretel's story.

GRETEL'S STORY

A YOUNG WOMAN'S SECRET WAR AGAINST THE NAZIS

GRETEL WACHTEL AND CLAUDIA STRACHAN

LYONS PRESS
Guilford, Connecticut

An imprint of Globe Pequot Press

To buy books in quantity for corporate use
or incentives, call **(800) 962-0973**
or e-mail **premiums@GlobePequot.com.**

First published in Great Britain in 2009. This edition of the U.K. original title *A Different Kind of Courage* is published by arrangement with Mainstream Publishing Co., Ltd., 7 Albany Street, Edinburgh EH1 3UG, www.mainstreampublishing.com.

Lyons Press is an imprint of Globe Pequot Press.

Library of Congress Cataloging-in-Publication Data is available on file.

ISBN 978-0-7627-6413-6

This book is a work of nonfiction based on the life, experiences, and recollections of Gretel Wachtel. In some instances, names of people, places, dates, sequences, or the details of events have been changed to protect the privacy of others and for artistic reasons. The author has stated to the publishers that, except in such respects, not affecting the substantial accuracy of the work, the contents of this book are true.

Printed in the United States of America

10 9 8 7 6 5 4 3 2 1

Those who think they would have done better in a similar situation may blame them.

—Golo Mann on the resistance
of the Kreisau Circle

CONTENTS

1

THE CANARIES

1940: The German Reich is at war. Poland, Holland, Belgium, and Norway have capitulated after German invasions. Paris is occupied, a truce has been agreed with France, and the Battle of Britain has begun. During the year, the city of Hamburg issues 123 bomber alarms and is the target of 70 British air raids, with about 700 people killed or wounded. Blackout is obligatory and food is rationed.

As the train pulled out of the station, it suddenly hit me. This wasn't funny anymore. The guards had made that more than clear. Now I had to be very careful if I didn't want to find myself in serious trouble.

Cautiously, I looked around. My fellow passengers were all female, but that was about the only thing I seemed to have in common with them. The others were dressed in loud clothes that left little to the imagination. Opposite me sat a slightly faded beauty wearing too much makeup and dressed in a short skirt and a tight blouse, neither of which I would have dared to wear. I was certainly no innocent, but the other women's outrageous clothes made me feel uncomfortable. They had noticed my more demure appearance too.

"Well, you haven't been pulled out of a window at St. Pauli, have you?" taunted the woman next to me, referring to Hamburg's red-light district, and the others roared with laughter. "Look at those fine stockings! Got your own *établissement*, darling, haven't you? Or why are you here?" Her voice grew a little sharper. After all, I could have been a spy for all she knew.

"I'm a danger to the young," I answered, half embarrassed, half proud. Again, there were gales of laughter, and I grinned. With my carefully chosen clothes, neat appearance, blonde hair, and young age, I could easily have been taken for a good BDM girl, a member of the Bund Deutscher Mädel, the girls' branch of the Hitler Youth. How could I have guessed that one careless remark would get me transferred to a new job for disciplinary reasons?

I saw that I was probably the only woman in the carriage who did not earn her money from prostitution. My initial anxiety gave way to curiosity as I listened to their talk. Although far from inexperienced, I had not heard anything like it in my twenty-five years, not to mention the language.

The guards, one at the front and one at the back of the carriage, stared bored into space, seeming lethargic and uninterested. However, I knew they'd wake up soon enough if one of us did anything unusual or even attempted to get out.

I forced myself to stop staring at the others and look out of the window instead. The train had slowed down. Were we nearly there? But then I noticed that we were passing what seemed to be a sort of building site. New railroad ties were being laid. But there was something unusual about the scene in front of us. Looking closer, I realized what was so strange. These were not your usual rail workers of the *Reichsbahn*. They were all women. They were working in groups of three. One lifted the heavy tie at one end with an iron bar, while the others stuck stones underneath. I couldn't imagine being able to budge any of the thick ties an inch, especially not with the rails still attached to them. It might have been necessary repair work—perhaps the whole route had sunk over time—but surely such a job should not have been imposed on women?

The workers wore ill-fitting striped prison uniforms. Most had dark hair and sad, heavy eyes in their pale, thin faces. One woman lowered her iron bar and put her hand to her back. The guard nearest to her started bawling at her. I couldn't hear his words but the woman's reaction spoke for itself.

Her face was gray and tired, so tired. I was beside myself with anger that these women were being made to do this work, especially as they looked completely undernourished. What I did next was an instinctive reaction rather than anything planned. I probably wouldn't have dared had I thought about it. I reached surreptitiously into my pocket until I felt the sandwich that I had hurriedly made before I left for the station that morning. As if to see better, I got up and stood by the window. Lowering it slightly, I waited for eye contact with one of the workers.

A face looked up—an exhausted face, without any expression, like a badly painted picture. Discreetly, I dropped my parcel. As the train carried on, I saw the woman pick it up, careful not to be conspicuous, and tuck it under her shirt. She didn't wave, she didn't speak a word or even look up, but in the flash of life that suddenly shot into her eyes, I read her surprise, her gratitude.

I dropped back into my seat, suddenly aware once more that I wasn't alone and unobserved in the carriage. The woman opposite me, who fifteen minutes ago had seemed to have nothing but contempt for me, studied me with open interest. As I raised my eyes to hers, half questioning, half defiant, she gave me a hint of a nod, got up with her handbag, and stepped to the window. To my delight, she waited for the right moment and, undetected, dropped her packed lunch at the feet of one of the workers.

At that moment, we became allies. She winked at me and bent over to whisper something in another woman's ear. Before long, about half of the women in our carriage had dropped their lunches out of the window, so carefully that the guards didn't notice anything. I was as happy as a child after a successful prank. My spirit was rekindled and the queasy feeling of anxiety I had had when I boarded the train was gone.

Up until that day, I had not been easily frightened. I was young and felt invulnerable; the word *danger* was not in my vocabulary. At the same time, I had not been unaware of the seriousness of the current situation, especially as Lydia, my best friend, was Jewish. Once, we had been sitting on a tram on our way home from school, when a repulsive man yelled at us, "Get up, you little Jewish pig!" Without hesitation, we stood up, leaving not only our seats but also the tram, and carried on by foot. Arguing would have done no good even if the tram had been full of empty seats. We knew who would lose out in the end if we confronted him, so we gave up straightaway. You had to choose your battles and try to resist where it might actually be effective.

By now, the train had picked up speed and we had left the rail works behind. My timidity toward the other women had changed to something like solidarity. Even though not everyone had joined in giving their food to the prisoners, no one had betrayed us either. As little as we might have in common, there was a certain bond between us; we were all on "the other side."

I let my eyes stray over the passing scenery, which grew increasingly rural after we passed the district of Rothenburgsort and the huge chimneys of industrial Tiefstack in the east of the city. The allotments, with their early-summer rows of cabbage and lettuce, created a cheerful impression, as if the city was populated by carefree weekend gardeners. At Bergedorf, there were simple houses with long gardens that gave way to wide fields, here and there dotted with fruit trees. A nice area for a trip to the country, I thought.

"Do you know how long the journey is?" I asked my neighbor after an hour or so.

"Not long now," she answered. "You can already make out the chimneys over there."

She was right. I could see the chimneys, along with large buildings and factory units.

The train must have been just for the transportation of workers from the Berliner Tor station in Hamburg to the works, as it stopped directly in front of a big factory building. As we got out, the excitement I'd felt about our act of defiance turned to a feeling of foreboding. I dreaded the thought of traveling to this grim place to do forced labor every day for the foreseeable future. I glanced around, looking for an opportunity to run off, but there was no chance. At the gate stood a guard with a rifle. In a sudden moment of naive pride, I felt very important being somebody who had to be supervised by people with weapons.

We were led in by a guard, a big woman in uniform who, with a great sense of her own importance, played with the big ring of keys at her waist. She too carried a gun, and it dawned on me that these weapons would really be used if one of us dared to run away.

The guard told us to follow her. We marched into one of the buildings and entered a washroom. It looked how I imagined the bathroom in an orphanage would—empty and sterile, with high ceilings, a tiled floor, and double rows of sinks, with poles overhead where we could hang up towels.

"Go on, get undressed!" I was surprised that we had to wash, but it didn't seem to be anything out of the ordinary. I was the new girl, so, as it was obviously routine to the other workers, I just followed their lead. The guard, who had not said anything except to hurry us up, had a go at me for not dressing in my uniform. "I'm new. I don't have one," I answered, trying not to stare at the wart next to her lower lip. She muttered some unkind words, disappeared for a moment, and came back with a bundle, which she threw at my feet.

It was an ugly gray uniform that fitted badly, but I knew better than to complain and just changed into it. There were no pockets in the trousers or the shirt, so that we couldn't smuggle anything in or out. Those who still had their lunch with them held it in their hands.

"What do we do with our clothes?" I asked my neighbor quietly. She gestured to a pile of dirty-looking sacks. "In there. You'll get them back tonight." I folded up my clothes and put them into a sack, tied it up, and left it in a corner, as the others did.

We were taken into a large hall with long rows of wooden tables. Next to the tables stood wooden wagons filled with piles of cartridge cases and ammunition. Lamps hung from the ceiling on different lengths of cables, probably to create the best possible lighting for the work. There were windows too, but they were so high up that it was impossible to see more than a fragment of sky. Most of the women knew where to go. They divided into their work groups and sat down at the tables without interrupting their talk. The guard shouted at me to take up my place at the middle of one of the tables.

Soon the traces of the work were visible. Our hands turned yellow; even our hair changed to yellow. No surprise really, I thought. The sign outside had read "Krümmel Dynamit Actien Gesellschaft," Krümmel Dynamite Company. This was the filling depot of an ammunition factory, and it was the TNT that turned our skin yellow.

"Welcome to the canaries!" grinned one of my companions.

Great, I thought. This is how I'm going to look from now on.

All we had to do was stuff the cartridges with powder, one after the other. I looked around, but I couldn't see far. At every table there was only a handful of women; maybe they could control us better like this.

I held up my hand and turned to the guard. "I need to go to the toilet." She scrutinized me skeptically, as I had only just started work (also, as I would find out, the tone the other women took was normally quite different, more like: "Hey! I need a piss!"). But the guard had no choice; she had to accompany me to the toilet. "This way," she barked, and led me through the hall.

As I followed her, I looked around to see whether any of the guards in the hall were men. With these female guards, I wouldn't get very far, but men I could handle. When I wanted to, I could wrap most of them around my little finger. Or maybe I just got my way because I was convinced I could do so. There! I was in luck. And he seemed to be in charge here—even better. I made eye contact, not too obviously but showing a spark of interest.

After that, I went to the toilet as often as I could. When I was sitting at the table, I tried my best to do everything wrong. Of course, it was no brilliant act of sabotage, but on the other hand I was convinced that even the smallest contribution could help in the fight against the system. The thought of producing weapons for the Nazis made me sick. So I either put hardly any powder in the cartridge, hoping they might be useless without much in them, or I simply worked clumsily, putting the cartridges upside down on the table, laying them down at the wrong angles, until the guard grew angry.

"My God, can't you do it? It's hardly difficult, is it?" she cried.

"No!" I said, putting on my most innocent expression, "I just can't manage it!"

By this time, she seemed almost relieved when I needed the toilet, because I was holding the whole group up with my apparent clumsiness.

Whenever I passed the male guard, I sought his eyes. The third time, I actually started to flirt with him. He seemed flattered, or at least he made it easy to catch his eye. "I'll get him to get me out of here," I determined, and I gave myself a maximum of twenty-four hours to achieve my goal.

The time crept by, despite my flirting and my occasional remarks to the other workers. I started to brood. Here I was, transferred for disciplinary reasons to an ammunition factory in Geesthacht, about 15 miles southeast of Hamburg. How had it come to this?

In the six years since I'd completed my apprenticeship in the textile business, I had already had ten different employers. In April 1940, I had started yet another position, this time in a gentlemen's boutique in Dammtorstraße. I didn't really fit in there. Everything was stiff and proper, from the clothes down to the employees. One day, a young man who worked as a decorator came into the shop.

I watched him for a while and decided that he wasn't "one of them." Somehow I thought I could sense who supported the system and who did not. We started a conversation and I asked, "Surely you're not a Hitlerite, are you?"

But that time I'd got it wrong. He must have reported me at once to the old ladies who ran the shop, worried that I wasn't on the right track. It wasn't difficult to guess where their loyalties lay—the whole day long, they greeted everyone who came in with "Heil Hitler"—and they were shocked by my remark. They considered it their duty to report me, and I was sacked with immediate effect. The reason: I was "a danger to the young, an anti-Nazi."

"You can pack up and go home," they told me. "And don't come back tomorrow. Don't come back at all." I was surprised, but then I realized that it must have to do with the question I'd asked the decorator. When I looked over at him, he avoided my eyes, which confirmed it for me.

"Fine!" I said cheerfully. "I think your shop is deadly boring anyway!" I picked up my few belongings and left, bought myself a sweet bun in the bakery, and went for a beautiful walk through the streets of Hamburg, sitting down on a bench at the Binnenalster, the Inner Alster Lake, and enjoying my sudden freedom.

While I watched the water and the boats, the mothers hurrying along with their children and the elderly gentlemen walking by, the sun suddenly broke through the gray cover of the clouds and made the waves of the lake glitter. On the banks, a duck waddled along picking at anything that looked edible. I ate my bun with a sigh of contentment in this picture of peace. I took a deep breath, stood up, and went to catch the ferry across the Außenalster, the Outer Alster Lake, instead of taking the Underground. In the summer, there was a ferry every half an hour, so I didn't have to wait long. I loved the journey on the white-painted boat, and always sat on the unprotected bench in the stern rather than in the sheltered bow, because there I could hear better the gentle lapping of the waves as the steamer chugged along. The steamers used to have girls' names, but under the current regime they had all been renamed after supposed National Socialist virtues, things like *Determination*, *Truth*, and *Loyalty*, which I found rather silly and unfitting for boats.

We passed the Alsterlust, the pier, where they were already playing music and where you could hire boats, then the Uhlenhorster Fährhaus, the elegant wine bar where the middle-aged middle classes mixed, and all the landing stages that gave the steamers their names, according to the district. I got off at the Krugkoppel Bridge, went down the steps and through the Alsterpark, and was already almost home.

When I arrived at our house in the Hochallee, I told my mother about my day. "You've got to look for a new job tomorrow, first thing," she told me sternly, shaking her head disapprovingly. "We will go through all the boutiques and make a list." But that wasn't to be the end of it.

Two days later, two policemen came to the door for me. I was making coffee (if you could call the chicory brew we had as a substitute "coffee") when they arrived at half past seven in the morning.

"Open the door!" thundered a voice outside.

My mother almost died on the spot. "For God's sake, child, what do they want? What have you done this time?" Neither she nor I thought of my remark to the decorator.

I went to the door and opened it. Police. I flushed in a sudden panic.

"Gretel Wachtel?"

"That's me."

"You are to report immediately to work at Krümmel AG in Geesthacht. The train is leaving at eight from Berliner Tor. Here is the letter of confirmation. Contravention is to be punished with imprisonment. You are coming with us."

Turning around, I quickly grabbed my slice of bread and butter and some paper to wrap it in and followed the officers along
the corridor and down the steps. Above us, I saw the curtains
move. At least the lodgers will have something to gossip about,
I thought as the men hurried me away. Then I realized that they
weren't wearing uniforms and my shock grew, because this must
mean that it was the Gestapo who had come for me.

I had often heard about people being taken. The ghost of the
Gestapo hung over every conversation, every disobedience, every
irregularity, no matter how small. In public and in all the institutions, it was already audacious to greet others with "Good morning" rather than "Heil Hitler." Nobody dared to ask any questions
about people who had been taken. If you asked questions, it meant
that you knew the disappeared well, and you were instantly under
suspicion. I'd always wanted to know what happened to those who
were taken. Was I about to find out? I wondered. Surely not for
an insignificant remark like mine?

Finally, a siren similar to a foghorn sounded and the day's
work at Krümmel ended. The women gathered in large groups
and streamed toward the washrooms. We had to get undressed
again and wash ourselves down, but before we were allowed to
change into our own clothes we were searched from top to toe.
The warder frisked me, checking every crease of my skin, under
my breasts, between my buttocks.

"What do you think I have hidden there?" I shouted, outraged.
"Do you honestly believe I squeezed a cartridge up there?"

The guard grew rough. "You will stop your insolence, you slut!"
she hissed at me, pushing me aside.

I was furious. No one had ever treated me like this. Who did
this woman think she was, just because she wore a uniform and
had found herself in a position of power over me? I held myself
back with gritted teeth. You wait, I thought. I'm getting out of
here quicker than you think! And I did already have a plan.

The return journey was much more relaxed than the trip there. The guards let us talk. We were in the same boat, the others and I, and after one day I felt as if I'd shared their lives for much longer. After we said good-bye, I left for home as quickly as possible.

All I told my mother was that I was working in a factory where there were good career opportunities. To my relief, she didn't ask any questions; I didn't want to talk about the whole uncomfortable truth.

The next day I knew what I had to do. First, I made a pile of sandwiches to drop out of the train window. Word must have spread among the rail workers, for today many worked close to the track and some looked up surreptitiously. One or two I thought I recognized from the day before. Our eyes spoke whole dialogues.

As I stood in the hall again, freshly washed and in my ill-fitting uniform, I marched off straightaway to the toilet. I had been given permission to go on my own, as the warder had grown tired of walking back and forth to the toilet all day. She was obviously disgusted by me, as I was clearly trying to make her life as miserable as I could in my pathetic situation.

I weaved my way among the tables, engineering it so that I would pass the man in command. I smiled at him and he smiled back, winking. That worked quite well, I thought, pleased by my progress. On my return, I slowed down to give him the opportunity to speak to me, which he seized.

"So, you don't seem to be in the right place here, do you?" he said, examining me carefully. Somehow I must have looked different from the other women, uniform or not; at least I believed so. Maybe it was my way of walking, my posture—whatever it might have been, he seemed to have the same impression. "What are you doing here?"

"That's a long story. I can't tell you in a sentence."

The way he talked to me suggested that he was not necessarily one of those who equated sporting a uniform with being above others and using their position accordingly. There were still people around who just did their work, no more, and I felt sure I had one of them in front of me.

"I suppose you've had quite a different education from the others. Could you do something like typing, in a different department?" he asked thoughtfully.

"But of course!" I beamed at him. "I can do that!" In fact, I had never so much as seen a typewriter up close, but at that moment I wasn't about to admit as much.

"Excellent!" he replied. "We desperately need people in administration. You'd better come along straightaway."

He walked over to the warder and told her that he wanted to use me for office work, whereupon she only growled, "Yes. Please get her away from me!" as if I were a piece of dirt. The man led me along to another building. It looked like an old manor house, three stories high with generous windows and the whole façade covered in ivy, with a big sign on the roof reading "Dynamit Actien Gesellschaft."

"Tomorrow, sit in the last carriage of the train," said my guard as we stepped into the building. "That's where the secretaries sit and the telegraphists, all the office folk."

"Will I be allowed, just like that?" I asked, surprised.

"If you show this card, yes. It's a sort of pass. You write your name on it, your address, and your position. That makes you one of them."

As I took the card, my stomach started to rumble loudly. "Was that your tummy?" he asked. "Well, I'm hungry too. Here you only get this strange brew—you can't even tell whether it's coffee or tea. But you all bring your own lunch, don't you? What did you do with yours?"

"I . . . I'll tell you tomorrow," I said, avoiding his look.

He tried to catch my eye but didn't say anything. Instead, he rummaged in his pocket and handed me two sweets. "I haven't got anything else at the moment, but it's better than nothing."

I took him up on the offer gratefully, as I had not had the heart to keep a single sandwich to myself that morning, which by this time I considered foolish.

We reached an office wing and went through corridors and a double door into a big hall. Everywhere sat women at tables with mountains of papers, each with a typewriter in front of her and hammering on the keys, all touch-typing at unbelievable speed. It clattered and rattled almost as loudly in there as on the factory floor. I racked my brains as to what I should do.

"Right! I'll hand you over to the man in charge. He'll show you your place and instruct you what to do," said the guard, who I realized had really grown on me. I bit my lip, but I didn't say anything, following him between the tables to meet the boss.

"Here's another typist for you, so you can stop your moaning once and for all!"

"Great! Then come along, girl. This way."

I said good-bye to my new friend and thanked him. As soon as he was gone, I turned to face the man in charge and cleared my throat uncomfortably. He looked at me, and I said, "I can't really."

"What?" he asked, perplexed.

"Well, type."

"No? And what am I to do with you? Is there anything you *can* do?"

I considered myself enormously lucky that this man seemed to be nice too, not at all like the female warder at the filling depot. "I can sell anything you want—ice to Eskimos! I can . . . I can make coffee! Tea!"

He looked me through and through. Then he sighed. "You're quite sweet, you are. Let's see if I can think of something. Maybe . . . I've got an idea. Wait here." He disappeared behind a door only to return a few moments later, signaling to me to follow him.

He took me to a small office in which huge shelves laden with folders and thick bundles of paper covered all four walls up to the ceiling. To one side, bent over a desk, sat an elderly man, gray-haired and wearing glasses, who looked up as we entered. "This is the filing office," the man in charge of the typing pool told me. "If you can at least read and write, I'll let you work here. Everything else, my colleague here will explain." He nodded to the man at the desk and left the room.

"What's your name, child?" the old man asked me.

"Gretel Wachtel. Please call me Gretel," I answered, glad that I was at last not just an interchangeable worker at Krümmel but a person with a name.

"Nice of you to help me, Gretel. My name is Mertens, Gottfried Mertens. Here the important documents are filed and kept safe. They all have to be sorted according to date and surname. This letter, for example, belongs with the ammunition orders. They go in this file here and then there on the shelf. Have you done anything like this before?"

"Not exactly, but it doesn't look too difficult. I'll manage!"

We looked at each other and there it was again, that feeling. Okay, once it had deceived me, with the decorator—that had been a grave mistake. But still I trusted my sixth sense again, and it told me that this man who sat before me was no Nazi.

I started work immediately, but I didn't follow my instructions at all. What should have been with the orders, I filed with the complaints; where I ought to have gone by destination, I filed by surname, and so on. It was almost fun messing everything up completely. After all, this place was making ammunition for the Wehrmacht. Every obstacle to its effective running was surely a good thing.

By the time I'd been there for three days, nobody could find anything. Herr Mertens was clear about my motives, but he didn't let me be removed from my post. I only hoped he wouldn't get the blame for it all. One day, after he had searched for an hour for a delivery confirmation and finally discovered it between the unchecked orders, he looked at me for a long time. I stopped in my tracks and returned his gaze. All he said was, "You've got to do what you believe to be right"—nothing else.

Meanwhile, I was still determined to get out. I had no intention of allowing myself to be forced to work indefinitely in an ammunition factory supplying the Wehrmacht. If only there was a way out! I thought it all through, but no solution came to me, and it wasn't until the spring of 1941 that a talk with my mother gave me an idea.

We were sitting at the table eating dinner—mother had managed to get hold, using our rations, of a piece of pork that was not completely riddled with gristle and fat. Seeing her sitting there with her straight back, her immaculately combed hair and spotless white blouse, we could have been in one of Hamburg's best restaurants. Mother took great care of her appearance. Letting herself go was unthinkable for her. A woman did not leave the house without a hat, nor without stockings, and at home you had to behave just as properly and dress just as neatly as you would in public.

Since earliest childhood, I had learned to live up to her principles. I was never allowed to get dirty, and looking smart was a priority. Now, she scanned me with critical eyes, but she didn't have any complaints about my appearance. However, she remarked worriedly, "Your appetite isn't what it was. If you carry on like this, you'll be looking like a stick soon."

"No wonder, with that stuff that we get on our rations," I retorted. "If I had a proper job, I could get us some things from the black market. Then we'd have something better to eat."

"If you would finally think of marriage, you wouldn't have to work at all," my mother replied, on her favorite subject. "You're already twenty-five and still you haven't tied the knot. Look at our neighbor Ilse. She already has the bronze Mother's Cross, with her five children. She doesn't need to go to work."

I put my fork down and stared at my mother. "Do you know what? That's not such a bad idea! If I marry, I won't have to go to the factory anymore. That's it! Where's today's paper?"

My mother didn't quite see what the paper could have to do with my marital status, but she went to get it for me. I browsed through it until I found what I was looking for: the personal ads. Most of them didn't pique my interest, and I had almost given up when I saw one that seemed promising: "Intelligent, handsome man looking for friendship/marriage with nice, educated woman between 20 and 30." That could be me, I thought.

I got my writing paper out of a drawer, copied the number of the advertisement onto an envelope, and started to write. It didn't take me long to decide what to say; I just wrote on a whim. What did I have to lose?

Dear intelligent, handsome man,

With reference to your advertisement in the *Hamburger Fremdenblatt*, I would like to introduce myself. I am 25 years of age, told I am good-looking, and most people who deal with me believe me to be nice as well as intelligent. If you would like to see whether you share this view, we could meet sometime to get to know each other. I look forward to your reply.

Yours sincerely,
Gretel

It was only a short letter, but I must have hit the right note, as I received an answer four days later. The advertiser, a Heinrich Lutz Öhlgart, suggested a popular café for our meeting. Luckily, he suggested Sunday, so I didn't have to try to rearrange the date.

The following Sunday I dressed as well as I could, although I had trouble deciding on the right thing to wear. Not only were clothes difficult to get these days, but I also had to take care to look neither vulgar nor boring. Makeup was out of the question for a "true German woman" of the time, so I decided on only a hint of lipstick—more would have been unwise.

The café was busy, as it was Sunday and many people who were out for a stroll were calling in for a piece of cake and a cup of real coffee. In spite of the crowded tables, I had no problem finding the man I was meeting. Perhaps as part of the sport, we hadn't arranged a sign to help us recognize each other, so I had to follow my instinct. At a table by the window, I saw a tall blond man, handsome and well dressed. He could have been the model for one of those "Aryans" described in the schoolbooks of today, I thought, marching straight toward him.

"Heinrich Öhlgart?" I asked, stretching out my hand.

"Lutz," he answered, rising from his seat and shaking my hand. "And you must be Gretel Wachtel. Please take a seat. What would you like to drink?"

I decided on a real coffee—pure luxury then. While I was analyzing his appearance, I ought to have spotted the severity in his steel-blue eyes, an unusual hardness that was striking, but that day I was far too impressed with his good looks to notice.

"Do you always read the personal ads in the *Fremdenblatt?*" he asked me.

"This was the first time, believe it or not, and only because my mother told me it was time for me to meet a man at long last," I replied cheerfully.

"So you don't know any men?" he asked provocatively.

"Let's just say no potential marriage material."

"And what about me? Am I potential marriage material?"

The conversation went well. He worked as an engine salesman and still lived at home, like me, where, as one of seven children, he contributed to the family income. There wasn't a lot of money, but then I wasn't after money. During our exchange, I tried cautiously to explore his attitude toward Hitler and the system, one of the biggest factors for me in a relationship. A good opportunity to investigate was to discover if he had been at the latest Nazi event. There were a lot of these—torchlight processions by the BDM or the Hitler Youth, parades, ceremonies, and the like—especially on certain dates, like Hitler's birthday or the anniversary of his seizure of power. So I asked if he had been at the most recent of these parades. "I don't normally go," he said airily, but as he said it he looked intensely at me and his eyes bored into me.

I nodded. "Me neither." There was no need to say more. We were in a public place and any further discussion could have been a fatal mistake.

Before an hour had passed, we left the café. He took me home, making no secret of his admiration for my address. I lived in one of the better areas of Hamburg, full of villas with art nouveau windows and well-maintained front gardens, set back from the quiet streets, which were lined with trees. It wasn't just an ordinary residential area; people came there to go for a walk, for pleasure. It was exactly to my mother's taste.

When we said good-bye at my door, we were still using the formal *Sie* for "you," but we both were interested in continuing our acquaintance.

"When do you next have time to see me?" Lutz asked.

I considered for a moment whether it was too early to talk about my transfer to Krümmel, but then I decided to lay my cards on the table. "I get back quite late in the evenings. As it happens, I've got to work in Geesthacht. I've been transferred for disciplinary reasons. If you still want to see me again, we can meet at eight during the week. That's when I get home." I looked at him inquiringly. Would he pretend to be busy now?

"Eight is a good time. I'll come and collect you on Tuesday evening and show you where I live. Don't worry, the house is full of family, it's all aboveboard. And then you can tell me how you ended up in Geesthacht!"

I agreed and let him go. It had gone much better than I'd expected. Lutz was nice, good-looking, educated, and interesting. He didn't seem to support the Nazis; otherwise, he wouldn't have agreed to another meeting. I skipped happily up the stairs to the

front door of our apartment. Farewell, Krümmel Dynamit AG!
I thought hopefully.

At work, I didn't let them see that I was counting the days
until I could get out. Unfortunately, as I had to travel with the
office workers, I wasn't able to drop any more food parcels out
the window without giving myself away. Most of the administration staff was working at Krümmel by choice and would have
denounced me at once—that much was obvious. So I couldn't
do my bit in that way anymore, and since I was determined not
to stay long at Krümmel, I wondered how much I could actually
achieve by creating chaos in the filing office.

Unmarried, I had no hope of being dismissed in the foreseeable
future. Only marriage could get me out. The Nazis encouraged the
growth of the "racially pure" German population; having children
was supposed to be a good German woman's duty and delight. I
did not waste a moment imagining myself as a mother, but the
thought of marriage appealed to me.

My neighbor Ilse had five children and had been rewarded by
the state with the bronze Mother's Cross. Bronze was awarded
for four children, silver for six, and gold for eight. I liked Ilse,
although she had no interest in politics whatsoever. Whether
the men in her life belonged to the resistance or the SS, she
didn't even care to inquire. At the beginning of our friendship,
I objected to what I called her irresponsible ignorance, but then
I started to appreciate her personality. You always had a great
time when you went out with Ilse. She was interested in theater,
the pictures, music, men. Even a trip to the baker's could turn
into an experience worth talking about. She managed to make
every aspect of life seem so interesting, as if it was the most
exciting adventure. When we talked, there was never a gap in the
conversation, no boredom, no empty phrases—time just flew by.

Once I grabbed her Mother's Cross, which she wore on a
golden chain around her neck. "What do you actually want with

this?" I asked, shaking my head. "It's not as if you can buy anything with it."

"I always get a seat on the tram," she answered defiantly, as if this was the greatest thing she could have wanted for herself. The way things were, I could see no point in bringing children into the world, only for them to be indoctrinated with Nazi ideology. And who knew how long Hitler's wars would last? I wouldn't have wanted any son of mine ending up as cannon fodder. Women would put announcements in the paper saying things like: "For the Führer, our people, and the Fatherland, my beloved son died the death of a hero . . ." All it meant for me was: "Children? No thanks."

But what I did hope to achieve by marriage was a new degree of liberty and independence. Staying out at night as late as I wanted without having to justify myself—that was how I imagined married life to be. Mother didn't really prevent me from living my life as I wished, but nonetheless I thought that life would change for the better when I was married. Wasn't it the ultimate step toward growing up? Maybe Lutz would be the door to this transformation.

2

LUTZ

1941: German offensives in Yugoslavia, Greece, and the Soviet Union begin. Hitler instructs his generals to suspend court-martial laws for the Soviet Union campaign: Crimes against civilians by German soldiers are not punishable, while any offense against the occupying power can be punished without trial.

On Tuesday, Lutz collected me from home. He lived in Hoheluft, a relatively deprived district, in a small apartment that wasn't nearly big enough for a family of nine. When he opened the door, I immediately smelled the whiff of cabbage that was omnipresent in poorer homes at that time. The apartment was so cramped that every corner of the rooms was filled with piles of washing, the younger ones' school things, papers and books. A single armchair and a threadbare rug told their own story, but everything was neat and clean despite the lack of space.

Lutz's mother was a small but sturdy woman, her head reaching only to my chin, her hair tied up in a neat knot. Her cheeks were ruddy and her friendly eyes blinked at me as I greeted her.

"So, you're this Gretel who Lutz has told us about. Nice to meet you!" she welcomed me. "I'm just making supper, if you don't mind. Lutz, go and introduce her to the others." I made the rounds. Only three of the six siblings were home, and their father was expected later. I asked Lutz's mother if I could do anything to help, and, after some initial hesitation, she assigned me to do a bowl of peas. I sat down on the balcony with the bowl on my lap and started shelling, looking down on the street below me.

Two girls were playing with a skipping rope, interrupted time and again by some boys who were tearing each other's hats off their heads and throwing them around. The walls of the surrounding houses had long since lost their paint, although here and there the remains of bygone days were visible—faded signs, patches of color, ancient-looking wooden doors leading to shaded backyards. In spite of the shabby surroundings, which I wasn't used to, the sight and sounds of the children playing had something familiar about them, as if it had always been like this and always would be.

"You're lucky to have grown up in a different area," Lutz remarked as he stepped onto the balcony to join me. I noticed that he used the familiar *du* for the first time, which seemed appropriate in the circumstances. "This is real life, I can tell you that. It's all about getting by—food, work, sleep—not like in your circles."

I looked up in surprise. Did he think that I was an upper-class snob, turning my nose up at people "beneath" me, without a clue as to what life was about? Did he think I looked down on him? His blue eyes were as cold as ice as he spoke. I almost felt uncomfortable.

"I have actually been living 'real life,' as you like to call it!" I told him, stung into defending myself. "My grandfather wasn't a socialist for nothing!"

"He was?" Lutz gave no sign of being impressed.

"Indeed he was!" I replied, flaring up. "He was a carpenter, and when the Nazis marched through the town on bank holidays, he hung the red flag of Hamburg out of the window, until the neighbors stormed in and begged him to take it down and replace it with the swastika. But he never did, even when my grandma almost died of worry on the spot!"

Now Lutz was impressed. "Did they take him in?"

"It never went that far, luckily. But he always swore that he wouldn't support that man in his ugly brown uniform, even if they did keep coming with their collections."

It was true. Even long before Hitler had come to power, the Brownshirts of the SA—the storm troopers who had in the earlier days of the Nazi Party aided Hitler's rise through violence and intimidation—had gone around rattling their collection boxes for this or that cause, spreading fear wherever they went. Everyone gave something, to avoid recriminations, beatings, or robberies. Granddad refused to offer so much as a penny; they'd never get anything from him, he vowed. My grandma, far too good-natured and without the strength of character to stand up for her beliefs, would tremble from head to toe and run into the kitchen, racing back with a few pennies and quickly sliding them into the box so they would leave us alone. Granddad would have a go at her: She'd give the shirt off her back to *them;* how could she? He'd get so angry.

Everybody knew what side Granddad Schulz was on. That he got away with it must have been simply because of his age and because he was so popular with everyone around him, being honest, straightforward, and charming. Too proud and independent to ever have been a member of a political party, he was nonetheless a socialist to the core. His village school had sent him to grammar school on an academic scholarship. He became a carpenter and specialized in the construction of gates and doors, which he sold to the rich citizens of Hamburg. I loved his workshop, the wonderful wood smell. As a child, I would watch him for hours—how he cut planks into shape with the big circular saw, planed, glued, and hammered. I believe it was his influence that saved me from falling for fascist ideology.

We were at a loss, at the time, as to how they could have seized power. Brawn should not win over brains, surely, and we'd believed the whole country must realize that. Of course, Germany's first-ever attempt at democracy, during the Weimar Republic, had not exactly been a success. Almost daily, there had been newspaper reports about another political murder; the victims were mostly well-known socialists, people we had huge hopes for. It was unthinkable that this could happen in a democracy. In this chaos, the government changed constantly, so we were certain that the Nazis would not last longer than a couple of weeks either. But they stayed. They constructed their dictatorship far too cleverly, right from day one. Three weeks turned into three months, three months into three years. What could not happen did.

As I talked of these things, Lutz only nodded; he had watched developments with the same horror. "And what about your dad?" he asked.

"My mother couldn't bear the poverty at home. Granddad was never interested in making big money, with his socialist ideas. Mother always paid great attention to her looks, wanted to be a lady and was drawn to high society. She wanted to get as far away as possible, so she applied for a job in Hanover, at Karstadt, the department store."

There, she worked in the lingerie department. She used to pass a tobacconist on her way to work, a picturesque and elegant wholesale firm. The owner, a man about twenty years her senior, developed an interest in her. He winked at her, then struck up a conversation with her, and finally they became friends. He was a widower with two sons, one of whom was only two years younger than my mother. Who knows what he must have thought, but his father married my mother.

However, the marriage didn't work very well. The older gentleman did not pay much attention to his young and pretty wife, not even when I was born in January 1915. Mother felt left alone; she was managing the shop almost entirely on her own by that time. She sold tobacco, kept the accounts, did the housework, and sent tobacco parcels to the front, taking orders from the parents and friends of soldiers.

One soldier fell in love with my mother's neat, dainty handwriting, which was not as surprising as it might seem. At the front, the faintest sign of normality from home was seized on like a lifebelt, offering an escape from the brutality of life there and, ultimately, from a potential breakdown. Hopes and dreams were important; a photo could offer a temporary release from hell. The soldier who received the cigarette parcel with my mother's note made it his mission to meet that woman. He clung to this vision and, feeling his hopes return, came on the first day of his home leave to find my mother. There he stood in the shop, flowers in his hand, and my mother was bowled over by the romance of it. Everything that was missing from her marriage was standing before her. The soldier became her lover.

One day, without much to-do, she left my father. She was deeply in love with Otto. Nothing else mattered to her. With me on her hip, she jumped on the train to Hamburg without even packing a bag. When she arrived in Hamburg, she moved back into her old room at her parents'. They were anything but pleased. Then, it was highly scandalous to run away from one's husband, let alone keep a lover. Otto, however, looked after us financially and gave us food, while meeting up with my mother as often as he could.

From then on, we lived with my grandparents in Hamburg. I was just learning to walk when we arrived, so I can't remember Hanover. I never knew my father. Once, when I was much older and full of questions, I saw a picture of him. But I didn't miss him. I had Granddad, whom I adored. He was my friend, my father, my teacher, and my idol. He was always there for me, whether it was a school event, a parents' evening, or my confirmation—Granddad was there.

Uncle Otto was a livestock commissioner. Once a year, we received a pig from him, which was duly slaughtered, and everyone

helped to prepare the meat. The whole house smelled of wonderful spices, ham was cooked, sausages and liver paté hung on
broomsticks—it was a feast. Granddad would share the meat with
all our neighbors, everyone would get something, but Grandma
wasn't to know about it. "There's another sausage missing!" I can
still hear her say, and Granddad's typical answer: "But that can't
be. There were only twelve, I'm sure." Pretending to go to the
chicken shed, he would have grabbed a sausage and taken it to a
neighbor, who would be asked under no circumstances to thank
his wife should they meet. He didn't leave it at the sausages either,
as I realized when I heard Grandma wondering why on earth the
chickens had stopped laying eggs.

My mother frequently went out with her rich boyfriend. Occasionally they traveled, always in style and elegance—bespoke
clothes and shoes, Pullman Express, no less—and Uncle Otto paid.

My mother's attempts to dress me in finery did not go quite so
well. Grandma was constantly trying to tidy me up when I came
home. "Let's see. Oh dear, what do you look like? What will your
mother say?" I had quite different ideas about how I should be
dressed. I'd have preferred to wear practical clothes that I would
be allowed to get messy. I was always picking flowers, getting
grass stains on my carefully chosen outfits. When Mother came
in, she would give me a slap and throw the flowers straight in
the bin, but I'd just wait for her to leave the room, fish them out
again, and put them in a glass of water.

When Mother returned from her travels, she would always
bring me "nice" presents, usually completely useless as far as I
was concerned—perfume, an expensive skin cream, a fine handkerchief, boring things like that. She took me along to the kind
of expensive cafés where you went to be seen. There, you had to
sit nicely and delicately eat cake, which I loathed. All I wanted
was a frankfurter with mustard or bread and dripping, but my
mother was appalled when I said so. "You can't possibly get that
here. What are you thinking of? Can't you behave just once in

your life?" I didn't care too much about her scolding. I found her hoity-toity ways extremely annoying, and knew that she only went to these places to flirt with other men.

"Don't get me wrong, I do love her!" I told Lutz, who had listened quietly to my tale. "But we couldn't be any more different, Mother and I."

Lutz nodded. "Have you never questioned her attitude?"

I thought for a while. "When I was about sixteen, seventeen, I started thinking about my mother. She was never accepted by the high society to which she so longed to belong. For the men, she was prey, and the women feared her, as it was known that she had left her husband for another man. But she was always smartly dressed, attractive and flirtatious. As I grew older, I didn't like that at all. I wanted a mother who was there for me, who gave me a sense of belonging, not a fine lady of high status who used me only as an accessory. We weren't a normal family who were friends with other families, who visited and were visited—we were never invited."

I didn't get to hear what Lutz thought about all this, because his father and his brother came home at that moment and his mother laid the table. Lutz greeted his father very briefly but took his brother to one side. "How did it go? All as planned?"

His brother shot a glance in my direction, which Lutz answered with a dismissive gesture and an "It's okay."

"Not quite to plan, but it went all right. Let's discuss it later and not bore our guest with shop talk."

"As you wish. This is Gretel. Gretel, Wilhelm, my brother, and that's my dad."

"Pleased to meet you!" We shook hands. "I hear you live in Harvestehude, child. What a nice area!" I nodded and smiled, although I wasn't so sure.

We sat down to eat: fried potatoes with bacon and the peas I had shelled on the balcony. I didn't like Lutz's father. Tall and haggard, with nickel-rimmed glasses and thin hair, he was a stark contrast to his wife, who was round and kindly. What I minded really were his eyes. Ice-cold, watery eyes in which I thought I could see a certain cruelty. With a sudden shiver, I realized that his eyes were like Lutz's. "Are you cold?" asked Lutz, but I just shook my head.

Over dinner, I tried to gauge the family's political attitudes. I wanted to find out whether, as I suspected, they too opposed the regime. "Did you read the paper this morning, about Poland?" I asked. "Did you see the pictures?"

Lutz's sister Gertrud, a pretty girl of about fifteen, knew immediately what I meant. "Terrible, how the Polish let their land get run down into such a state! The harvest figures are barely—"

She didn't get any further. Lutz shouted her down. "You don't really believe this rubbish about the Polish mismanagement, do you? That's such typical, evil propaganda shit—"

"Lutz!" hissed his mother, with a terrified look at me.

Lutz didn't flinch. "What do you think, Gretel?" he asked. All eyes were on me.

"It's easy to condemn the Poles as incompetent when you compare such pictures. Who knows where they took those shots? This wasteland without trees or shrubs is in Poland, and then next to it, this lovely village, with its rolling countryside in the background, is in south Germany. That doesn't seem like a scientific proof to me."

"Quite right!" Wilhelm said triumphantly. "And the harvest figures are complete rubbish. I don't believe a word of it. It's only another attempt to justify their hideous *Lebensraum* policy!"

"But it's quite possible that the Germans really are able to work the land better," Gertrud argued, defending herself. "Only on Friday, I read how they—"

Again, she got cut off. "Don't you believe it!" said Lutz. "We all know that the papers are forced to toe the party line. All they do is boast about the Nazis' achievements, supporting the machinery of war." Turning to me, he explained, "You've got to excuse Gertrud. She has joined the BDM, where they're brainwashing her."

Once more, I noticed the hard look in his eyes. Alarm bells should have rung, but, with my usual stubbornness, I saw only what I wanted to see, and that was an anti-Nazi, handsome and with a friendly, homely background. Also, his brief exchange with his brother had been an indication that not everyone in the family merely watched what was happening and shrugged their shoulders, and I liked that a lot.

After the meal, we sat a while at the table, talking about harmless, uncontroversial topics until Lutz's parents and sisters had left their places. Wilhelm asked me what I did for a living. I talked openly about my work at Krümmel, in which both men showed great interest. They exchanged meaningful glances, hardly able to contain themselves as I talked about the documents I had to file.

"Did you ever check out where most of the ammunition deliveries go?" Wilhelm asked. I shook my head. It hadn't occurred to me to do anything with the information I dealt with. "Next time you read something about a large-scale delivery, make a mental note of the place it's going to. All you have to do is tell Lutz about it."

"And what will you do with that information?" I inquired curiously.

"Don't let that trouble you, love. Those who don't know anything can't get caught up in anything," Lutz said, putting me in my place.

I didn't let him see how annoyed I was about being talked to like that. "I'll see what I can do," was all I replied.

At this point, Wilhelm, who had coughed repeatedly during the conversation, was seized by a coughing fit and began choking and spluttering. I jumped up to get him a glass of water, but his mom came in from the kitchen with a bottle of medicine. He was coughing up blood, and I felt very uncomfortable watching him wiping his mouth with a blood-stained handkerchief, trying to stop the coughing by pressing it hard against his lips, while more and more blood appeared. The rest of the family seemed used to this, but his mother's worry was heartbreaking.

Lutz steered me toward the door and pointed at my jacket. "I think we've got time for a walk before I take you home." I nodded, stuck my head through the door of the living room to say good-bye, and followed Lutz.

"It's quite useful, Wilhelm's sickness," he said when we were outside. "It means he can do more without seeming too suspicious."

What was that supposed to mean? I wondered, whistling in the dark. How could he consider sickness to be an advantage? But I just asked, "What has he got?"

"Consumption. The doctors don't give him long."

I felt as if he had hit me. How could he talk about his brother like that, so completely detached and emotionless?

"What do you mean by 'do more'?" I asked him.

Lutz looked me up and down, then pointed at the wall of the house we were passing. I didn't see a thing. Questioningly, I raised my shoulders. Lutz nodded toward another wall. All I noticed was flaked-off paint and the remains of a poster. Shreds of an old poster clung to the wall of the next house we passed, and Lutz pointed again to this. Slowly, it dawned on me what he meant. I realized that the posters had all been propaganda: "Germans, beware! Don't buy Jewish goods!" and the like. I opened my mouth to speak, but a man was walking past us and the look Lutz gave me made me shut up.

When the stranger had passed, I exclaimed excitedly, "You're tearing them off! Great! That's absol—" I didn't get any further. Lutz snatched me into his arms and planted a kiss on my mouth. Surprised, I didn't even struggle. Then I saw out of the corner of my eye the reason for his spontaneity in the form of two brown uniforms. However, as the metallic steps faded, he didn't let go of me, and I wasn't keen to free myself. Someone knows what he's doing, I thought contentedly.

We stood for a long while leaning against the wall. He held me tight, and in his eyes glowed a desire for more.

"You're not doing this for the first time, that's for sure!" he murmured into my hair.

"Well, if you'd prefer a virgin, then you'll have to write another ad," I replied.

He got quite excited, but I felt exposed on the street and fended him off with at least some degree of conviction, looking pointedly around us.

Lutz urged me to spend an evening alone with him, and I thought feverishly. Of course, it was too early for this, but I wanted it myself. I had hardly ever felt desire as intense as this. Maybe it was because of his confidence, his maturity and his assertiveness, which I interpreted as strong masculine character. His good looks didn't do any harm.

"Have you got time tomorrow?" he asked.

"Come for me at eight. I'll tell my mother you invited me for a meal."

He put his arm around my shoulders and took me home. I flew up the stairs and went straight to bed, hoping to make the time go by more quickly.

At work the next day, the hours passed unbearably slowly. What helped was my mission to keep an eye out for orders for large-scale deliveries and remember their destinations. I looked very closely at every letter I had to file, until one caught my eye. It was a big delivery to Warnemünde, to the northeast on the Baltic coast. I was tempted to pocket the whole letter, but I didn't dare. Instead, I noted the place and time of the delivery, rubbing my hands together with excitement, thinking of how impressed Lutz would be with me.

Most of the day I spent in wild imaginings about how the evening would turn out. When the doorbell finally rang, I was ready and waiting. I was wearing the dress that my mother considered "far too revealing." It emphasized my figure and suited me well. Lutz held out his arm, I took it, and we headed off.

"Where are we going?" I inquired.

"I have a friend who's got an apartment in the Wandsbeker Straße. He's away at the moment, on business in Leipzig, and I've got his keys while he's gone. And we won't starve either." He showed me the brown paper bag he was holding. "Bread, cheese, and wine."

It was a mild spring evening, the air pleasantly fresh, and I enjoyed walking through Hamburg's streets. The apartment was on the fourth floor of a run-down apartment block. The stairway was dark and dingy, but when Lutz opened the door I was relieved to find the apartment itself clean and bright. I looked around while Lutz put the food on the table and went to get glasses from the kitchen.

I looked out the window. The street was quiet at this time. Lutz stepped up behind me and put his arms around my waist. "Did you see anything interesting at Krümmel today?"

The whole day, I had thought of nothing but how I would tell him about the delivery, and now I had forgotten all about it! Quickly I made up for lost time and reported my discovery proudly. But how disappointing his reaction was! "What sort of delivery exactly? And what's the transport like—train? Truck?"

"I'm not sure. I thought you—"

"Your information is completely useless if you don't remember the details. What we need is figures, dates, transport details, exactly what sort of ammunition, all that!"

Neither he nor Wilhelm had said so. My hurt feelings must have shown, because Lutz calmed down. "Now, don't make such a face, it wasn't your last day at Krümmel, was it? There's still plenty you can find out, and not only from them . . ."

He started to seduce me expertly. This shows experience, I thought with a shiver; he must have had a lot of practice. I didn't hold back for long and I enjoyed it thoroughly. We didn't even take the time to move into the bedroom.

The wine was not a good choice, but we enjoyed the food nonetheless, talking about the cultural program Hamburg had on offer at the time. Everything was full of Nazi propaganda: In the theater, the plays were threaded with anti-Semitic messages; at the cinema, they played only schmaltzy films supposed to reinforce German patriotism, with a lot of singing and "true Aryan talent."

"I wouldn't mind the new Curd Jürgens film, though. Sometimes I do feel like a bit of schmaltz," I admitted.

"If you want, we'll go sometime soon. I'll find out when it's on from the paper." Lutz was in a good mood. "But when the news comes on, you've got to cover my mouth to stop me shouting out loud!"

I had trouble enough keeping quiet myself. You always had to endure the awful propaganda clips with ear-piercing trumpets and speeches by the Führer, watching the good workers building highways, admiring the progress on the Eastern Front. If the aim was to get the whole cinema to jump up and cry "Heil Hitler," it didn't work. Hamburg wouldn't toe the line quite so easily; at least, the audiences never did when I was at the cinema. You had to be very careful how you reacted to the propaganda, however. There were spies and informants everywhere, and the slightest remark could lead to serious consequences.

Before we left the apartment, we were gripped again by desire and threw ourselves into each other's arms. I loved Lutz's recklessness and gave in to my own body's demands, enjoying every minute. On the way home, it was completely dark, the streets empty and quiet. When I spotted a shopfront with a poster saying "If you buy from Jews you betray your people," I jumped up and tore it down. Lutz immediately started berating me, his face contorted with anger. "Not like that, you idiot! You've got to make sure first that no one is in sight. You have to be on your guard. It's not a kid's game! You should know that much. If anyone sees you, you've had it. Don't you understand?"

Guiltily, I listened to him. The next time, I looked all around me first, but Lutz was still not happy. He elbowed me, pointing his face upward. Of course! In my excitement, I hadn't thought of the windows. But it was late and the blackout curtains were all drawn. We managed to get about eight posters down before we drew near to my house.

"Tomorrow evening?" asked Lutz. I nodded. "Oh, no, wait," he said. "Can't do tomorrow. Day after that? Same time?" I didn't ask him why he couldn't make it the next day. He seemed suddenly quite closed-off. If it had been nothing important, he would have told me straightaway, so it could only be something big, something dangerous. We said good-bye with fierce kisses and I watched him walking down the road. I suddenly felt a strong wish to do something big and dangerous against the Nazis too—without knowing how to go about it.

3

LYDIA

Under the Nazis, anti-Semitism had turned to open persecution, with racial laws placing greater and greater restrictions on the rights of Jewish citizens. Their businesses were taken over by "Aryans"; Jewish children were no longer allowed to attend schools, and students were barred from universities; Jews were not to have any relations with "Aryans"; Jewish doctors and lawyers were stripped of their qualifications and forbidden to practice; Jews were not allowed to employ "Aryans" or to use public transport or public institutions. They were forced to sell their property at low prices to "Aryans." Contravention of these laws would result in imprisonment or the death penalty.

Jews, effectively deprived of their citizenship altogether, were subjected to attacks by individuals and a number of pogroms, often organized by party officials and ending in murder and deportation.

From autumn 1941, Jews were officially deported to ghettos and concentration camps and were forbidden to emigrate.

Returning from work the next day, I decided on a whim not to go straight home but to the Alstervorland, a green space with lovely views of the Außenalster, where steamboats went peacefully by. The weather was beautiful. It hadn't rained for days and it seemed a pity to go inside.

As I walked through the park, I saw in front of me a familiar sight. The plump, short figure with only a few hairs left on his head that could only be . . . "Dr. Manes!"

When he turned around, his face was a mixture of delight and worry. "Child! Don't—please don't talk to me! What if someone sees you?"

I was very fond of Dr. Manes. He was a lovely man, highly intelligent and kind. Not only had he cared for me throughout my childhood, but he had also looked after my grandparents' health—until they forbade him to treat "Aryans."

"I don't give a damn," I told him, walking alongside him. "I haven't seen you in ages, so I'll talk to you as long as I want to. How are you?"

He sighed. "How am I in these times? Do you want the honest answer? My patients diminish by the hour. I'm only allowed to treat Jews now, and they vanish one after the other. But I have to count myself lucky to be able to still practice. Financially, I'm on the verge of ruin. They have taken everything away from me."

I was enraged. "Did they come and loot your house as well?"

"What do you think, child? They won't leave the villa of a Jewish doctor be when they organize attacks throughout the country! And that wasn't all."

"What else?"

"First, I had to pay 4,000 marks Reich Flight Tax, because my house was estimated at the value of 16,000 marks. Having said that, this was quite a while ago. Now, because I'm Jewish, I wouldn't even get 200 marks for it."

I didn't understand. "What's this Reich Flight Tax? Didn't you say last time I saw you that you didn't want to follow your son to Johannesburg?"

"It has nothing to do with whether you want to emigrate or not. If you are Jewish, you have to pay in any case. Meanwhile, it got to the point where I couldn't have left anymore even if I'd wanted to. Have you heard how long the lines in front of the American embassy were? Even if you stood there overnight, you wouldn't necessarily get to see anybody. Everyone wanted a visa and no one wanted too many Jews in their country. I'd never have thought it would come to this. If only I'd listened to my son."

Dr. Manes had told me about his son's constant pressure: "Come with us, Dad, please! Don't you see what's going to happen? Come while you still can leave Germany!" He didn't listen, though. He had fought in the Great War, had received a medal in 1915, a hero of his time. "They won't do anything to me," he insisted. "I was born and bred in Hamburg. Nothing will happen to me."

I remembered how sad he had been about his son's departure to South Africa. However, not long afterward he had received good news. His son had started up a factory over there, producing ties and cravats, and had established a new life. That had helped Dr. Manes to accept his decision, although, of course, it did nothing to bridge the long distance to his child.

"And then, they confiscated 20 percent of my assets to pay for the damage of Kristallnacht. What they estimated them at was simply a joke, a huge amount more than what I'm really worth."

I felt terribly sorry for him. I had heard that the insurance companies would not pay for the damage inflicted on Jewish property by the fascists during Kristallnacht, "the Night of Broken Glass." Instead, the victims had been obliged to "re-create order in the Reich." It was an outrageous injustice, and I was still fuming with fury when I thought about it.

"Sorry to go on like this," said Dr. Manes, "but there is no good news at the moment, I'm afraid. What about you? How are you and how are your grandparents?"

"They're both dead," I told him sadly. "Not long after you had to stop treating Grandma, she went downhill really quickly. The cancer just consumed her. Granddad didn't survive her for long. He couldn't go on without her."

"I'm so sorry to hear that. Your grandparents were great people. You would have to search far and wide to find a couple as kind and honest as they were. I'm sure you miss them terribly."

I did. Their deaths had left a huge gap in my life. I hadn't felt I truly had a home since they'd gone. Although we'd moved out of their house when I was fourteen, I'd continued to spend time at their place every day. Grandma would always make me something to eat right away, and I would discuss everything that mattered to me with Granddad. My address was Caspar-Voghtstraße, where we'd moved to initially before taking the apartment in the Hochallee, but my home was still the gray block of apartments in the Horner Landstraße in Horn, the suburb of Hamburg where I'd grown up.

Dr. Manes took my hands in his, pressed them firmly, and looked into my eyes. "You are strong!" he said. "Don't let them get you!" To hear this from him, who had to suffer so much under the restrictions on Jews, was almost absurd, but it was typical of his kindness. "I've got to go. A patient is waiting for me. So nice to have talked to you. Take care!"

I stared after him for a long time. There was nothing I could have said to him, as much as I wanted to, nothing I could do. I hoped he would escape the grasp of the Nazis and somehow manage to get his emigration sorted out with the authorities.

The high spirits I had been in lately because of my dates with Lutz were dampened by the encounter. Slowly I walked on, staring at the water. Hamburg was my hometown and I had always loved living here. What was happening in the city now made it hard to know whether I could really still call it home.

For years now, the façades of buildings that housed Jewish-owned businesses had been marked with the word "Jew"; shops had displayed posters saying "Buy only from Germans!" or "Germans! Defend yourselves against the Jewish atrocities propaganda!" In shops run by "Aryans," signs proclaimed "Jews are not served here."

Sometimes in town I passed a jeering crowd gathered around one or several Jewish citizens—men or women—forcing them to scrub the road or to run around with signs around their necks bearing degrading slogans. I never knew what was better—to hurry on so as not to be among the onlookers, or to stay and try to give the victims a compassionate glance, which would not have helped a lot either. Had I tried to do something to stop the mob, I would have suffered the same treatment as a "Jew-lover."

Passing a park bench, I sat down, deep in thought. All of a sudden, a hand was placed roughly on my shoulder and a voice hissed into my ear, "What are you doing here without your star, you little Jewish slut?"

Shocked, I looked up into a face distorted with hatred above an SA uniform. "I'm sorry to disappoint you, but I am neither a slut nor am I Jewish."

I'd hoped to embarrass him but my words had no effect. "If you are an Aryan, you're not allowed to sit on a Jews' bench. Haven't you got eyes in your head? Get up at once. Or are you actually waiting for a Jew? If you are, then I'll get you done for race crime."

He was utterly serious. There was no hope of making someone like that see sense. As furious as I was, I kept my thoughts to myself and reluctantly got up, shaking my head. Indeed, the bench was painted yellow, a clear sign that it was to be used solely by Jews. I turned my back and started to walk off, but he stopped me. "Papers!" he demanded, in a voice hoarse with rage. Luckily, I had my identity card with me and showed it to him. He let me go with a muttered, "Don't let me catch you again."

No longer in a mood for walking, I hurried home. I had just poured myself a cup of tea when the doorbell rang. Worried that my sin of having sat on a "Jews' bench" might have further consequences, I quickly smartened myself up and went to the door. Outside stood no uniformed soldier, but an unshaven man in a threadbare jacket, with unkempt hair and a hunted look in his eyes.

"Gretel Wachtel?"

"That's me!" He looked me up and down, then rummaged in his pockets and pulled out a crumpled letter. Nonplussed, I took it. "Would you like a cup of—"

"From France!" he interrupted me in a low voice, without listening. He glanced around furtively, turned, and ran off.

"But wait! Where . . ." He was already around the next corner. I tried to go after him, but couldn't see a trace of him. One block further along, I gave up and, shrugging, returned to the house. He'd looked as if he needed more than just a cup of tea, and I would have been happy to feed him. Why had he run away? Did he think I was dangerous?

Curious, I tore the envelope open. The letter consisted of only two words: "I'm alive." Nothing else, no matter how long I examined it. However, what gave me goose bumps was the handwriting. I knew this handwriting—how well I knew it! For years, I'd copied algebra homework and sometimes even whole test papers written in this hand.

I grabbed the nearest chair and slumped into it. For about two years, I had tried to get it out of my head, with little success, and now it was back with a vengeance. Lutz's presence had helped me to break from my constant worry about Lydia. In fact, I hadn't thought of her for some days now, I realized, feeling guilty.

Lydia I missed almost more than Granddad. She had been my best friend since I was nine years old. We had been classmates. I was all right at most subjects, except algebra, which I just couldn't get into my head. It bored me to death. Lydia, bright and academically gifted, had no trouble with any subject, and certainly not algebra. One day, she just came over to me asking if I would like her to help me a bit, and we were best friends ever after.

Lydia helped me with my homework and I trained her in athletics, ball games, and gymnastics. As she was not as sporty as me, we complemented each other extremely well. She often invited me to her home, where I was soon treated like a family member. The Seligmanns lived in an area where a lot of Jewish families had their homes, at Graumannsweg in Uhlenhorst.

Lydia's father was a famous chamber musician and director of a conservatoire, a small musical academy, at his huge white villa, which was built in the typical Hamburg style, with big double doors connecting the rooms. The family lived downstairs, and upstairs they taught music. From every room drifted the sound of a different piece; whenever I visited I was fascinated by the vibrating atmosphere. Lydia herself was a fantastic pianist. When she played "Hungarian Rhapsody," tears always came to my eyes. I was sure that not even Liszt could have played it better.

Her mother was a lovely, open-minded woman. With her cuddly figure, she embodied for me everything I longed for—family, home, hospitality, and togetherness. It was never boring in the Seligmann household; friends came and went all day long. Usually, students from the conservatoire would eat with the family, and Lydia's sisters Helga and Lucy brought their friends as often as she brought me. Frau Seligmann fed them all; everyone was welcome.

I had never eaten kosher food before I met Lydia, but there was nothing I didn't like. Most meals consisted of chicken of some sort; it was unbelievable how many recipes Lydia's mother had for chicken. My favorite was chicken soup with *kneidlach,* small homemade dumplings. At Lydia's, you could just help yourself from big bowls to whatever you liked most. In my own home, everything was put on your plate and you had to eat what you were given with great decorum, but here meals were fun. For me, a lot of the dishes were unusual, and I tried a wealth of new culinary treats. A meal might consist of cholent, a sort of beef stew, gefilte fish, rice, and a lot more, always accompanied by green or black olives, which I loved, and a deliciously soft white bread called challah, in

the shape of a plait, so different from the hard, grainy rye bread
with which I had grown up. At the table everyone was always
talking and laughing, and I quickly got used to family life at the
conservatoire. Occasionally, I took Lydia home to my mother's,
but not very often, especially in later years. Not long after we left
school, Hitler came to power and the restrictions began, and Lydia
became reluctant to stray far from the Jewish quarter.

At school, we had been lucky; nobody cared about race or nationality at the private school of Maria Busse at Uhlenhorster Weg,
which we attended from the age of about fourteen. Our classmates
were from Czechoslovakia, Greece, America, and we even had a
girl from Persia, who was very popular until her father arranged for
her to be married at thirteen and we lost contact. She had to move
away, and we were completely at a loss as to what it would be like
for a girl of our age to be married, even having children herself.

From school, we could walk home to Lydia's, but if we wanted
to go to my place, we had to take the tram, number 27. My
mother and I had only recently moved out, so I usually took my
friend to my grandparents' if she came with me. There she would
happily tuck in to liver sausage sandwiches, which contained pork
and were, of course, not allowed. "Please don't tell my mom,"
she would beg me. "Otherwise I'll have to sit a whole day at the
synagogue and ask pardon for not having eaten kosher."

When I asked my granddad whether I ought to persuade her
not to eat them, he simply answered, "Let her be. Let her do
anything she wants to do," with a note of foreboding in his voice.
And so it stayed our secret.

After school, Lydia couldn't find a position as an apprentice
because she was Jewish. Wherever she went, they asked for her
papers and that was it. The best-case scenario was a polite apol-
ogy: As she was not "Aryan," there was nothing one could do.
However, far more often she was insulted or even threatened. I
felt somewhat guilty about the unfairness, as I easily got a place
as an apprentice to a textile retailer.

Then, after my apprenticeship, I got a job straightaway, at a clothes shop in Spitalstraße. The owner's name was Berg, and the shop was called Blusen-Berg. Again, I felt he was one of the good ones, but I wanted to know more about his attitude to the whole situation in our country. Before long, there was a special day in the Nazi calendar and the whole city was given a half-day holiday to celebrate and join a parade. All the shops were to be closed. The Führer himself was to parade through the streets and the masses were invited to cheer him along.

I stood by the door of the shop, looking at the crowd that was flocking toward the parade route. Berg came to stand next to me. "Don't you want to go?"

I shook my head and looked into his eyes. "Why aren't you going yourself?"

He returned my look, saying simply, "For the same reason." From then on, we both knew where we stood. "However," he told me, "you have to go. If not, we'll be suspected. It looks better if we're not both in the shop."

I understood. Unwillingly, I made my way along the route, always following the crowds to the Rothenbaumchaussee, where I found a space from where I could see the road. As the first cars with leading Nazi figures arrived, a murmur went through the people. At the sight of Hitler himself, everyone suddenly behaved as if they had lost their mind. There was shouting and screaming—"Heil! Heil!" and "My Führer! My Führer!"—arms waving in the air, women hysterical, children crying. It was unbearable.

The moment his car had passed the spot where I was standing, I turned around and fought my way back to the shop. I had had enough. I had seen him all right, the Führer, for whom a whole people behaved like that, and his staring, steely eyes had sent a shiver down my spine. When I arrived back at the shop, Berg was already expecting me, knowing that I wouldn't stay any longer than I had to. He didn't ask about it or make any comment. He

just said, "I think we'll go for a drink, shall we?" I nodded, still
a bit dazed from the raging crowd.

We went to a café and ordered real coffee. Sitting there, we
still didn't talk about what we were really thinking; there was no
need. After that day, I had a great time at Blusen-Berg. He let
me deal with his best customers and never criticized me, even
when I came in late.

I still met up with Lydia, although not as often, of course,
as when we were at school. She was helping her father in the
conservatoire. The whole Jewish community had grown closer.
I might have felt uncomfortable to be a privileged "Aryan," but
my friends didn't blame me for it. Still welcome, I visited the
Seligmanns regularly, although by now I could get into trouble
for maintaining such "contacts."

The atmosphere in the conservatoire had changed. It was not
as happy and relaxed as we were all used to anymore. All too
often, new anti-Jewish measures were discussed, the disappear-
ances of whole families reported, degrading experiences of friends
recounted. Over everything hovered a fearful anxiety about how
things would progress.

"Why don't you go abroad?" I asked Lydia worriedly one day.

She smiled sadly. "It's absurd, but as much as they hate us, they
make it so difficult for us to leave the country. First, you need an
emigration permit, then a visa from the country you want to go
to. You only get a visa once you've paid the Reich Flight Tax, and
that's terribly expensive. It wouldn't be easy for my dad to find a
job as director of a conservatoire in a new country, so he would
have to be able to prove that he was financially independent.
And on top of all that you need money to bribe people with, or
you can forget it. We are constantly talking about it, but it's just
impossible. And where should we go? This is our home."

"What about Palestine? I've heard that many of those who
leave go to Jerusalem."

Lydia shook her head. "The British hardly allow anyone in anymore. The Arabs revolt nonstop, so they've put strict controls on the number of immigrants. Now you only get a visa if you have family who already live there or if you can prove you have a job organized there. The only other option is to get a capitalist certificate, which proves that you are able to live independently from the state."

"Can't you do that? Just sell the house!"

Lydia told me that if you were Jewish you would get only a fraction of the real value of your house. "Believe me, if it was any easier, we wouldn't be sitting here and letting all this happen to us."

I stared at her in disbelief. I couldn't grasp the fact that it had been made impossible for the Seligmanns to emigrate. But it was true. The family were reasonably well off, but Lydia had spoken of enormous sums of money. And even if they could have sold the house for a fair price, there would be no chance of getting the whole family to Palestine. Other countries had similar restrictions, according to Lydia, because there were already streams of refugees trying to escape Germany.

Naturally, I would have preferred Lydia not to have to emigrate at all, as she was my best friend and I would miss her terribly, but it was obviously the only solution for her. If only we had known how deadly serious the situation would become not long after our talk, we would not have spoken about the bureaucracy of emigration but packed the whole family's belongings immediately. Not even our worst fears anticipated what was coming.

The nightmare started after an attempt on the life of a German embassy employee in Paris. On November 7, 1938, Herschel Grynszpan, a Jewish student, shot Ernst vom Rath. The papers reacted hysterically and the Nazis screamed for revenge. All over Germany, "spontaneous" demonstrations against the Jews were held; I was not the only one to doubt whether these were really unplanned and unprompted. For many, these rallies seemed like a promise that more violent action was to follow.

Three days after the assassination attempt, I left the house in the morning as usual to go to work. At the time I was working at Möhring and Co., a shop selling linen, bedding, and trousseaus. The Hochallee, our street, was in a calm residential area; there were no shops and hardly any people about. But as I neared the city center, my eyes took in images I failed to comprehend. The streets were littered with shards of glass, debris, broken pieces of furniture. People stood around staring, shouting anti-Jewish slogans; others were trying to clear up, boarding up broken windows or repairing smashed doors. The smell of smoke was everywhere.

I couldn't understand what was going on. All I could gather was that something must have happened in the night. Wherever I looked, I saw complete chaos. As I passed a jeweler's shop, I saw a group of Hitler Youth boys helping themselves from the shop window. Nobody stopped them. A woman even picked up her child to let him have a better look, and another stepped forward and grabbed something from the window herself. Angrily, I looked around for a policeman, but there was none to be seen, although you would have thought that in such a chaotic situation the state would be trying to restore the order on which it usually liked to congratulate itself.

It was obvious that only Jewish shops had been vandalized and looted, which, I realized, explained the absence of the police, and the scene shocked me. All the department stores—Robinson, Dyckhoff, Franz Fahning—destroyed! The sight of the mannequins sent a shiver down my spine. The looters had undressed them and thrown them through the windows. They looked like people in heaps of rubble, covered in glass shards, here a leg, there an arm. It was a horrible sight, hinting at what might have happened to the owners of the shops and their families. I hurried to the shop, sick with worry, but I should have known that it would be unscathed, as the owner was "Aryan." A lot of my colleagues were strong believers in the current political system, but not Herr Mohn, my immediate superior. When I arrived at work, his brow was furrowed with concern.

"There have been riots all night," he told me. "The Nazis have published the names of all the streets where Jewish families live. For the streets with the most Jewish households, they have listed names and addresses."

I turned white. *Lydia.* "I've got to go, right now!"

I turned on my heel and dashed to catch the next tram to Uhlenhorst. Out of the window, I saw further horrific sights. I had never seen Hamburg in such chaos before. Chanting men went in groups through the streets; boys in Hitler Youth uniform shouted anti-Semitic slogans; everything was in an uproar.

It didn't occur to me how futile my journey to Uhlenhorst was. Obviously, the address of the famous chamber musician Raphael Seligmann would have been on the list issued by the Nazis. The family couldn't possibly stay in that house, was all I could think. I was determined to take them all to my apartment. I didn't have much of a plan, and the idea that they might not come with me didn't even enter my thoughts.

When I finally arrived at the conservatoire, I knew immediately that I was too late. The doors stood open; the rooms had been ransacked; everything was broken. I picked up a shard of porcelain, a piece of a plate that Lydia's mother had loved, an old family heirloom. My fingers closed into a fist around it until blood dripped onto the floor.

I leaned against the wall. My knees gave way. I wasn't brave enough to walk through the house. I just stared into space. How long I sat there I couldn't say, but eventually I forced myself to get up. My eyes fell on the piano, Lydia's piano. The stool was lying on its side on the floor, the once beautiful instrument shattered. I picked up some music, and straightening the sheets, as if it would do any good, put them in an orderly pile and placed them on top of the broken piano. On top was Chopin's "Raindrop Prelude," and when I saw that, for the first time the enormity of what had happened hit me.

Tears streamed down my face, soaking my blouse as I stormed out of the house. I ran as if I was hunted, finally slowing down when I lost my breath, looking for a tram. When I got back to Möhring & Co., I didn't have to say a word; Herr Mohn just took me in his arms.

It wasn't possible to find out anything about the Seligmann family. I couldn't ask anybody; that would have been too risky. All I could do was buy every newspaper, especially the ones I wouldn't normally have used for toilet paper. Herr Mohn and I read, appalled, what had happened in the night, sickened by the satisfaction the articles took in the events. We read them all: the *Neue Hamburger Presse*, the *Hamburger Tageblatt*, the *Anzeiger*, the *Hamburger Zeitung*, the *Nachrichten,* and the *Hamburger Fremdenblatt*, the one I usually read.

Finally, I found the article I was looking for. Among reports of other atrocities, I read about what had supposedly happened at the conservatoire. The official version was that Herr Seligmann had thrown himself out of the window and Lydia's mother had drowned herself in the bath. Two daughters had been taken away; one had escaped. I felt sick to my stomach. Never would Herr Seligmann have thrown himself out of the window, not in a thousand years. He would have defended his family to the last, I knew that. And as to drowning oneself in the bath—how could anyone drown themselves in a bath?

There was no thought of work on that day. I was totally horror-struck, my thoughts circling around the same thing over and over again. If only I knew where the girls had been taken to and who had escaped. Was it possible that Lydia was alive?

Herr Mohn didn't even try to comfort me; any attempt would have been in vain. But when, over the following days, I didn't stop talking about it, still serving customers listlessly and without concentrating, bursting into tears at the slightest thing, he took me to one side. "Listen, Gretel," he said. "I know what you're going through, but this doesn't get you anywhere. It doesn't help your friends if you live your life in misery, grieving nonstop. This is not Lydia's friend Gretel, is it? They liked you because of your cheerfulness and your determination not to let anything get to you. Cling to the hope that it was Lydia who escaped. Pull yourself together. Maybe you can actually help somehow, somewhere, at some time, so that others won't suffer the same fate. Keep your eyes open!"

He had hit the right note. I managed to do as he said, to pull myself together. I thought about his words and determined to undertake something against the regime, however small, at the first opportunity. I would suppress my own fears and do what I could, even if it wasn't much. I would keep that resolution in years to come, and it would lead me in unexpected directions.

Kristallnacht, as the events of November 9–10, 1938, came to be called, I never forgot, but individual sights I had seen, I tried to dismiss. Particularly, I tried not to think too much about what Lydia and her family suffered and what they felt before and while they were murdered or carried off. I didn't want to turn it over and over in my mind. It would have cost me my sanity. What stayed with me was the gnawing concern about Lydia, Helga, and Lucy.

As I now held the piece of paper with the message in Lydia's handwriting, telling me that she was alive somewhere in France, I broke down in tears. I told myself that the man carrying the letter probably didn't know any more either, and that it didn't matter that I hadn't had the chance to speak to him. I would have given anything to find out more, where she was, how she was—would I ever get to see her again?

For a long time, I wondered through what elaborate underground route she had managed to get her message to my house.

I would have loved to have talked to the man who had given it to me, to have offered him something to eat and maybe my help. But he couldn't have known what it meant to me, and in that world no one took any unnecessary risks. After all, a word could mean the end of someone's life.

4

HARVESTING

1941: Hamburg issues 78 bomber alarms and is the target of 42 air raids, with some 2,500 people dead or wounded. More than 7,000 are made homeless and more than 10,000 have to be relocated. There are ruins and burned-out buildings in every district of the city. The weekly meat ration is reduced to 400g, the number of calories provided by rations per person per day to 1,928.

I could hardly wait to tell Lutz about the letter when I met him the next evening. He came late and seemed nervous, constantly looking at his pocket watch. Something was bothering him, and I wondered when he would be ready to trust me enough to confide in me.

"You'll never believe what happened today," I started to say as we walked together along the Hochallee. Lutz listened—I hadn't told him about Lydia before—but his interest seemed to be focused more on the messenger than the Seligmanns. I couldn't answer many of his questions. All I remembered was the man's ragged clothes and unkempt appearance. I hadn't gotten a good look at him at all.

If Lutz suspected which organization the man belonged to, he didn't tell me. "How do you think he knew? How did he get my address? Do you think he came straight from France?"

Lutz shook his head. "Surely not—at least, not just to bring your message. He is probably just a link in a long, long chain. His job almost certainly was or is to do with something completely different. You can count yourself lucky to have heard anything at all. The net only needs to tear in one spot and all the information vanishes."

"What net? Can't I do something?" I now asked directly.

He looked somewhat annoyed. "If something crops up that you can help with, I'll let you know. At the moment, information from your archive is important—looking out for that, you're more useful than you think."

That day, though, I had had nothing of significance for him. The folder on the major delivery about which I'd so proudly told him during our last meeting was still in the office of my superior, and I hadn't had the opportunity to look at any details.

"Do you know what?" I said. "I feel like celebrating! I'd like to drink to the fact that Lydia is alive and safely in France."

"Hope you're right. France isn't that safe either," Lutz replied, dampening my enthusiasm. "But celebrating sounds like a great idea. Let's go to Schwartz's. He's a business acquaintance of mine, and there's always something going on at his place."

I didn't hesitate to agree; private get-togethers were usually far more fun than the beer cellars, where you had to weigh every word in your mind before you spoke in case you caught the attention of a political spy. Lutz's acquaintance lived in a ground-floor apartment in Gellertstraße in Barmbek, not far away. All we had to do was cross the Krugkoppel Bridge and we were practically there. However, after we rang the bell, it was ages until the door was opened; we almost gave up. Schwartz, a stocky, balding man in his late thirties, quickly waved us in.

"We've got something to celebrate and so we thought we'd look in on you," Lutz told him.

"Sure! In you come. Down here."

He led us down a staircase to his cellar. The room didn't look comfortable at all. It was filled with bottles and sacks with what seemed to be various different contents. In the middle of the room was a wooden table with a naked lightbulb hanging above it; two men and a woman sat on wooden boxes or sacks, the air filled with cigarette smoke. I found this strange environment exciting and immediately went to sit down at the table without waiting for an invitation.

Schwartz pushed a bottle of red wine in my direction—there didn't seem to be any glasses—asking, "And what's there to celebrate?"

Lutz shot me a warning glance, so I answered, "My sister's had a baby!" As I told them more about this imaginary birth, having a vague idea of the right sort of thing to say because of my neighbor Ilse's pregnancies, I caught Lutz grinning out of the corner of my eye.

The evening was loud and happy, and Lutz's advances toward me grew less subtle with every sip he took from the bottle. First, he looked me up and down and when our eyes met, he raised his eyebrows in a meaningful way. Then he started to touch me, at first as if by chance, but more and more frequently. The others weren't exactly struck by blindness, but I didn't care about their comments—the atmosphere allowed for unconventional behavior.

Lutz moved nearer and I didn't object. Again, my body took control over my mind, and I felt only the heat of desire. We got up at the same time and said our good-byes quite hurriedly, to roars of laughter from the others, who could see what was going on. On the street, Lutz had his hands everywhere, and as he pushed me into a doorway, I just giggled. "What—here?" Forgotten were all precautions, let alone nosy neighbors, but then we weren't tearing down posters—only our clothes.

It was over in a flash. Out of breath, I smoothed down my skirt and giggled again.

"Do you want to go home?" asked Lutz.

"Not really, but I suppose I should."

He walked me back and we arranged to go to his house for a meal the next day. I was so tipsy that it took me quite some time to open the door. Inside, the light was still on; my mother, who had been in bed, came downstairs. Lutz blew me a kiss and went before she could blame him for my condition.

Mother regarded me sternly, shaking her head. She thought such behavior was common, but she wouldn't have made a scene in the hall in case our lodgers heard. She always waited until we had shut the door to our apartment. Underneath us lived Walther Gernot, a factory worker with a wooden leg, whose wife I couldn't stand. Frau Gernot's conventional, nosy ways had gained her the position of "block warden" for our area. She was a minor party official, tasked with checking up on us and reporting anything unusual to the authorities. She was always trying to get us to go to official party events or to sell us some terrible fascist propaganda magazine. The role made her feel very important, and her presence was a constant reminder that it wasn't safe to say and do what I wished even in my own home.

Our other lodger, Herr Mengel, was very religious; he wouldn't have approved of a daughter coming home in my state either. He belonged to a group founded by the American evangelist Billy Graham. When he wasn't roaming the streets preaching, he worked at Gunkel, a fish factory. We got mountains of tinned fish from Herr Mengel; I particularly loved the herrings in tomato sauce he gave us. I wasn't very keen on him, but since he ate with us, I couldn't avoid him altogether. He was big to the point of obesity and it was a chore to watch him eat; the only food we got plenty of from our rations was potatoes, and he'd stuff enormous amounts of them into his mouth.

Apart from the lodgers, I loved our house. We had moved there because of my Aunt Netta, who had looked after the handicapped child of the previous owner. When the owner died, the child was put into a home and Aunt Netta married. My grandmother urged my mother to have a look at the house before anyone else snapped it up.

We had been delighted with it. A grand villa, it was nicely situated in Harvestehude, one of the best areas of Hamburg. There was a cellar, once the living quarters of the servants, then the ground floor, with an imposing living room divided from the dining room by big pillars. From there, an iron staircase led down to the back garden. We liked the rooms on the first floor best and decided to live there. As it was too big a house for just the two of us, we looked for lodgers. Those who wanted to could have their meals cooked and washing done by my mother, an offer gladly accepted by Herr Mengel.

About a week after we moved to the Hochallee, a bomb hit our old house in Caspar-Voghtstraße. For some months, there had been air raids as the British responded to the German offensive on England. I had been beside myself with fury when I read about the Battle of Britain in the papers. Not England as well, was all I could think. Having learned English at school, I had always dreamed of going to London one day. Now I read in the papers how the Germans were turning this beautiful city into ash and rubble. The damage caused by the British bombers I blamed solely on our own government, although I would never have dared to speak such thoughts aloud.

Almost every night since early in the summer of 1940 the air-raid siren had howled, but it did not always mean that planes were actually coming. We had been told to move immediately to a shelter or to our cellars when the alarm sounded; these were, in accordance with the rules, equipped with food and first-aid equipment. Somehow, though, I hadn't initially felt threatened by the attacks, not anticipating that we might get hit ourselves. That was something that happened to other people, the aftermath of which you might pass the next morning on your way to work, full of pity for the victims and shocked by the scenes of devastation.

However, when Caspar-Voghtstraße was hit, it dawned on me
for the first time that this was not necessarily something that happened only to others. My attitude started to change. The whole
area where we had lived until recently, including our old house,
was reduced to rubble. Mother and I were unbelievably lucky
still to have a roof over our heads. Many of our old neighbors
had been hit, and it suddenly brought the danger home to me.
It was sheer chance whether you were hit or spared. After that,
I ran down to the cellar whenever the alarm sounded. Sometimes I ran to the nearest public shelter; I preferred these, as I
considered them safer.

Our immediate neighborhood had not been badly hit, but
some houses were severely damaged. Some had no roof, others had lost their façades, but the residents of these buildings
somehow managed to carry on living there despite the damage.
The unpredictability and the hardship created a new solidarity
between people who once would have barely said hello in passing.
Ilse, our neighbor with five children, soon grew used to my help
carrying the little ones as we rushed to the shelter to the sound
of the howling sirens.

Everyone tried to help those who had been hit. Cooking was
one of the greatest problems for those who had been bombed
out. Conversations in the public shelters revealed other people's
misfortunes, and soon Mother and I cooked not only for our
lodgers but also for two or three local people whose homes had
been damaged, and everyone would bring something along for
the pot. It was interesting to see what each dinner turned out to
be. Everyone contributed what food they had been able to get
hold of with their rations. One might bring a loaf of the crumbly bread that tasted like sawdust, another a sausage that looked
and tasted like a tube of sand; with a little bit of luck, someone
might have a real bone and some half-fresh vegetables, and then
we would eat a proper soup. Mother would put it all into the
huge pan in which we used to cook fruit to make preserves for

the winter. Our soup kitchen helped us to get to know a great many people, and meals were always big gatherings.

Although I did not like Frau Gernot, our house spy, I was quite fond of her husband. He worked at a factory in which they produced chocolate shells for pralines. Sometimes he managed to sneak some chocolate shells home and he was happy to share them. What a delicacy! Grateful, I would stuff myself with them, and eventually I asked how he managed to smuggle so many out. He laughed and, to demonstrate, pulled up his trouser legs. Confused, I stared down at his ankle and the end of his wooden leg, both half-covered by his long johns. He pulled at a string he had fastened at the seam, and I began to understand. By tying up his long johns at the ankles, he could secretly stuff them with chocolate shells. I was very impressed.

Under normal circumstances I might have hesitated to eat chocolates that had been transported in a man's undergarments. But for us, living off rations, with hardly anything available, chocolate was an unbelievable pleasure. If we had found a proper praline lying in a cowpat in the road, we would have picked it up, washed it, and eaten it happily.

The extreme nature of life in wartime had a strange influence on me and some of my peers. Everything could be over and finished with the very next day: A bomb could hit you, or the Gestapo could take you for whatever reason. The streets you walked could change from one night to the next; what was there yesterday might be gone tomorrow. This strange situation suddenly rendered traditional values less important. If I did not survive tomorrow, I told myself, then I would at least have lived today to the full, without doubt or regrets.

This also meant that I had no wish to spend the rest of my possibly short life at Krümmel. I couldn't stand it for much longer, and I saw Lutz as the solution to my problem. Our relationship was developing excellently. If it carried on like this, we would soon be married and I could bid farewell to Krümmel. As a potential mother, I wouldn't have to work any longer. The thought stopped me from looking too closely at Lutz's personality; I closed my eyes to his faults and trusted my basic optimistic attitude.

The day after the party in Schwartz's cellar, a Saturday morning, Lutz came over unexpectedly and briefly spoke to my mother. I couldn't hear whether he apologized for my condition the evening before. In her eyes, it was up to the man to make sure that nothing happened to a girl, and if I returned home drunk, it was he who was to blame as much as it was my own fault. He must have said something to mollify her, though, as my mother let me go out with him.

Lutz greeted me with a kiss and told me, "Pack a few simple things. We're going to the country overnight." I was taken aback and gave my mother a sidelong glance. Lutz must have informed her of his plans, as she gave a curt nod of agreement, so I went to pack. I didn't want to spoil my own surprise, so I didn't ask any questions, I just went along with it.

We took the tram to the main station, where Lutz bought tickets and led me to the train. As he stowed our luggage in the carriage, I realized that he had brought some empty sacks. I raised my eyebrows as it dawned on me what we were up to. "We're going harvesting, aren't we?"

Lutz nodded. "I hope you didn't imagine a romantic weekend as invited guests at a country house!" he joked, upon which I vigorously shook my head, because I had indeed thought of something along those lines. "You'll get the benefit of it yourself, you and your mom. You'll see."

A little chastened, I looked out of the window. I knew this route. It was the way to Geesthacht. We didn't go far. We got off the train at Bergedorf, to the southeast of the city. Lutz took my arm and we walked along the road until a car came by and gave us a lift.

We were in Vierlande, an area well known for fruit and vegetable farming. Big fields of apple and plum trees stretched to the horizon; in others, runner beans or potatoes were grown. Half-timbered houses were dotted around. It was a peaceful setting, as if the world was still wholesome. Before long, our journey was over. Lutz asked the driver to drop us off, and we thanked him and got out.

Lutz took his things, I shouldered my backpack, and we walked toward the nearby village. By the side of the road, we saw a sign proudly announcing: "This village is Jew-free!" I sought Lutz's eyes, enraged, but he just shrugged his shoulders. "What did you expect?" he asked. "Did you think only the cities harbor Nazis?"

As we arrived at a farm, Lutz pointed to a cardboard sign saying "Seeking pea pickers." He asked me to wait in the shadow of a tree while he went up to the farmhouse to introduce himself. I had a look around. The house seemed old. It sheltered under some enormous oak trees. Chickens pecked around the yard, some ducks waddled over the cobblestones, and a dog on a chain lay in the sun. There was an open shed filled with various handcarts, a plow, a harrow, a roller, and other machinery. A bit further along were stables for horses.

Lutz came back from the house with two big willow baskets. He seemed to know what he was doing, as he led the way straight to a field where other workers were already busy. "Off we go!" he said cheerfully, so I took a basket and started picking peas.

In all my life, I had never really done any manual work; my mother had brought me up as a fine lady (or so she thought), not as a farm laborer. Soon, my back started to hurt from the constant bending. The sun beat down and I wished I had brought a hat with me, like the other workers. I stretched, wiping the sweat from my forehead and holding my wrist to my aching back.

Lutz was quite a distance away and he didn't seem to be particularly worried about me. Not once did he so much as turn around to check on me. At first, I was annoyed, but then I started to see this unusual situation as a challenge. I'd show him! There was nothing that would get me down, and certainly not "proper" work.

I approached one of the other harvest helpers, a strong young girl roughly my age. "Haven't you got a sun hat?" she asked. I shook my head, whereupon she motioned to me to follow her. At the edge of the field, where we had all left our belongings, she went to a basket of cutlery. She pulled out a tea towel, knotted its edges together and handed it over to me. "Not very fashionable, but it should help!"

Grateful, I took it and my mood improved instantly. We got to talking. The girl told me that she regularly helped on the farm, taking whole sacks of fruit and vegetables home as payment. I understood that Lutz had also arranged to be paid in kind. Money wasn't worth much anyway. The girl told me how people paid the farmer for food: "Most people take the contents of their houses to him. He's got the nicest carpets, he's got jewelery, he's got the best china. Last week, I saw a man bringing his wardrobe, a beautiful piece of furniture. Soon, he'll be able to open a shop!"

We speculated on how rich the farmer might be by now, working along the rows deep in conversation, so that I didn't notice my back aching anymore. Finally, it was time for our lunch break, and we all sat together in the shade of a big oak tree.

The farmer's wife came with bread, butter, cheese, sausage, and homemade cider. It had been a long time since I'd enjoyed a meal so much—I was ravenous—and the cider lifted the atmosphere considerably. Lutz and I sat back to back, as the tree trunk had been taken, and occasionally his hand wandered back, an indication of what was to come in the evening.

To my relief, we didn't have to pick peas in the afternoon; now it was plums. More helpers joined us. Altogether, we made a crowd of about fifteen to twenty pickers. The plums were yellow, sweet and juicy, and they tasted absolutely delicious. For every two plums I put in the basket, I ate one.

We had a lot of fun as we picked; jokes went around and a lot of nonsense was talked. I was enjoying our trip to the country more and more. In the evening, we went tired and sweaty to an old barn, where all the harvest workers would be staying overnight. Washing facilities were not provided, and we had to make our way to the hedge if we needed to go to the toilet.

Lutz hooked his arm into mine and gave me a look. "Shall we go for a walk?" he asked. Truth be told, I was actually too tired, but I let him persuade me. As soon as we were out of sight of the others, he pulled me down into the grass, burying his face between my breasts and his hands under my skirt. I didn't find the setting very romantic—the grass scratched me and I was stung by some insect or another—but Lutz was adamant. "Come on," he murmured, "you want it as much as I do. I know you!" He knew enough tricks to get me going. I soon forgot how uncomfortable I felt and we both enjoyed rolling around in the open air.

Back in the barn, we didn't look any more disheveled than the others. We were all dirty and ragged, and we sat together for a long time talking and laughing, until one by one we withdrew to find a place to sleep in the hay. Lutz and I found a spot up high in the barn, made a cozy nest, and fell asleep within minutes.

My rest did not last long. Suddenly, my bowels moved, and quite forcefully so. The plums! If I had only stopped eating those plums! Desperate, I looked around. It was pitch black, the whole place was littered with sleeping bodies, and there was no toilet. In any case, I wouldn't have had time to pick my way down the ladder and out of the barn.

In despair, I threw myself to a window high up in the wall of the barn, tore my skirt up, and hung my bottom out. Lutz had woken up. "Gretel? What on earth are you doing?"

I groaned and said, "Don't ask! These goddamn plums!"

Lutz understood the situation and stumbled through the hay to hold my hands, to make sure I wouldn't fall backwards out of the window. At that moment, nothing mattered; dignity was not up for discussion.

"You don't happen to have a newspaper on you?" I asked eventually. Lutz rummaged in his bag, where he managed to find a piece of paper, and I thanked the Lord.

"I hope you don't need it anymore," I said shyly.

"So do I!" answered Lutz.

I started to giggle and couldn't stop. Lutz joined me and we roared with laughter until the people around us started to complain.

5

GRÖMITZ AND SYLT

When Lutz and I arrived back in Hamburg on the Sunday evening, we were laden with peas and plums, our reward for picking. Most of them went to Lutz and his family, but Mother and I still had some for our soup kitchen, so our bombed-out neighbors would benefit too.

Lutz and I met regularly now. Mostly, we went to his house. When we wanted to make love, it would happen in the most unusual places, wherever the urge took us. After it had happened once in a doorway—mind you, not while I was sober—the idea didn't seem so awful anymore. It created a strange type of excitement to think that we might be spotted at any moment, and we felt terribly daring.

About nine weeks after our first rendezvous, Lutz suggested that we spend a weekend at the seaside. As we were not married, it was out of the question to go unaccompanied, so we arranged for Lutz's brother Wilhelm and his wife, whom I had never met before, to go with us. We set off by train on a Friday evening to Grömitz, by the Baltic Sea.

The journey didn't take too long. We passed through the towns of Lübeck and Neustadt and soon saw the Bay of Lübeck. Grömitz turned out to be a lovely little village. I loved it at first sight.

There was no comparison with the upmarket resorts like the Timmendorfer Strand. Here in Grömitz everything was unfussy, simple, and down-to-earth, just to my taste.

At once, I forgot hectic daily life in Hamburg. The war didn't seem to have reached this village. I didn't even see any anti-Semitic signs. The air smelled of the sea, the houses were plain, long brick buildings, blending harmoniously into the landscape. The cobblestoned streets were lined with lime trees, and at the edge of the village proud old beeches stood by the seaside. Between their trunks, the water glistened. It was quite different from the North Sea, where you had to walk for miles through sand dunes to get to the water's edge.

The locals were the epitome of the typical northern German— dressed simply, straightforward both in appearance and character. They seemed to shy away from any unnecessary word, greeting us with the northern dialect salutation *Moin!*, but otherwise keeping themselves to themselves. However, they were friendly enough, and one local directed us to the guesthouse that Lutz and Wilhelm had chosen before we left.

I had been introduced to Wilhelm's wife, Margot, a bony creature who looked older than me, at the station. Her haggard appearance didn't say anything about her personality, I told myself sternly as I walked toward her with an outstretched hand. Instead of taking my hand and saying hello, however, she only nodded curtly and spoke solely to Wilhelm.

When we arrived in Grömitz, she seemed no more relaxed or friendly. She had shown no sign of appreciating the beauty of the landscape. Now, she bent down to inspect her shoe, grumbling, "Of course, with these cobbles, no wonder I've broken a heel. How irritating!" I prepared myself for a difficult weekend. And yet I had grown almost fond of Wilhelm, with his quiet but determined ways, so I resolved to try for his sake to get on with Margot.

The guesthouse turned out to be a farm in the center of the village, where we got two sparsely furnished rooms and breakfast, nothing more. Lutz had signed us in as a married couple. I liked that. "We'll unpack first and meet down in the courtyard, all right?" asked Lutz. All agreed, and we went to our rooms. I was making for the window to look at the view when Lutz threw me onto the bed. "Finally! In style, like normal couples," he grinned. No longer than ten minutes later, we began unpacking and I got my chance to admire the view, which wasn't of the sea but of the village itself.

"Let's go down!" I said, and we ran down the stairs and stepped out into the yard. It was a liberating feeling to be in the country-side. I literally shook off the stress of the city and stretched. Lutz watched me coldly as if I was a passing pedestrian in the city; no emotion showed on his face. "You look like a cantankerous block warden who noses about to see whether anyone listens to the enemy on the wireless," I observed.

He was annoyed. "And you behave like a child," he retorted.

I wasn't prepared to let him ruin my good mood. Let's go to the seaside, I thought, that's what we're here for. Reluctantly, he let me pull him toward the beach, constantly turning around to look for the others. Finally, they appeared and hurried to catch up with us. "You're not going without us, are you?" Wilhelm asked in a mock-threatening voice. "That'll cost you a beer!"

In high spirits, I ran on toward the beach, which was quite a walk away from our guest house. We had to follow the cobble-stoned main street, where we saw that Grömitz even had a real hotel and a health spa. We went up a hill and then had to walk through a cemetery to get to the sea. When we got there, we took our shoes off and ran into the sand. Lutz and Wilhelm fell back a bit, and I managed to talk with Margot for the first time.

"I do hope that the sea air will do Wilhelm's lungs good," she began. "It's high time that he got a bit better."

"Is it that bad with his health then?"

Margot nodded sadly. "The doctors don't give him very long."

"Oh shit!" Commiserations were not my speciality; I usually just said what I thought. "Couldn't he stay up here a bit longer if it helps him?" I suggested.

Margot sighed. "He won't. He's far too involved in his business in Hamburg. I wish he'd take a step back, but he uses his illness for cover and it works ever so well."

I was puzzled. At first, I'd thought she meant Wilhelm's work when she spoke of "business," but this was obviously quite a different matter. "Cover?" I asked curiously.

"Don't you know anything?"

"Well, Lutz doesn't tell me anything, although I said that I wanted to help," I replied crossly. "At least Wilhelm confides in you. Maybe he even lets you join in . . ."

Margot hesitated to tell me more, but I pushed her to carry on after glancing behind us. The men were still some distance away; maybe I would finally get to hear something of Lutz's activities. There was no way I was going to miss this opportunity. "I wish someone would let me know what's going on," I told Margot. "This is driving me mad! All that Lutz lets me do is tear down posters and get information from Krümmel, and I would love to do something real."

Margot saw that I could only be on the right side of things. Maybe I had misjudged her; at least she seemed a reliable confidante, her lips sealed. "I can't tell you much," she said, "only that they help where they can. They pass on information. Usually they don't even know themselves who's behind it, what it's about, or who finally ends up using it. Nobody knows more than is strictly necessary. That's sort of their safety net in case someone gets caught. Sometimes it's flyers, sometimes oral messages—anything really. If they can, they also organize passports or money for fugitives."

"And who are their contacts?" I asked. Margot didn't feel comfortable, that much was obvious, but I was determined to find out more.

"You've got to ask Lutz for yourself. They only know a few. They arrange different meeting places each time so that the authorities don't become suspicious. I don't know any more, and to be honest, I don't want to either."

I had to be content with that. I wouldn't get any more out of Margot. I doubted that I could get any more from Lutz, either. He always clammed up completely when I asked him any questions. But what did I want names for, anyway? What I knew was enough. Lutz was on the right side. That was all that counted. He was even actively involved against the system, which was better still. I wondered whether he would propose during the weekend away and dug my feet deep into the sand.

The next day, Lutz did indeed propose, but it was much less romantic than I had imagined. We were sitting under a beech tree looking at the waves, glad to be on our own for a while. The others had settled down in the local pub, but I had insisted on going for a walk, and Lutz had joined me.

"I want to marry you!" he blurted out suddenly. "There—I got you a ring!"

Although I was prepared for it and ready with an answer, I hesitated a moment before replying. Was escaping Krümmel really reason enough to agree? After all, I would have to live with my future husband. Maybe I shouldn't . . .

"All right, then!" I said, despite my doubts, reaching my hand toward him so he could slide the ring on. I scanned his face for signs of affection, but all I could see in it was a kind of relief, as if he had taken a deep breath after holding it for a long time. Perhaps he had feared that I would say no.

"All's well, then!" was how he acknowledged my answer. The sun made his hair shine a bright blond, and I realized again how handsome he was. But handsome or not, had I made the right decision? Did we actually love each other? He didn't seem very loving, not even as he sealed our engagement with a kiss. There was no warmth in his eyes at that crucial moment.

Warmth. Did I have any feeling of warmth myself when I looked at him? If I was completely honest, not at all. Heat, yes, when we were gripped by desire, but not real affection or a feeling of belonging—that just didn't come into our relationship.

But I was capable of love—and how much so! Three times I had been madly in love, but it had never turned into a real relationship. Maybe that was my destiny—not to be with those I really loved. Maybe I had just been too young. The first time, certainly, I was only seventeen. I had fallen in love with a fellow student, Arthur Korell, who was nineteen at the time. He lived with his mother and two brothers, married very young, and died early in the war.

Arthur might have been a teenage crush, but my second love, Kurt Hansen, surely was not. Never in my life would I forget him, I was certain. It had hit me at first sight; the whole thing was truly romantic.

I had been in the theater with my mother, and we went to the Boccacio afterward. The Boccacio was a restaurant with a bar, where tea dances were held in the afternoons. For 1 mark 15, you could get a coffee and a piece of cake. As I was only nineteen and an apprentice, I couldn't afford much more, apart from about six awful-smelling American cigarettes. In the Boccacio, however, I would have the opportunity to meet somebody who would enable me to extend the evening, taking me for a meal or to a nightclub.

My mother came along quite willingly, and we found a table where we could eat something. At the table next to us sat three young men, one of whom was extremely good-looking. Absent-mindedly, I scratched my back; I was wearing a lovely green wool dress, which, unfortunately, itched terribly. The handsome young man at the neighboring table happened to look at us at the very moment I lifted my arm awkwardly to scratch, and he raised his eyebrows in amusement. Caught in the act, I froze and looked away, fussing with the dotted veil that was fastened to my white straw hat, vowing that I would never again wear a wool dress.

As the music began to play, the man jumped up and came straight over to our table. He bowed to my mother and asked, "May I have this dance with your daughter?" Mother was enchanted. This kind of behavior she usually looked for in vain when it came to my admirers.

He introduced himself as Kurt Hansen, and we danced to every song they played, without a break, all evening. Never had I encountered such stimulating conversation; never had I danced so naturally with anyone. It was as if we each knew the other's slightest movement in advance; we were totally in tune with each other. I forgot everything around us. On the way home, Mother grumbled, "Great evening for me, that was!" But in truth she didn't begrudge me my happiness.

After that, Kurt and I went out together frequently. He was a dream of a man: sporty, intelligent, kind, and very attractive. Twice a week, he collected me from work and we went to the Binnenalster, where he kept a rowboat. On the water, we would unpack the sandwiches his mother had made him, usually cheese with prawns and mayonnaise. He was a member of a social club called Blumenpott, which held dances and boating trips on the Alster, and he had countless friends whom I liked a lot. Once we went to a fireworks display. The entire youth of Hamburg, or so it seemed, watched it from boats on the water, with Kurt and me right in the middle, completely overwhelmed with love.

One day, Kurt came to our house to speak to my mother. My heart was in my mouth; I painted the future in the brightest colors. But when he had finished talking to my mother and came to my room, the expression on his face shattered my illusions at once. He looked into my eyes, took my hands, and said gravely, "Gretel, I have just explained to your mother that I cannot see you again. I should have told you right from the start that I am promised to someone else. I am to marry a girl whom I don't love. But it has been arranged for a long time now, and I can't go back on my word. I am so sorry, Gretel. Please believe me.

We just can't see each other again. I am far too much in love with you."

It took a long time for my broken heart to heal. Day and night, I cried my eyes out. When I finally got over it, something in me had changed. As much as I had loved Kurt, he had never touched me—I was still a virgin. Now, something shut down in me. Suddenly I felt like running wild; honorable men were of no interest to me anymore.

First, I slept with a stepbrother of Arthur Korell. It was no fun whatsoever, but I had decided to lose my virginity. As it couldn't be Arthur, I made do with his stepbrother. After that, I developed a kind of hunting instinct. Whenever I wanted a man, I got him. I would be the one who ended the relationship, and usually quickly. I had it all under control.

During all these affairs and flirtations, I hardly ever felt anything more than lust and a sense of taking all that was on offer. I had no fear of disease or pregnancy, and I should have counted myself lucky that I didn't have anything to regret.

My impulsive personality was reflected in my working life, too. I never stayed long where I didn't like it, and my worker's book filled up quickly with a variety of stamps. My time at Blusen-Berg was the longest I stayed in any job, at more than two years. I left in 1936, and then only because Herr Berg was arrested. He, unlike so many, did not go to prison for political reasons, but because he had run over a child, who did not survive. As Berg was not a member of the Nazi Party, and hence his political attitude was in doubt, he had no chance of avoiding jail.

I found work in a warehouse where life was very strictly regulated. The supervisors were old hags who seemed determined to eliminate any fun. We had to clock in, which I hated, so I pushed my card again and again into the machine, so that the time on the stamps was illegible and yet nobody could blame me for not stamping it.

Not long after I started work there, I stormed out of the building at lunchtime, furious over yet another unjust and disrespectful scolding, and decided spontaneously not to go back. I knew I would lose my wages—I hadn't even got my worker's book stamped yet—but I simply didn't want to see the building ever again, and in fact I worked myself into such a rage that I wanted to leave the city altogether. Away from here, to another part of the world, just off and go, I brooded.

I searched the job listings in the *Hamburger Fremdenblatt* until I found something that suited my mood. The silk boutique Brandt in Mönckebergstraße was looking for slim models, for whom they wanted to create bespoke dresses to be shown at a major fashion show in Westerland on the island of Sylt, where all of high society went on holiday. Just the thing for me!

Sure that they would take me on, I introduced myself at Brandt and got the job straightaway. Of course, I had quite some competition; the most beautiful women in Hamburg had come to apply. But I was certain that I too had my advantages, despite my nose, which I didn't like. I had a slim, sporty figure, didn't need to wear a bra, and had quite a pert bottom.

Possibly due to my pertness, I packed my bags the same day and headed off to Sylt. At first, I shared a room with a colleague, but she was too single-mindedly after men. This was not the pot calling the kettle black; for me, there was a difference between us. I chose my lovers carefully, while this colleague of mine was indiscriminate in her choice and therefore, in my eyes, without class.

As soon as I arrived, I began exploring the island, which was beautiful. During one of my excursions, I met a locomotive driver who lived with his wife in a delightful little house in the dunes and who offered a bed-and-breakfast for tourists. To my surprise, it was vacant, and I didn't hesitate to move in that very day. I loved my new accommodations and was treated by the couple as if I were their own child.

I told my mother in a letter about my luck, and she decided spontaneously to take a four-week holiday and join me. We had a fantastic time together, taking our breakfast in the summerhouse, looking at the sky, which seemed so much bigger than it was anywhere else we'd been, and listening to the constant singing of the larks.

I soon realized that the fashion shows in the spa hotel would not be enough to keep me busy. I didn't want to just lounge around and wanted to earn a bit more, so I looked around for a second job. On a noticeboard at the hotel, I saw that someone was looking for a salesperson in a souvenir shop called Teapot. I went straight there, found that I got on like a house on fire with the Polish owner, and was soon working by night as a model and by day in the shop. I was needed there only in the mornings, so I still had the afternoons to explore the island and enjoy my summer on Sylt.

After the shop closed at midday or after the catwalk show was over, I would go for a walk in the dunes. I felt that life could not be any more delightful than this. The inhabitants of the island seemed quite apolitical, and I found Nazis only among the tourists. I would watch them sticking swastika flags into the sandcastles of their children, without apparently feeling ridiculous about it, spoiling the nice clean air of Sylt with their very existence.

Once, after a show, I ran down to the beach to enjoy the summer night when I caught a melody in the air, so beautiful that it sent goose bumps all over my arms. I followed the sound through the dunes, until I saw a tall man sitting peacefully in the sand and playing the flute while watching the sea.

I could barely control myself. Without a word, I walked over and sat down right next to him, listening intently, as if it was the most natural thing in the world. We grew to be close friends, and were inseparable for two weeks. We swam, went for walks, watched the moon and the stars, and felt very close to each other. This man was completely different from my usual prey, and I fell in love.

His name was Wolfgang, an American with a German mother, and as much as I wished he would, he didn't touch me once. "No," he said sternly, "because I can't marry you. I have to go back soon and leave you. Then you'll be sad and I don't want you to be." As if it mattered! I was distraught when his train left. Again! Twenty-one years old, and every time I really fell in love, I couldn't get the man I wanted. I just must not fall in love, I told myself.

Wildly determined, I fell back into my old ways, and met a funny, wealthy man by the name of Fritz Müller. Fritz, the proud owner of an automobile, helped me to get over my broken heart by chauffeuring me around in his fancy BMW, and he invited me to visit him in Berlin during the Olympics, which were to take place that summer.

I accepted his invitation gladly, having dreamed of witnessing the Olympics. By that time, it would have been impossible to get accommodation anywhere in Berlin even if I could have afforded it, so I was grateful for the offer. I worked until the last day in July 1936, took the train to Hamburg, and a couple of days later one to Berlin, to stay with Fritz and see the Olympic Games.

6

THE OLYMPICS

When I got out of the train at the main station in Berlin, I was swallowed up by an enormous crowd of people, all of them talking in different languages from every corner of the world. I was no country bumpkin, but the variety of faces, clothes, and languages almost made me feel dizzy. Luckily, I saw Fritz almost straightaway, and he walked through the crowd toward me with remarkable speed and without bumping into anybody. "There you are!" he grinned, gave me a big kiss, and took my suitcase, leading the way down the stairs and to his car.

On the way to his apartment, he took deliberate detours to show me the city. He obviously intended to impress me, and he succeeded. I gazed around me, looking in every direction, amazed. The streets were teeming with people; cafés had tables and chairs outside; everywhere was humming and buzzing with entertainment, music, tempting food and drinks, souvenirs, and cultural events. Despite the mobs of people, the streets were clean. What I liked best were all the gigantic trees, many more than I was used to in Hamburg.

Fritz explained that a lot of what I saw had been conjured up just for the Games. The Nazis wanted to impress not only us Germans but the whole world, and they were pretty successful about it. The organization was indeed outstanding, as Fritz showed me on a special events map: The layout was very well thought out, the Olympic village with the athletes' accommodations a designer's masterpiece, the public transport carefully organized, and prices for transport and food were very reasonable, even on my budget.

Fritz's apartment, situated in a good area of the city, was spacious and bright. From the windows, I could look down on a green courtyard; I should have felt quite at home, but something wasn't right. I spent a while by the window, trying to work out what it could be, but I couldn't put my finger on it until Fritz said, "So, do you want to explore Berlin now, or do you want to stand all day by the window and watch the sky?"

That's what it was: the sky! For my taste, there just wasn't enough sky in Berlin. I was used to more space in Hamburg. The canals and the Binnenalster created a certain feeling of space and freedom that I missed here. Not even the many beautiful trees lessened my feeling of being caged in by all the buildings. I definitely wouldn't want to live in Berlin, I privately decided, but it was certainly worth a visit. I took my jacket and answered quickly, "Coming!"

Fritz showed me everything that was worth seeing. First, we went to a café right in the center of the city, where we sat outside and took in the bustling atmosphere over a plate of sausages with potato salad. Afterward, we dived into the crowd and went for a tour on foot. Fritz showed me where people met in the evenings, where the best breakfast places were, where I might see celebrities, and where the athletes went in their leisure time. Had he asked me half an hour later where I'd find which bar, I wouldn't have been able to answer him. I let myself drift with the flow of the crowd, speculating about people I'd never seen before and probably would never see again, completely living in the moment.

Generally, Fritz tried to keep his Berlin accent to a minimum in my presence when he was not too excited. Why he did it, I couldn't say, but I noticed that he frequently changed his tone, demeanor, and even pronunciation depending on whom he was talking to. In a café full of Berliners, his dialect would be very strong, while he spoke almost High German with me when we were alone.

My host pulled a program for the Games out of his pocket to help us decide which competitions to watch. I was most interested in the athletics, which I knew so well from our sports lessons at school. I wanted to see the hurdles, the relay, the long jump, and the 100 meters.

"What about swimming?" Fritz asked. "They've built a new pool. You'll be amazed by it all!"

"I'm not that keen on swimming, but they mention the high dive here. We could watch that if you like."

Fritz nodded vehemently. "Of course!"

"Oh, look, the men's 100 meters final is this afternoon. We've got to see that! I've read about Jesse Owens in the papers. He's said to be simply fantastic. Has he made it to the finals?"

"Indeed he has. I'm sure he'll get a medal. You can see him all right, we'll make it in plenty of time—that's at five. But we'd better take the Underground. It'll take us straight to the stadium."

We headed off toward the Underground and the Olympic Stadium, the biggest of its kind ever built, with ten athletics grounds, playing fields, a huge outdoor swimming pool, a diving tower, equestrian grounds, and last but not least, the huge Mayfield, built especially for parades and shows. It was almost too much, everything as new and perfect as could be.

"The athletes are not badly off either," Fritz told me. "They get everything they need—street maps, an Underground map, the best accommodation. That's what they've built the Olympic Village for. They've built real houses with double bedrooms, showers, and toilets. For every house there is an interpreter to help the athletes, and it's said that they even have dentists at their disposal. The women are housed quite near the stadium, and Baroness von Wangenheim is looking after them personally. It's said that they've even built a sauna for the Finns, as they are so used to having one. The rowers are the luckiest ones of all—they're in Köpenick Castle!"

Fritz was unstoppable, and I was impressed, although I had my reservations. "You missed quite something in the opening ceremony," he told me. "What a spectacle that was."

"I'm sure it was. I can imagine," I growled. "Demonstrations of the 'godlike Aryan body.' Thanks but no thanks."

Fritz looked at me, astonished, the enthusiasm on his face changing to surprise. We had not spoken about politics so far, and he didn't pursue the subject. Luckily, we had just reached our destination.

The stadium was full to the brim. A constant flow of spectators came and went. We took our seats right at the top of the stand and took turns with a pair of binoculars. We were just in time for the 100 meters. The starting positions were marked with spoon-like little spades in the cinder track, ready for the athletes to dig their feet in. All the men were dressed in white shorts and vests.

Fritz turned to his neighbor to inquire about Owens's time in the heats. "Exactly the same as Ralph Metcalfe's world record," came the answer, "10.3 seconds. And Metcalfe is also in the race!" It promised to be exciting. I fidgeted impatiently in my seat, trying to make out which of the two black men was Jesse Owens. "Is he the one on the inner or the one on the outer lane?" I asked eagerly.

Fritz took the binoculars. "Inner lane. The other one is Metcalfe."

"My goodness, what a perfect, well-proportioned body!" I remarked, impressed.

"Steady on!" Fritz answered, pretending to be jealous.

Meanwhile, a man dressed in white and carrying a pistol approached the starting positions and stood near the athletes. "On your marks . . . Get set . . ."—*bang!*

Owens shot off like the pistol itself. Metcalfe's start was not quite as perfect, and Owens took the lead in a flash. Metcalfe gained on him but didn't quite catch up. Owens ran like clock-work. Only his arms and legs moved, nothing else—quite different from the others whose bodies and heads bobbed forward and back. Owens reached the finish line almost half a meter before Metcalfe, the others following further back still, his victory clear and well-earned. I jumped up and shouted with the crowd: "Jes-se! Jes-se!" It was wonderful to see the sour faces of the Nazi bigwigs on the balcony. The best German runner had just about made it to fifth position. I was elated.

We stayed a while to watch the women's 100 meters semifinals and then some 3,000 meters hurdles heats. Fritz looked pleased by my enthusiasm. The atmosphere had completely enveloped me. Letting my eyes wander around the stands, I saw how involved the audience was. They suffered and cheered with the competi-tors, whatever their nationality. They sang, they screamed, they laughed and cried.

Above us, all around the stadium, the flags of the participants were flying in the wind. The scoreboard was decorated with the flags of those countries that had recently won gold, flapping in front of the Olympic rings, which looked as if they were floating unsupported in the air.

After Owens's victory in the 100 meters, I was keen to see him in his other disciplines, too. On the following day, the long jump finals were, luckily, in the afternoon, so I was able to explore Berlin in the evening with Fritz, have a nice lie-in, and still not miss anything.

Lutz Long, a German, contested for the gold medal with Jesse Owens. Hitler was in attendance, and I couldn't stop myself from focusing the binoculars on him occasionally. Long jumped first: 7.54 meters. Owens followed with 7.74. On the second jump, Long manages 7.84 meters, but Owens surpasses him by 3 centimeters. Hitler rubs his hands over his trouser legs, wipes his face—almost a sign of emotion, I think sarcastically. The third is Long's best jump: 7.87 meters, exactly the same distance as Owens's second.

Now it all hangs in the balance—will Owens succeed? The stadium is silent, tense, as he collects himself and concentrates, bent over. His hands run down his hips, over his face, down his hips, then he remains stock-still for a moment, runs up—jumps.

It's 8.06 meters! The crowd is roaring. Everyone is out of their seats. The Americans shout for joy, waving their flags madly. It's my turn again with the binoculars, and I study Jesse's face. There is no sign of self-importance or conceit, just a beaming smile; you couldn't help but share in with his joy.

In the evenings, we dived into another world. Fritz showed me around Berlin, and I was happy to accept his generosity. He always paid, whether for entry or for food and drinks in the restaurants, cafés, and dance bars. I didn't find that in the least troubling; even if I had had money, I wouldn't have thought of paying when I was with a man. I was a child of my generation. Anyway, he was well enough off with his posh BMW, and he loved to show off. "Look, do you want that?" he would ask, pointing at something or other in a shop window, and always within earshot of other people, but I just laughed and waved him off, not wanting to owe him too much. His business supplied butchers with materials they needed for making sausages, and he always introduced himself to people as "F. Müller, Spices and Intestines," which drove me crazy.

On my first night in Berlin, I avoided going back to Fritz's apartment for as long as possible, not unaware of the fact that he had certain expectations of me. He was great in bed, but I didn't like his hairy body. He had thick hair on his arms, legs, shoulders, chest, and back—everywhere. His bed was far from comfortable, and he didn't change the sheets once during the whole of the Olympic Games. Once he asked me, "Do you always have to be drunk when you go to bed with me?," whereupon I swallowed, got into an almost dangerous coughing fit, and luckily he forgot his question as he had to pat me quite vigorously on the back.

On the whole, I had the most wonderful time in Berlin. I enjoyed every single hour. I attended all the events that I was keen to see; Fritz let me decide what we went to. "They've overdone it a bit with all their predictions of German victories, haven't they?" I crowed, browsing through the papers during breakfast, reading about the supposed sporting supremacy of the Germans. I realized that it must sound as if I didn't want my own country to win, but I was annoyed by the arrogance of the propaganda, which had nothing to do with true sporting spirit. Fritz preferred not to discuss my opinions in detail, staying on the safe side and trying not to spoil the visit.

Hitler, present at many competitions, largely declined to congratulate the winners; at least, I never saw him doing so. It was rumored that in this way he avoided having to shake hands with a black athlete, which would have been unavoidable given Jesse Owens's successes. Instead, so some said, he personally invited chosen athletes to private celebrations with senior Nazis. How much truth there was in these rumors, I didn't know, and I had better things to do than brood over it.

It was not even necessary actually to attend the competitions. If we weren't in the mood to make our way to the stadium, we could sit in one of the cafés at the Ku'damm and listen to the loudspeaker reports. The whole city was caught up in the Games; if we'd wanted to escape them, we would have had to stay in bed all day—not a prospect I fancied. In the evenings, we could also have gone to the pictures to see the daily newsreel, featuring the day's action from the Games, but we skipped that. We preferred to go out, throwing ourselves into the international hordes, talking, laughing, drinking, smoking, dancing. It was a dream.

The most unforgettable event of all was the women's relay. At the previous Olympics in 1932, the German women hadn't won a medal, but now, in the heats, they had broken the USA's world record of 47.0 seconds with 46.4. We were all convinced that they had the relay victory in their pocket. Hitler posed on his balcony with a triumphant grin on his face. As the starting pistol sounded, he got carried away enough to cheer, leaning over the balustrade.

The German women did indeed take the lead, which kept increasing. The whole stadium was cheering; the German spectators were beside themselves. Even I was on the German athletes' side for once—maybe because they were women. Everybody was standing, hopping with excitement. Marie Dollinger, the second-to-last runner, was in the lead by about ten meters. The last pass was to Ilse Dörffeldt. Then the unthinkable happened: Dörffeldt let the baton fall. A murmur went through the audience; *ooooh's* and *noooo's* could be heard all around. Poor woman! She was holding her head in her hands. She looked as if she couldn't believe it; she broke down in tears. Hitler slumped back into his seat, punching his knee with his fist, but even his disappointment didn't cheer me up.

I felt for Ilse Dörffeldt, who looked as if she wanted to dig herself a hole in the ground. Helen Stephens had shot past her to the finishing line, but this American victory was no triumph. Luckily, Ilse's comrades seemed to feel more solidarity than anger; at least, they took her into their arms and talked to her. I bit my lip. I had experienced the full range of emotions during the Olympic Games; what with the emotional extremes, the full use we'd made of the city's nightlife, and the time spent talking to countless strangers, by the end of the trip it felt more like two years than two weeks that I had spent in Berlin.

Having said that, the second week was less frantic than the first, as the events taking place then were less interesting to me. We saw a couple of football games and watched the high dive; the grace and elegance of that sport was a nice counterpoint to the hectic excitement of the athletics events the previous week.

I packed my bags on Sunday, August 16, and I found it easier to leave than I'd thought it would be, as I was suddenly overcome by a longing for Hamburg. All at once, I was tired of the buzzing crowds. I didn't even want to attend the closing ceremony; I just wanted to be back home. Fritz drove me all the way to Hamburg in his car. He might have had hopes for a steady relationship with me, if not more, but I blocked any movement in that direction. We had had a wonderful time in Berlin, and that time was now over. Life carried on. I needed a job, and Fritz would get over it. I really didn't want to spend my life with him. Wolfgang—that would have been different. I would have married Wolfgang on the spot. But that was not to be.

7

MARRIAGE

"What's that song?" Lutz asked, interrupting my thoughts. I surfaced from my memories, only now realizing that I had been humming Wolfgang's favorite flute melody.

"I don't know," I evaded. "Shall we have a drink to our engagement?" Lutz agreed, and we ran back to the pub where Margot and Wilhelm still sat, told them of our plans to marry, and raised our glasses. After many more drinks, Lutz and I went to bed to seal our promise. It was neither romantic nor exciting, but I didn't allow myself to dwell on that.

My mother was outraged when she heard of my plans. "How can you marry that man? You don't know him at all!"

If I'd stuck to the truth, I would have found it hard to justify my decision to her. As it was, I answered shortly, "Well, I love him!" Lutz's attractive, handsome appearance made it possible for me almost to believe it myself.

As soon as my mother accepted that we were really going ahead with it, she threw herself into the wedding preparations. A great deal of organizational talent was required, not least because food was so scarce. After all, a big celebratory meal did usually involve meat. Meat, however, like everything apart from barley and rutabaga, was strictly rationed, the allowance being 250g per person per week, and the quality was hardly ever satisfactory, to say the least.

Luckily, we had Uncle Otto, who managed to get ahold of a huge calf's tongue. Auntie Frieda, having worked as a cook for years, turned it into the finest meal of the year—tongue ragout in Madeira sauce—which meant that Mother had her hands free to organize everything else.

She arranged for the wedding to take place in a church in the Eimsbüttel area of the city. We were to be taken there in an open carriage drawn by two white horses. It was summer, the weather fine. I wore a white organza dress and Lutz a light suit. He looked marvelous, but during the journey I didn't look at him much, only at the nodding necks of the horses. The rhythm of their hooves seemed to clatter *big-mis-take-big-mis-take-big-mis-take.*

I shook myself and tried to block out my doubts; there was the church—no turning back now. Anyway, I could always get a divorce if things went wrong. With that thought, I entered the church.

The wedding ceremony was considerably delayed when the priest found out that Lutz was not a member of a church. He hadn't mentioned this before, and I stared at him in disbelief. Suddenly, a triumphant idea flashed through my mind: This is it, this is the solution. It's not going to happen after all. I hadn't reckoned with Lutz, though. In his determination, he promised the priest he would join a church as soon as we were married. The waves calmed, the storm was over, and we were soon pronounced husband and wife. The tongue ragout was consumed by about twenty guests, all family members, at our house in the Hochallee. It was all over very quickly, and suddenly I was a married woman.

Our honeymoon consisted of a week in Grömitz, during which we rarely made it out of bed. I would have preferred to go for a walk occasionally and see the sea, but Lutz's interests were quite restricted. If I managed to drag him outside, he still thought of only one thing. I constantly felt his hands all over me, and it began to seriously annoy me.

"Can't you leave me alone at least for five minutes?" I demanded, flaring up, pushing his hand off my bottom. "We've only just got out of bed!"

Lutz's reaction was rather abrupt. "What's the fuss about? You're not normally so hoity-toity! After all, you're my wife now, and there is such a thing as marital duties."

I exploded. "And what's that supposed to mean? That I've got to spread my legs every quarter of an hour? You can stick your marital duties! We're not living in the Middle Ages anymore!" Enraged, I stormed off. Great start, our honeymoon. We had our first argument, and it wasn't to be the last by a long stretch.

Back in Hamburg, we moved in with my mother to begin with while we looked for somewhere to live. It was not an easy time; Lutz and my mother constantly picked at each other. It became more than clear that they didn't get on, and I found it increasingly difficult to stay on my husband's side. The tension became unbearable. Lutz behaved very provokingly, expecting to be waited on hand and foot, and seemed to think that my mother and I were his maids. We were both infuriated by his behavior and joined forces to find a place for Lutz and me as quickly as possible.

We moved to an old-fashioned house in the Immenhof in Uhlenhorst. It was an idyllic setting, by the Kuhmühlenteich Lake and right next to the Gertruden Church. Our small, partly furnished apartment had a fairly spacious living room and an outdated dining area made of oak. The nicest thing about the apartment was the balcony off our bedroom. Unfortunately, we didn't have our own bathroom, and had to share the kitchen with the other residents of the house, too. The others turned out to be a relentlessly arguing lesbian couple whose disputes invariably ended in a fight.

To begin with, I minded these frequent quarrels; I tried to settle their arguments while being careful not to overstep the boundaries—I didn't normally poke my nose into other people's business. It took me quite a while to figure out that the two of them had a sadomasochistic relationship; they both enjoyed the continual fights. So I let them be, although I found it difficult at times to ignore their outbursts.

Lutz didn't leave me alone one single day; he seemed to be obsessed. What I had enjoyed before our marriage, since we hadn't met daily, became more and more of a nuisance. Whether I felt well or not, whether I had my period or a headache, or was simply tired, Lutz insisted on getting his pleasure, with or without my consent. Perversely, my increasingly reluctant reaction seemed only to spur him on. More often than not, he would hold me down with an iron grip and force me into intercourse.

As he never hit me, it didn't occur to me to think of what he did as rape. All I knew was that I had an ever-increasing feeling of revulsion and, ultimately, hatred toward him. *You bastard!* was all that went through my head. If I said it aloud, he reacted as if I had paid him a compliment.

As a married woman, I had finally been able to leave Krümmel, so despite the situation I found myself in, I had at least fulfilled my original goal. To stay employed, I started as a secretary in Lutz's business. He dealt with tool machinery, which he sold on, chiefly to Saxony.

In the evenings, Lutz frequently disappeared; often he didn't come home until the next day. My initial curiosity gave way to a great sense of relief at being free of him for a night, so I didn't ask much about where he went or what he was doing. However, when on one occasion he hadn't returned after several days, I did start to worry. After all, I knew about his illegal activities, if not in detail, and I wouldn't have wished the Devil himself in the hands of the Nazis.

Eventually, one evening about four days after he'd gone out, I heard a key in the lock. Lutz dragged himself into the apartment, staggering, and slumped onto the bed. He was completely disfigured, his normally handsome face so swollen that his eyes were just slits. He was covered in yellow and black bruises, with scratches and stab wounds all over his body.

I sat down next to him on the bed, shaken by his appearance. "What in heaven's name has happened?"

Lutz turned slightly to his side, which seemed to cause him enormous pain. He swore loudly. "You know exactly what's going on. Why do you ask such stupid questions?" he shouted. That was as much of an answer as I could expect.

So, I surmised, the Nazis had got him. How had he managed to get away, though? Why hadn't they locked him up or sent him off somewhere? Were they following him? Did they hope to get more information that way?

I began to speak my thoughts: "You don't think they want you to—"

"Of course they do. Do you think I'm retarded?"

I just couldn't talk to him. "If you want, I could run some errands for you," I offered, despite his harsh, dismissive demeanor.

"You must have lost your mind," he answered. "If they know about me, then you're just as much under suspicion. Why don't you think for a change!"

Shrugging, I stood up. Fine; as he wished. I'd find a way to do something. What did I need Lutz for?

"Hang on!" he commanded in his usual domineering way, unbuttoning his trousers, swearing at the pain.

I looked down on him, full of hatred. "You're not thinking . . . in your condition?"

But he had already grabbed me by the wrist and pulled me down onto the bed. "You've still got your hands, haven't you, darling?"

Our marriage turned from bad to worse. Hamburg was being heavily bombarded, particularly at nights. The Battle of Britain was over. We understood that London had not capitulated and Hitler had withdrawn his air force, so now Britain did not have to defend itself and could go on the attack. And that was exactly what they had been doing since May 1941, often sending a hundred planes at once, bombing both strategic and civilian targets.

The continual air raids and the threat of the bombs, as well as the howling sirens at night, were not without effect. We were tired and tense, shouting at each other, or not speaking at all. I never went to the cellar with Lutz. We were lucky not to get hit. Large parts of Hamburg were shattered into ruins.

On the night of July 26–27, 1942, the sirens began howling just after midnight. This time, the raid sounded worse than any I'd experienced before. For two long hours, we listened to the drone of the planes, together with the terrible sound of the antiaircraft guns and the hissing and whistling of the bombs before they hit their targets with enormous crashes.

When they eventually sounded the all-clear, I went to the window and loosened the blackout curtains to have a look outside. The sky had taken on an unreal-looking gray-orange color. Everywhere, huge fires were burning, especially toward the northeast, only perhaps one or two Underground stations away. "Barmbek's burning!" I shouted to Lutz. Suddenly, I was overcome with fear. *Mother!* What would I do if she'd been hit?

I ran to the phone. Would it be working? With shaking hands, I pulled the piece of paper on which I'd written her number out of my pocket. Lutz watched me suspiciously and asked: "And what are you planning on doing now?"

"Well, phoning my mother, of course, to see if she's all right," I answered.

"Nonsense!" Lutz said angrily, slapping the phone out of my hand. "I've told you a million times that the phone is only there for emergencies or business, so leave it!"

I was beside myself. "What's this if it's not an emergency, Lutz? She could be dead for all I know!" I picked up the receiver again.

"Which would not be the worst thing that could happen . . ." muttered Lutz, walking toward me, holding my wrist with his left hand and forcing my fingers open with his right to get at the piece of paper with the number. He tore it into tiny pieces, threw them to the floor, and pulled the phone cable out of the wall. "We'll see if you disobey my orders!" he said coldly.

I saw red. Without another word, I turned on my heel and stormed out of the apartment. First, I headed toward Schwanenwik as usual, to take the pedestrian ferry over the Alster. Then I realized how confused I was. It was still nighttime and the ferries wouldn't be running. I changed direction and ran all the way to Harvestehude, passing burning houses, the ghastly skeletons of their façades towering above me in the flaring light of the fires. There was so much rubble on the streets that I had to pick my way over and around heaps of debris.

It was almost dawn when I finally arrived in the Hochallee. The journey had never felt so long before. The last part I ran as fast as my feet could carry me. I saw the house as I shot around the corner. From afar, it looked intact, and as I got closer, I could see that it was indeed undamaged. I dashed up the stairs and into the kitchen. There was my mother, as if nothing had happened, preparing breakfast. With an enormous sense of relief, I threw my arms around her neck. I hadn't realized till that moment that not only had I been anxious about her safety, I had also simply missed her a great deal during the past few trying weeks.

After some days' refuge in her house, she sent me back to the Immenhof. Despite her dislike of Lutz and despite her own past, she was convinced that a married woman should stay with her husband. "Don't you make my mistakes," she told me. "Go and give it another try."

I looked at her for a long time without speaking. It had been great to be able to just stay at home with her for a while. Even if I didn't take the opportunity again, the fact that I'd realized I had the option did perk me up. I felt strengthened. All right, I would try again. Maybe our marriage still had a chance. I nodded and got up.

"There you are!" Lutz snorted as I entered the apartment. "Did you think you could just run off? You're not going to carry on like that. Something's wrong with you, but we can do something about that."

"What do you mean?" I asked warily.

"Well, all your belligerence toward me. You've become so difficult, and frigid as well. Before we married, you were completely different. All you wanted was a husband. As soon as you've got him, you turn into a fishwife. I know what you're missing, apart from a regular walloping. You're no good in the office anyway, so it's time you turned to what women are here for anyway. I've waited long enough. Now we're going to see if there really is something wrong with you!"

I couldn't believe it. "Children? You want us to produce children? In this day and age, when you're not sure if you'll still be alive tomorrow? You're not serious!"

"Of course I'm serious! Why do you think I married you?"

I tried to appeal to his anti-fascist attitude. "You want to hang the Mother's Cross around my neck? Lutz, either you've completely changed or I've completely misjudged you."

But Lutz was adamant. "You don't see it, do you? A better camouflage than a 'true German family' is hardly imaginable. Just think!"

So that was what this was about. I turned around to hide my face, and went to make a start on the mountain of dishes that had grown in my absence. While scrubbing the crusted food from the plates, I took stock. If I was quite honest with myself, I had married for purely selfish reasons. Why, then, did it hurt me to know that Lutz had done the same? Was it simply injured vanity, or was I upset by my own foolishness in having married this man?

He was a good-looking Resistance fighter—how could it have gone so wrong? Weren't all those who stood on the same side desperately trying to fight the system, united? I scraped agitatedly

at a burned pan, as if I was trying not to clean the object but to
scrub away my own naiveté. Behind me, the door shut with a bang.

What had I imagined? That through Lutz I would gain access
to circles where people met at night, planning sabotage against the
Nazis? That I would meet exciting young men and women hatch-
ing thrilling plans, that more and more daring missions would be
entrusted to me, that my life would be bristling with challenges?
I probably had secretly hoped I'd be celebrated as a heroine one
day. Gretel and Lutz, the infamous, attractive couple, admired by
the crowds. Instead, here I stood in the kitchen, scrubbing dishes
for a sadistic, egotistical, chauvinistic, sex-obsessed pig.

When Lutz returned, he threw a coat at me and led me out of
the house. My questions were answered only by harsh remarks.
He pointed out that he'd told me already that something was
wrong with me. He was dragging me to a doctor to get to the
root of my inability to conceive, and to arrange help. I was curious myself as to why I had never fallen pregnant, never having
taken precautions, so I didn't object to the examination. The
doctor, who bustled around in his white coat, trying to create
an impression of cleanliness and vigor, discovered that there
was a problem with the position of my cervix and suggested
an operation. I listened to Lutz's steps as he paced impatiently
up and down outside the consulting room, looked the doctor
in the eyes, and said, "Please, take the money and just don't do
anything. Our marriage won't last. Don't tell my husband about
it, though!"

It was sheer luck that I got my way, because medical staff in
the German Reich were obliged to make their patients' fertility
a priority. Lutz would never learn that he could have fathered
a child by me had I wanted it. In my mind, however, we were
already separated; it was just a matter of making my getaway.

Three times, I fled to my mother; three times, she persuaded
me to go back and try again. The fourth time, I left for good,
with all my things. In retrospect, the incident that led to the

final separation wasn't even that extreme. Lutz had been abusive, but not any more so than usual. He had tried to throw a vase at me, and I'd ducked just in time. Half an hour later, I'd already forgotten what the argument was about. It was as insignificant as always.

I went straight to the phone and asked the operator for a moving company. "Come to Immenhof 5 at ten o'clock in the morning. I'm leaving my husband." During the night, I locked myself in the bedroom after packing everything that wasn't rented with the apartment. For Lutz, I left a spoon, a knife, and a cup—nothing else. Throughout the night, he raged like a lunatic. He screamed and thundered his fists on the door, but suddenly, his behavior didn't frighten me anymore. Since I'd taken steps to leave, a certain calm had come over me. I even thought idly about the lesbian couple in the other apartment, wondering if they thought we were taking after them.

In the morning, I unlocked the door at two minutes to ten, walked past my still-raging husband to the door, and let the removal men in. I knew that Lutz wouldn't dare to attack them while they were doing their job. In his situation, he couldn't risk having anything to do with the police. Powerless, his hoarse attempts to intimidate were his only weapons, but I was unperturbed. "Do ignore that maniac, please," I told the movers. "All this is going with me."

When I'd moved to the Immenhof, my mother had rented out my old bedroom straightaway. Because of the houses damaged and destroyed in the air raids, the state ensured that all possible accommodation was used. Those made homeless had to be squeezed into properties that were still intact. Accommodation was allocated by the council, so it was a lottery; you had no choice about who came to share your life with you. The only space available for me at home now was the loft, and I took to it at once, loving the tiny window and the steeply sloping ceiling. As soon as my furniture was installed, I came down to the kitchen and drank a toast with my mother. We emptied two bottles of wine, talked and laughed, and I felt wonderful.

Lutz did not give up easily, though. Almost daily, he came to the Hochallee to shout slander and abuse from the road. I was a whore, frigid, a lazy bitch, a calculating cheat . . . the accusations were endless. "I know how you're earning your money!" he shouted, his voice loud and clear in the street. "And what do they pay you, your customers? Do they pay in kind or in hard currency? No wonder your own husband is too much for you when that's your business!" This seemed to be his explanation for my loss of interest in our sex life. He hadn't reflected at all on his own conduct, that much was obvious. It could only be my fault, because of my abnormality, that I had left him.

As much as I tried not to listen, I couldn't escape the feeling of being under siege. I caught myself standing by the window, searching the street for a sign of him. If I saw a shadow in the distance, I would freeze, hurriedly stepping back. However, I did manage not to respond. Not once did I shout any form of abuse back at him. Eventually, the nosy woman from downstairs, Frau Gernot, proved herself useful for the first time since I'd known her. Tired of the constant disruption, she bent out of the window and threatened Lutz with the police, so that every time she poked her head around the curtain, he would instantly disappear.

His "visits" became less frequent, but his slander had potential consequences. One of his accusations, shouted out at the top of his voice, was that my mother received black-market meat from her lover, which was true. Although almost everyone got something or other from the black market, it was nevertheless highly dangerous to be caught, as you would be denounced as a traitor to your people.

"We've got to be cautious for the next few weeks," my mother warned me. "As long as we don't throw that horrible stuff we get on rations in our own bin where they can find it . . . just lob it into a public one when you're out and about." I nodded.

A common way of identifying black-market dealers or customers was to search their bins. If there was anything edible there,
the inhabitants had evidently found a different source of supply.
Those who bought food only on rations would not be so wasteful
as to throw anything away.

And yet, despite the efforts of the authorities, the black market
blossomed, and it wasn't long before I was right in the thick of
it. It all started with Herr Mengel's tinned fish. At first, I gave
some of the smoked herrings that he brought back from work to
acquaintances, feeling I should share. As a thank-you, I usually
got something back: a vegetable here, some home-baked bread
there, and if I was lucky, an egg.

I got quite excited about my swapping, until I discovered that
most of my friends could hardly stomach any more of the fish.
"God, Gretel," sighed Frau Petersen, Mother's seamstress, "my
husband and I cannot possibly eat another smoked herring for at
least a fortnight, and we have nothing else in the house. Don't you
have a bit of meat for a change?" I promised to have a look around.

After racking my brains, I wondered if maybe Willi Calsen
could be of help. He was a farmer's son, and I liked his honest,
straightforward ways. He worked in the clothing industry, and
I'd met him when I'd asked for work in his fashion boutique.
Occasionally, he let me help out and paid me for it, and slowly
a friendship had developed between us.

I discussed the problem with Willi, and we met that very
evening to view his cache of food. Overjoyed, I decided on cutlets
and some sausages, gave him a large amount of money, and went
to call at the Petersens' house. "Was it meat that you asked for?"
I said, dangling my bag under Frau Petersen's nose and grinning.

Her jaw dropped. "You're not saying . . . come in, quick!" She
was completely beside herself. "Now what can I give you for that?"
she asked. "Hang on . . ."

After a while, she came back from the cellar with a basket of
bottled plums and pears. She explained that her aunt lived in Altes

Land, the great fruit-growing area. I took the basket gratefully and headed off with a plan. I already knew somebody who would bend over backwards to get hold of some bottled fruit.

Before long, I knew the game. When you swapped, you could get hold of anything, and if you swapped cleverly, you could earn a fortune. If you had bacon, you could get eggs. If you had eggs, you could get cheese. Some people paid in kind, most with money. My mother was terrified that I might get caught, but as she did quite well out of my business, she held back on critical remarks and turned a blind eye as I got more involved in it.

8

THE BLACK MARKET

1942: At the Wannsee Conference, the "final solution of the Jewish question" is outlined to the Nazi leadership. The systematic murder of Jews in the death camps begins.

Cologne is largely destroyed by British air raids. The German 6th Army is encircled by Soviet troops at Stalingrad.

Hamburg issues 65 air-raid warnings and is the target of 15 attacks. More than 2,000 inhabitants lose their lives or are injured. The worst bombing attack so far happens in July, when almost 70,000 incendiary bombs leave 15,000 homeless.

My little attic room became more and more like a storeroom. I liked things in tins and jars best, as I didn't have to get rid of them immediately but could wait until it suited me. Fresh food, of course, had to be moved on without delay, and even then the strangest smells sometimes emanated from under my bed.

My mother's new lodger, bombed out and sent to live with us, was not uninterested in the goings-on. One afternoon, he knocked on my door and I let him in without having hidden my produce. Leaning on the door frame, both hands in his pockets, he took in the tins and packages. "Could you use schnapps as well?" he asked.

I examined him closely. Dark curly hair, nice friendly brown eyes—just how I imagined Italian men to look. I liked what I saw. "Depends. I'll have to see," was my reply.

To my surprise, he turned and left, but he soon came back with a strangely shaped brown bottle, from which he poured some clear schnapps into two test tubes. He offered me one of them, saying, "You can call me Kuddel. That's what my friends call me."

Without hesitation, I downed the contents of the test tube, which burned my throat. "Not bad!" I coughed, and Kuddel laughed.

We instantly became the best of friends. Kuddel was roughly my age, came from south Germany, and had not been called up because he'd had polio as a child and his leg was stiff from the hip down. He worked as a chemistry lab assistant at Hamburg University. That was where he secretly distilled the schnapps. After we'd been chatting for a while, I noticed him repeatedly looking at his watch, getting fidgety. "Do you have an appointment?" I asked curiously.

"Not exactly. I mean, not one that I'd have to leave the house for," Kuddel answered, glancing at my little wireless on the shelf.

"Good!" I said. "Come on!" I stuck the radio under my arm, climbed into bed, and lifted the covers invitingly.

Kuddel scrambled in and I threw the quilt over us. After a while, we heard it clearly, even though the reception wasn't too great. "Germany calling! Germany calling!" sounded from the speaker. "Not that one!" Kuddel raged. "That's the Nazis!"

"I know, I know. It's okay. Just wait." Soon, I had the BBC news. We lay still and listened. Sometimes the news was followed by a program called *War Commentary*, which kept us up-to-date with the news from the front lines and enabled us to work out what was really happening—which was generally far removed from what the propagandist German programs told us. We could also find out when the British were planning to drop more pamphlets from airplanes, so that we could be prepared to pick them up.

It was highly dangerous to pick up these pamphlets, let alone be seen reading them. If you knew in advance that they were to be distributed, though, you could wear a coat with big pockets or take a shopping basket that wasn't open or see-through so you could quickly pick up a leaflet and hide it. Back at home, unobserved, you could read what was happening on the front lines and then pass the information on to reliable friends. Sometimes the pamphlets gave quite different statistics from our German newspapers, stating how many bombs had fallen on German cities and giving their weights in tons and kilograms, which lent credibility. Usually, the messages ended with encouraging sentences like "It won't last much longer!" or "Your hopes will soon be heard!"

I told Kuddel about my marriage, and he suggested I should hurry with my divorce, even if it meant I'd have to work wherever I was sent again. I agreed. In fact, by this time, even married women were legally obliged to work if they did not have children, so it would be of no use to me to stay married to Lutz on paper. I might as well be officially free again.

An acquaintance had recommended a solicitor from Wansbek who I was told would be good, quick, and successful. I made my way to his office to find a sympathetic, understanding man in middle age. After I'd told him in detail about my marriage, we carried on talking about more interesting topics. We liked each other and each found the other physically attractive. I realized that I was falling back into my old ways. I flirted and laughed, threw my scruples to the wind, and acted as I had before my marriage, spontaneously deciding to sleep with him and enjoying myself enthusiastically.

He gave my case priority, refused any form of payment, and in no time I was a divorced woman without even having had to appear in court. I kept Lutz's surname, Öhlgart, as everyone had started calling me "Öle" instead of Gretel, and I'd grown used to it. I also thought of the changed name as a part of my life and history.

"Whether I made a mistake or not, after all I did marry, and I don't mind acknowledging that," I explained to Kuddel one evening.

"There aren't any mistakes anyway," he said wisely, "just experiences."

We had got the test tubes out again, philosophizing until, as so often, an air raid tore us from our conversation. Kuddel usually stayed in the house, out of a fatalistic attitude more than laziness. "You can get hit anywhere, here or there, and particularly on your way between them!" he said. "But you run off before you wet your pants!" I jumped up, snatched my overnight bag, which I always kept packed and ready, and raced down the stairs.

My mother was already waiting for me, holding the cellar door open and calling me impatiently, but I ran past her. I wasn't in the mood to spend hours in a confined space with our lodgers. Experience had taught me that it could be mind-numbingly tedious. "I'll go to the public shelter with Ilse," I shouted as I ran out the door.

Ilse had her arms full with children and bags, as I knew she would. I opened my arms to take the little one from her and we ran in a stream of people to a nearby street called Jungfrauenthal. There, beneath an elegant four-story block of apartments, were huge cellars that were open for the public to use during air raids.

The lobby looked grand with its tiled floors and the beautiful cast-iron lift next to the stairs that led us down to the cellars. The shelter was quite well equipped; it even had some beds, which were usually allocated to children. The best places were taken by the inhabitants of the apartments. After that, it worked on a first-come, first-served basis. Normally, we found a place somewhere in the middle. The beds always went first, then the corners, and finally the walls, so we often had to make do with just a bit of space on the concrete floor.

Ilse spread out a woolen blanket to get the children comfortable. This time, we hadn't made it in time to get them a bed. She and I sat back to back, so that we could at least lean against each other, nursing the children's heads in our laps. The atmosphere wasn't too bad, as we all felt relatively safe down there. No one had any inhibitions about sleeping next to complete strangers. We were all in the same boat, and all constantly overtired because of the relentless bombing raids and disrupted nights. Usually, the alarm sounded late at night. We were lucky if it started before ten o'clock and we were not yet in bed. Often enough, though, it howled us out of sleep, sometimes at two or three in the morning. In their haste to get to safety, most people dressed hurriedly, sometimes running down to the shelter in their nightclothes.

Sighing, I looked around. Children cried and their mothers tried to calm them down. An impertinent old man stared at us from a distance, as if he was trying to catch a glimpse up my skirt.

"The cellar is crammed full again," I commented over my shoulder.

"How long do you think it'll last this time?" Ilse asked. "Hopefully only a couple of hours, so I'll get at least some sleep."

"As long as it doesn't start up again once you're tucked up in bed. That's the worst," I answered.

"Hmmm, especially after half an hour . . ." Ilse's head fell onto her chest. She had fallen asleep mid-sentence.

She was a good-looking woman, blue-eyed with dark blonde hair, very tall and leggy. She was not sporty, rather feminine, which was reflected in her dress sense—all frills and jewelery from top to toe. Men found her stunning, and she in turn loved men. They lined up to visit her at home, and probably not to play Ludo. She didn't seem to worry that she was married, but who was to say what agreement she might have with her husband? Anyway, it was none of my business, I told myself. I had great conversations with Ilse. She was cultured, kind, and witty. I liked her.

I stroked the sleeping head of little Helmut. He was a cute child who had only recently started to walk. I really liked him a lot. Watching him sleep helped me to forget my own anxiety and fear. Nonetheless, I planned to shelter somewhere different during the next air raid, to get away from this cramped cellar—maybe in the cellar of the Catholic church on the other side of our house.

The following night, I didn't forget my plan. I was awake and still fully clothed when the sirens began. When I had shot past my mother and the cellar door, I looked out for Ilse, but couldn't spot her. Maybe this time she'd gone to the public bunker earlier to get a better place and some sleep. The thought eased my conscience, and I headed for the church.

The St. Elisabethkirche was a modern building in the classic style of the '20s, built from big sandstone bricks and with the pointed copper roof on the bell tower that was typical of Hamburg churches. Around the heavy oak door were figures chiseled into the stone, but otherwise the building was simple and plain, which I felt made a refreshing change for a Catholic church.

Surprisingly, the cellar was situated underneath the parsonage, an old villa, rather than below the church itself. It wasn't a designated public shelter, but the priest, Monsignor Bram, welcomed anyone who needed a refuge with open arms. I had been there a few times before. I liked the atmosphere; the people seemed more interesting than those at Jungfrauenthal, and it wasn't as overcrowded.

I hurried up the curved stone steps and through the paneled entrance hall, with its beautiful parquet floor, toward the cellar door. Monsignor Bram was already down there, involved in a lively conversation with a group of men in front of a niche with a built-in wine rack. When he saw me, he smiled and gave me a friendly nod before turning back to his group.

The others sat on the old pieces of furniture stored in the cellar or stood in small groups together, talking in subdued voices. The priest himself was a picture of kindness with his bald head, pink skin, glasses, and gentle eyes. Like the host at a party, he looked after everyone's needs, whether it was a place to sit, something to eat, or simply the company of others.

I got talking to someone but couldn't shake off a thought that had crossed my mind before. As during my previous visits, I didn't recognize a single face apart from Bram's, and I was quite good at remembering people. Their conversations often indicated that these were well-educated and interesting people, doctors, lawyers, and the like. Deep in thought, I looked around until my eyes met those of the priest, who considered me just as thoughtfully.

As soon as the all-clear sounded, he came toward me. "Why don't you join me for a glass of wine upstairs?" he asked me in his usual friendly voice. I followed him up, curious about what he wanted to discuss with me.

"You're not particularly religious, are you?" asked Bram, pouring red wine into a glass. I shook my head. "It's not what really matters, anyway, my child. What's more important is your attitude. You're not in the Party or interested in joining them?"

I burst out, "Is it that obvious?"

Bram smiled. "I meet a lot of people. You learn to judge these things. Let's be open with each other—you want to ask me something, don't you?"

Out with it, Gretel, I told myself; if not, you'll choke with curiosity. "Why do I never see the same people down there? I mean, it's always interesting and I have some really good conversations, but I do ask myself why I never meet the same person twice," I blurted out.

"I can't say much about it, only one thing: The people you see here are on the run. They hide here for a night, there for a day, until at last they have made it and left Germany behind. If they stay, they won't survive, not in these times." He took a mouthful of wine and rolled it in his mouth, gauging my reaction, looking calmly at me. My face must have mirrored my thoughts, for Bram asked, "Do you want to help us?"

Did I want to? What a question! Of course I wanted to help. For so long I had wished to do something useful, considering myself a coward, powerless and weak. How I had badgered Lutz to give me a task, but all he had wanted me to do was immerse myself in the role of a housewife and mother so that he'd have the perfect camouflage for his own actions. Yes, I'd torn down posters, but I felt that in truth I hadn't done a thing to help—nothing. "What can I do?" I replied.

Bram looked delighted by my enthusiasm. "The biggest problem is the organization of food," he replied earnestly. "Do you think you could help us with that?"

I looked him in the eye. "You bet!"

Had he learned about my black-market activities? If so, he didn't say. But he must have gathered something, otherwise he wouldn't have asked. It was highly dangerous for him to share his secret with others. Surely he wouldn't have risked it if he hadn't been certain that I would be able to help.

"Where do they all come from?" I couldn't help asking. "And where are they off to next?"

"It's better if you don't ask. I don't know much myself. But where we can, we ought to do something to help those in need. That's our duty before God. If you feed someone, give them shelter, pass on information for him, it may seem a small thing to you. But when we help others in this way, we are like a link in a chain."

I would remember his words for a long time. How I admired Bram for his zeal! On my way home, I planned feverishly. What could I get ahold of? The people in the cellar had no ration books, of course, if they were on the run. That meant they didn't even have bread, flour, potatoes—nothing at all.

The next morning, I went straight to Willi Calsen. "Listen, I need a lot of meat. What do you have most of at the moment?"

Willi didn't seem to find my inquiry strange, and he didn't ask any questions. "I've got a calf's tongue—would that do?"

I didn't hesitate. "Okay. You'll either get money for it or a bucket of condensed milk."

"I won't be able to move a whole bucket," Willi pondered, "and I'm not bothered about money. But if you don't have anything else at the moment, fine."

At home, I unpacked the enormous calf's tongue under the unbelieving eyes of my mother and started to prepare it. "Not like that!" she scolded me. "You've got to cook it first before you can skin it. What do you want with all that meat anyway?"

As grateful as I was for her help, I refused to answer that. "Don't worry, Mother. I've got my reasons."

She must have felt like I did when Lutz gave me such answers, but it was for her own protection. My mother worried first and foremost, as did most people in these times, about the survival of family and friends. She wouldn't have denied help to a stranger who asked her for it, but she wouldn't risk anything of her own accord, especially not if it could have fatal consequences. "Just be careful, child," she told me. "You'll bring us all down if you don't watch out."

For me, it felt wonderfully exhilarating, reckless, and heroic to do something against the hateful regime. The thought of being a part of saving people's lives gave me an enormous feeling of pride, mixed with the thrill of not getting caught, of having to plan carefully—it was the ultimate challenge. I was twenty-six, feeling invulnerable, and I shook off any worries about the danger that came with it.

Monsignor Bram helped me not to become arrogant with the sense of my own heroism. The following night, the air raid I had hoped for came, giving me the opportunity to take the calf's tongue, wrapped in a blanket, to the parsonage. I could already picture the looks on the faces of the fugitives when I unwrapped my parcel. Bram led me in, cut up the tongue without delay, handed slices to the people, and took me to one side.

"You have helped us a lot, and it would be great if you could get food for us on a regular basis. You can imagine how grateful we are. But think of the word of the Lord when He says, 'Don't let the right hand know what the left is doing.' That's advice with a double meaning for us. First, nobody needs to know about it; second, beware of pride and self-importance. We are all just tools of the Lord."

I nodded guiltily, and he took my hands in his, rubbing them kindly. Then he got up to bring the others some bread and wine. The bread was pitifully crumbly, baked from rough corn flour, falling to pieces when sliced. The wine was better. Bram took it from one of the niches in the cellar. It had probably been stored there for years, kept for a special occasion.

I was already planning the next delivery. I felt sure that Herr Mengel's smoked herrings would finally find grateful customers. And if the bucket of condensed milk was poured into jam jars (an ideal job for my mother), I could swap them for some tinned meat.

9

DR. MANES

My mother wasn't exactly delighted that I'd stepped up my "business," but she didn't refuse to help me either. Although she warned me to be careful, she did enjoy the things that I managed to get for her on the black market. It was fantastic to rediscover the taste of real coffee or to hold half a dozen eggs in your hands. Sometimes it was hard not to invite friends and family to a party when you got ahold of something really good. However, one had to resist the temptation, because everyone would have been suspicious right away.

I found it particularly difficult to wait patiently to find customers when I managed to obtain a whole wheel of Roquefort cheese. I had to cut the cheese up and wrap the pieces in newspaper. Because of its smell, I couldn't take it out of my room until I knew I had customers for it. For about a week, I put up with the most terrible smell around my bed, about which Kuddel, naturally, made some cheeky remarks.

One night, when I had just crawled back to bed after the all-clear sirens, falling asleep immediately, I was suddenly torn out of my dreams by a strange noise. At first, I tried to ignore it, exhausted as I was, but it kept going on, and I gradually recognized the sound for what it was. Someone was throwing stones at my loft window. Who could it be, and what could they want at this time of night?

I sneaked to the window, loosened the blackout curtain, and looked from the side of the window down onto the street, but I couldn't make out more than a faint shadow, someone darting back to the shelter of a tree. It couldn't be Lutz, I thought; he was finally leaving me alone. Ilse? No, she would knock at the door if she needed my help. It had to be somebody else, someone who needed to hide—from my mother, our lodgers, or even the police.

Cautiously, I opened the window a little and stuck my head out. A figure materialized out of the shadow of the tree and hurried underneath my window. "Gretel?" came a hushed, familiar voice.

"Wait, I'm coming down," I whispered, before tiptoeing downstairs and opening the door. No one was to be seen. Had I dreamed it? Then, as I stepped out—barefoot, in my nightie—to have a look around, the figure appeared once more from the shadow of the tree. "Dr. Manes!" I breathed, but stopped myself instantly, pressing my hand over my mouth, afraid of attracting the attention of our block warden, Frau Gernot. "Quick! Come in!" I whispered.

We sneaked soundlessly upstairs to my room. I carefully closed the door behind me, turning the key just in case before leading our old family doctor to my bed so that he could sit down. He was almost unrecognizable. He looked completely exhausted, his hair had turned snow white, and his breathing was labored. "What's happened?" I asked.

He just shook his head, buried his face in his hands, ran them through his hair, and stared at the floor. I knew that he wouldn't have come to me in the middle of the night without a good reason. Something terrible must have happened, and I wasn't sure if I wanted to hear about it. "If only I had listened to my son," was all he said, murmuring that one sentence over and over. "If only I had listened."

I stood up, put a hand on his shoulder, and offered him a cup of tea. Had he even heard my question? He looked at me without seeing me. I slipped out of the door, crept as quietly as I could down to the kitchen, and returned after a while with a cup of hot herbal tea and a slice of bread and cheese. I had to literally press it into his hands before he surfaced from his trance.

"I'm so sorry, child," he said. "I think it's the feeling of being safe for a moment."

I feared the worst. "You're on the run, aren't you?"

Dr. Manes nodded sadly. "I didn't believe what my son predicted. They won't hurt me, I told him all the time; I'm a respected GP, I fought in the Great War, all for the German Reich. But no—I'm just a Jew, so off with me and with all the others. And nobody can do anything about it. Cattle wagons! Cattle wagons! Maybe they're all dead by now!"

Dr. Manes was a kind, intelligent man. He was not very tall, rather a little stocky. His hair, until recently streaked with gray, was now completely white, and his eyes behind his steel-rimmed spectacles strangely expressionless. It wasn't like him to speak so confusedly. He must have been in a deep state of shock. Cautiously, I began to try to find out what had happened. "What cattle wagons? What have they done? Do you want to talk about it?"

"They put us in cattle wagons, like cows or sheep. Those who weren't quick enough jumping in were shot and then thrown in. There were far too many of us, with nothing to eat, no sanitary facilities, not even seats. We weren't allowed to take anything with us. All we had was the clothes we were wearing. We didn't even have water. Then they locked the doors. We couldn't see anything. It was dark inside. The only light was what came through the cracks in the wood. When the train jerked or braked, we fell all over each other. There wasn't enough space to sleep."

"That's impossible!" I exclaimed.

Dr. Manes gazed at me. "You don't believe me? I probably wouldn't have believed it myself if someone had told me."

Of course I believed him, as horrendous as his story was. The Nazis were capable of anything. If anyone doubted that, all they needed to do was look at the propaganda papers like *Der Stürmer* and *Der Angriff.* They were drenched in hatred and spite, both the illustrations and the articles, reflecting the brutality with which the Nazis treated the Jewish population. "Where were they taking you in these wagons?" I asked.

"Somewhere in the east, a camp of some sort. They didn't tell us a thing. They just came and ordered us to go with them. First, we were taken to a sort of collection point in Vierlande, a camp. Some of us had been in quite a few other camps; the conditions are dreadful. They said that they only wanted people who are fit to work; what they're planning to do with the others, I dare not imagine."

"They wouldn't . . ."

"Of course they would! They know no mercy. I won't forget those faces for the rest of my life."

I shivered. Spontaneously, I jumped up and hugged Dr. Manes. "God, I'm so glad you're here! How did you escape from the wagon?"

"The train had stopped again, and some of us rattled at the door. Somehow, the locks must have come loose and we managed to ram it open. The train started to move again as the first man jumped. I was right by the door, so I threw myself out as well. How many got away, I don't know. We just ran as fast as we could."

Dr. Manes had walked the rest of the night to get back to Hamburg. He oriented himself by the train tracks, traveling in the opposite direction from the transport he had been on, being careful not to be seen. When he arrived back in Hamburg, he ducked from doorway to doorway. "I couldn't think of anyone else to go to. All my friends have gone, and you are the only 'Aryan' who dared even to speak to me. What happens now, I don't know. You'll have hell to pay if they find me here. I'd better be on my way."

"That's out of the question!" I cried out. I felt so angry to think of what he'd been put through. "I'll think of something. I've got some connections. Something will turn up. First, though, we've got to hide you. It's getting light outside." The dark crack in the blackout curtains was starting to turn gray. "Please come with me. It won't be the height of luxury, but at least we'll have you safe for the time being."

I took him to our coal cellar. The other cellar served as our air-raid shelter and was therefore out of the question. Quickly, I sneaked upstairs to fetch some more food. I took it down to the doctor together with some woolen blankets and a jug of water.

"Child—" he began, but I didn't let him finish.

"I don't want to hear anything. Please don't worry."

As I hurried back up the stairs to get a cushion, a candle, and maybe a book or something, I bumped into my mother in the corridor.

"What are you doing up so early?"

I stood as if turned to stone. "I . . . I was hungry, so I woke up. I was just about to make breakfast."

I couldn't have sounded very convincing, as my mother pushed past me, shaking her head. "If it's anything to do with your 'business,' I don't want to know. One day you'll get taken, and it'll be for that!" she warned me.

Best to retreat, I reflected.

"I thought you were hungry?" she called after me as I went up the stairs.

"I could eat a horse! I'm just going to get changed!"

I was on edge, thinking about Dr. Manes and how I could help him. It was obvious that I had to confide in Monsignor Bram, but could I wait until the next air raid? Eventually, I came to the conclusion that I had to visit the St. Elisabethkirche straightaway.

I marched in and sat down on one of the benches at the back, hoping Monsignor Bram would appear before long. To begin with, I was on tenterhooks, fidgety and anxious. Then I calmed down, taking in the atmosphere. It was so peaceful and quiet, a true refuge from the chaotic world outside. I wasn't a believer, but as I stared at

the altar in front of me, I imagined that there must be some kind
of higher power. If I'd been religious, I might have believed that my
prayers to be able to contribute something to the Resistance had
finally been heard. I watched an elderly lady kneeling in a pew in
the middle of the church, her hands clasped and her lips moving
relentlessly. I wished I too could pray; but then, maybe my thoughts,
hopes, and wishes were not so different from prayers anyway.

I must have fallen asleep. I woke suddenly, my neck hurting.
I didn't know how long I'd been there. I could see somebody
moving around at the front of the church. I got up, stretched,
and walked slowly toward the altar. I was in luck. It was Monsignor Bram, putting new candles into the holders. He looked
up and saw me. Whether it was the fact that I didn't normally
visit the church or the look in my eyes, I don't know, but he
knew at once that something was up, and that I needed to talk
to him. He came toward me, saying, "I'm glad you're finally
ready for confession." For a moment, I was slightly baffled, but
I caught on. I followed him and sat down in the confessional.

"Monsignor, I have someone I need to protect, just like you!
In our coal cellar. He escaped from a transport and now I don't
know what to do next to help him. Shall I bring him to you
tonight?"

Pastor Bram cleared his throat. "No, don't do that; that's too
dangerous. Don't do anything. Leave it to me. Tell him to be ready
to go and leave the door open at night. It could be that nothing happens tonight. It may be tomorrow. How do you get from
your front door to the coal cellar?" I explained which door was
the right one. "Does anyone else know about it? Your mother?"

"No, no one but me."

"That's good. You mustn't tell anyone. That's very important.
Don't worry, we'll try everything we can. Now go back and act
as if everything is normal."

I felt ecstatic with relief. However, as I had just come out of
the confessional, I tried to cast down my eyes and walk with

dignity out of the church. Even here, you could be observed, I reminded myself. Spies aren't prevented from entering churches.

Our doctor would escape, I knew it; I felt that all I needed to do was believe strongly that things would turn out well in the end. No qualms now, I told myself; follow Bram's example of discretion and nothing will happen to Dr. Manes. The priest hadn't asked any questions, no who, why, or where. You can learn a lot from this man, I thought, determined not to tell even Kuddel about the situation.

Back home, my mother sent me shopping. She gave me the ration cards and I prepared for a long day. In fact, I was already a little too late—the baker surely wouldn't have any more bread. However, we had to be seen to line up like everybody else. For black-market dealers, the daily trudge around the shops wasn't simply to get food, but also a necessary deception. And, after all, we didn't get everything we needed from my bartering. What you could get that way was, whispered hints and rumors aside, unpredictable.

About four and a half hours later, I returned home. Most people started to line up before dawn; if you had a grandmother or young children, they would be sent out to line up, as they were less sorely missed at home. Some would bring something to sit on—an old piano stool or just a wooden box—so they didn't have to stand all day long. My legs were aching by the time I got home, and I flung myself gratefully onto a kitchen chair.

"What did you get?" my mother inquired. I showed her my pathetic haul: a bunch of carrots so soft that you could bend them in half without breaking them, an onion, a tiny pat of butter, and a stone-hard piece of crumbly bread. "Don't worry," I promised, when I saw her disappointed face, "I'll go again later." She knew that I meant I would get something through my contacts. With a sigh, she started to prepare the vegetables, cutting out the rotten bits first.

I went back out, making my way to the vegetable market where I had started to help out. If I gave a hand for a couple of hours, I could usually take home more than we'd eat ourselves, and the produce was at least fresh. On the way back, I was able to swap some for other things. If I was lucky, I'd get cigarettes. They were in great demand and useful to exchange for more-unusual items. Often, I was simply given money for them. For us and the refugees in the church, I kept two cauliflowers, three bunches of carrots, and a few leeks; the rest I disposed of by calling in at an acquaintance's house "for coffee."

In the evening, I waited impatiently for the house to go to sleep. Unsettled, I took up a book only to put it away again. I tried to count the money I had accumulated on the black market, carelessly stuffed into my pillowcase, but after the third attempt I gave that up as well. Eventually, I had a better idea. I went through my wardrobe looking for clothes that a man could wear. The only trousers I owned were too long and tight; my blouses were too feminine, and the jackets were unsuitable too. I went to pay Kuddel a visit.

"Hey, you're after some schnapps, are you?" he asked good-humoredly, but I just pulled the door closed behind me and blurted out, "I need some trousers, Kuddel, and a clean shirt. Could you give me some underwear too, and some socks?"

Kuddel knew to expect the unexpected from me, but this did confuse him a little. "I don't think you'd get much for them on the market . . . Just look at my clothes. You can't offer those to anyone, I shouldn't have thought!"

Without answering, I began rummaging in his drawers and held a couple of items up. "Can you spare these?"

"Sure!" laughed Kuddel. "They'll suit you just fine! Here, have the long johns, too. And hang on . . ."

We had a lot of fun sorting out clothes. As I was obviously not prepared to explain what it was all about, Kuddel didn't ask.

I appreciated it. Like Bram, he understood that one didn't ask any more questions than strictly necessary.

By the time we'd finished, I felt I'd waited long enough. It was safe to assume that everyone else was fast asleep. I prayed that the sirens wouldn't sound while I was going about my business. Quickly, I stuffed the clothes into my mother's shopping bag and heated some of that night's soup on the stove. The biggest challenge was not to rattle the crockery. Finally, I sneaked down into the coal cellar, the bag on one arm and the food in the other. This time, I had remembered to bring a candle too.

"Dr. Manes!" I whispered into the dark, hoping not to make him jump.

"Gretel! How kind of you to come!" He sounded relieved.

"God, it must have been awful to stay down here the whole time without any light or any idea of the time. Are you all right? Did you manage to sleep?"

"I slept like a log. I finally felt safe for a while. Don't worry about me. I listened to the noises of the house and knew that night had come when it all went quiet."

I gave him the soup before it got cold, along with a half-full bottle of wine I had found in the kitchen. While he ate, I showed him Kuddel's clothes, telling him about the laugh we had had choosing them in an attempt to cheer him up. Dr. Manes took them gratefully, and I could even make out a hint of a smile on his drawn face.

Then I told him about the goings-on in the church next door, my conversation with Monsignor Bram, and that someone would come to fetch him.

"You are 100 percent sure that this man is trustworthy?" he asked.

I could have been quite offended by the question, but of course I had not suffered a fraction of what he had lived through in the last weeks, and I understood his cautiousness. "Yes, 100 percent!"

I assured him. "You can trust Bram with your life. The only thing is, we don't know when exactly they will come."

I suddenly remembered something. "The door! Damn it! I should have unlocked the door. Wait, I've got to go upstairs quickly. How could I forget?" Like the wind, I flew up the steep steps, unlocked the front door, and tiptoed back down. I hoped I would wake up before the others, so no one would become suspicious about the open door. I was exhausted from lack of sleep, and there would probably be an air-raid alarm again. Every hour's sleep was precious, but I didn't want to leave Dr. Manes on his own. He had been down here all day without a soul to keep him company. I hadn't reckoned on him, though. After all, he was our family doctor. Maybe he saw me suppressing a yawn, or perhaps he just noticed how tired I looked, but he said, "Time for bed now, young lady! Thank you so much for all you've done for me. I won't ever forget it."

Moved, I retired to my bed. When the alarm sounded at half past three, I grabbed my bag, in which I'd packed vegetables and bread, and ran over to the parsonage. Ilse must have been starting to wonder why I never went with her to the public shelter anymore, so I planned to join her at the Jungfrauenthal shelter next time.

That's what I did when the sirens sounded the following night. I'd brought Dr. Manes some food again earlier, and we'd had a conversation about his hopes of joining his son one day in Johannesburg. It was nice to talk about South Africa, something different from the usual wartime topics. In his letters, Dr. Manes's son had given the impression that he was doing quite well. His tie factory was going strong, the scenery was absolutely stunning, and he couldn't wait for his father to leave the hated German Reich and move in with him. "I don't need any persuading now," sighed our doctor. "I've finally realized how right he was."

When the sirens began to howl again, I wanted to stay and carry on talking, but Dr. Manes shooed me upstairs. "Quick, your mother will get worried if she doesn't see you!" He was right, of course. I pressed his arm and flew up the stairs, just in time before the others appeared. My mother tried to insist that I stay in the house for once, but I convinced her that Ilse needed my help with the little ones. This time, I was able to get some sleep in the shelter, and after the all-clear sounded I stayed until morning. Ilse tended to do that quite often; it was too much for the children to be carried to and fro during the night.

The next evening, I was looking forward to continuing my conversation with Dr. Manes. At long last, the house settled down for the night. I waited another half-hour and then went down to the kitchen. I made a sandwich with some leftover sausage. This time, I'd brought my school atlas so that we could look at South Africa together. I went down the stairs to the cellar and whispered, "Dr. Manes!"

I was waiting for a reply when I heard a noise above me. I froze. Then a voice said, "Got you! Let's see then what you're playing at when other people are sleeping! Something's going on here. I've had my eye on you for a while now."

The spy from the first floor! I had to think fast. "What do you want? Don't you know this is the coal cellar?" I asked, speaking loudly to tip Dr. Manes off and give him a chance to hide in the coal. I turned and went up the stairs toward Frau Gernot, but she stood firm. She had a triumphant expression on her face, which looked strangely distorted in the candlelight. Old witch! I thought, enraged. What good did it do her, poking her nose into other people's business? What satisfaction did she get if people were caught? Did she hope for a medal, or did she simply enjoy getting others into trouble? This was no game. It could cost Dr. Manes his life if she betrayed us.

In desperation, I told her, "You don't have any right to sniff about down here! I'll tell my mother all about you, and then you'll have to look for another landlady!"

She didn't pay me any attention. She just pushed me aside determinedly and went down the stairs and into the cellar, confident of victory. "Ha!" she called out, while I feverishly tried to think up a Plan B. She held up the woolen blankets I'd brought Dr. Manes and pointed to last night's soup bowl. "I knew something was going on! Come out, wherever you are!" My legs turned to jelly as she shouted into the room.

Receiving no response, Frau Gernot began to search through the mounds of coal. She placed the candle next to the soup bowl on a wooden crate and started to rummage in the increasingly dusty blackness. "I'll find you!" she called out. "You won't get away!"

"Now stop it, Frau Gernot, this is quite intolerable!" I had regained some courage and decided to try to get her out of the cellar. "Stop that digging. You'll get all dirty."

But she had worked herself into a rage. "Do you think I'm too stupid to grasp what's going on? I'm not block warden for nothing, you know! All traitorous activities have to be reported, and if there isn't something fishy here then I'll—"

"What's going on here?" My mother's voice suddenly thundered down on us. "Frau Gernot? Gretel?" she called as she came down the stairs. "I'm waiting for an explanation!"

Quickly I preempted my enemy. "I just set myself up down here because I didn't want to get out of bed when the alarm sounded, and Frau Gernot seems to think that I'm not allowed to do that!"

"Complete nonsense!" Frau Gernot snorted. "Someone is being hidden here. A blind man could see that!"

My mother looked at me. "Well, I can't see anyone, can you?"

Frau Gernot, having searched the room, was forced to shake her head. "But I am certain—"

My mother cut her off: "Gretel, did you bring these things down here?"

I nodded humbly and began folding up the blankets.

"Then tidy up the mess. In future, you stay away from the coal cellar, and if you make yourself something to eat, have the decency to bring the dishes back to the kitchen. Can we all go back to bed now?"

I could have kissed her. Even I couldn't tell whether my mother was covering for me or whether she really didn't realize what was going on. Frau Gernot hissed at me: "This will have consequences!" before sticking her nose in the air and marching past me up the stairs. I wasn't too worried, though. She couldn't prove anything. There was no evidence.

Once she was out of sight, I mimed wiping sweat from my brow, murmured something like "Silly bitch!," and took the incriminating dish and blankets back upstairs. Without another word, my mother and I went to our rooms. That really had been close!

So Dr. Manes had escaped, then. I had unlocked the front door straight after my mother had gone to bed, but I hadn't expected him to be fetched so early in the night. I'd thought they would come for him in the early hours. Maybe it had happened the night before, during the air raid, as I was sleeping next to Ilse in the Jungfrauenthal shelter. In any case, he had escaped our spy. I fervently hoped that luck would stay on his side during his journey. I had learned tonight how easily he might be discovered.

10

THE WEHRMACHT

1943: The uprising in the Warsaw Ghetto is brutally crushed.

The 6th Army surrenders at Stalingrad. In the wake of the defeat, Goebbels calls for "total war." Mussolini is overthrown and the Allies sign a truce with Italy.

Hamburg issues 89 air-raid warnings and 112 alarms; the city is the target of 21 bombing raids, 7 of which are part of Operation Gomorrah, which kills about 40,000 people. Fewer than 16,000 can be identified. Statistics report 50,000 wounded, but some estimates are as high as 125,000. More than 80,000 buildings and 100,000 apartments are destroyed or heavily damaged.

At Christmas 1942, we received special rations, as we had done in previous years. We had real coffee and almost enough eggs, sugar, and flour for a proper cake. The "German woman," of course, was skillful enough to conjure the loveliest meal out of the most meager ingredients, and the tabloids printed recipes. It was still difficult to get used to the constant scrimping on ingredients, and it was a real treat to have something more than barley and rutabaga without having to sneak around to get it.

My mother and I spent some pleasant days together. We went out wherever and whenever it was still possible. We saw *Der Rosenkavalier* at the State Opera. When New Year's Eve came, I found myself brooding over my future. I had to go to work again, before it was discovered by the authorities that I was divorced and without employment. As a matter of fact, I was rather keen to start working again. I was beginning to feel bored and claustrophobic even without the help of the nights in the air-raid shelters.

I went around to all the shops that were still selling clothes, but there weren't a great many left. The majority had been under Jewish ownership and were now destroyed and looted; others were bombed out. Also, fabric was even more strictly rationed than food, and very few clothing retailers had been able to survive. In the windows of Karstadt, the department store, were woolly hats and scarves, ready to be bought and sent to the boys at the front, who were in bitter need of them. I had learned to advise customers on what to wear depending on their size, shape, and personality, but the time for choice was over. My trained eye spotted many a refashioned curtain in the dresses of the ladies I passed in the street.

Since I couldn't find anything suitable, I carried on helping at home and at the vegetable market. There was plenty to do. Then, in February, I received a letter stating that I had been summoned for service. When I saw where my new workplace was to be, I shot upstairs with a scream to my mother, who was making the beds.

"Mother," I panted, out of breath, "you'll never believe where they're sending me to work! On April first, I'm to start at the Wehrmacht."

Mother dropped the pillow she was holding. "But what can they possibly want with you there? Isn't that a job for men—officers, people with careers in the military?"

"It's not only for men. They'll need secretaries and all that. They've called me up to work on the telex machines. Do you think I'll have to wear a uniform?"

My mother thought a lot more practically than me, as usual. "The telex machines? But you can't even type! What do they want you to do?"

I wasn't so sure myself. At Krümmel, I had just about got away with pretending to be able to type. I didn't think I'd be so lucky this time, not in an institution like the Wehrmacht. But then the letter did mention a six-week training course at the post office before my start date, so I supposed I would be taught how to type there.

But did I really want to work for the Wehrmacht, in the lion's den?

"Boy, all the senior Nazis will be running around there. You won't last for two days, I reckon," was Kuddel's comment. We were sitting on my bed drinking chicory coffee and discussing my situation.

"Well, I won't have to worship the Führer, will I? Only work there. Just think what information I might get ahold of!"

"Oh, yeah! Especially as you know the right kind of people to pass it on to—like your heroic ex!" Kuddel teased me. "I'm sure the war will be all but over once you're one of the telex girls!"

"Now stop talking rubbish!" He had really wound me up. "Surely it's better if there's someone like me in there than if it's all people who are sworn to the Führer! And anyway, I don't exactly have a choice here. I've been called up."

Kuddel had to admit that. He looked at me, suddenly sympathetic and worried. "Look after yourself, will you? Once you're in there, you've got to watch your tongue or we won't see you again."

"Don't fret," I told him. "I'm not a complete imbecile. Still, I'll be interested to see whether there's anyone there who thinks rather than just obeys."

"And how exactly are you going to find out?"

"I'll have to see. They can't all have their heads stuck in the sand. Some of them must see that Hitler is destroying everything."

"Obviously not!" argued Kuddel. "They're all in it together, otherwise they'd have done something ages ago. One of them could have finished Hitler off long ago, maybe with a bomb, like in Munich, or just by shooting him with a pistol. Like that, see." He mimed loading, cocking, and shooting a pistol. I played mortally wounded, falling back on the bed and breathing raggedly.

Two days later, I was on my way to the post office, where the training course for the *Nachrichtenhelferinnen des Heeres*, the telex machine operators of the army, was to be held. Although I was ten minutes early, there was already a line of women in front of the steps.

At twenty-eight, I seemed to be one of the younger ones. Not all of us had been unemployed, I gathered from the conversations going on around me, but the others had all been called up like me. We had no choice in the matter, as we were obliged by the emergency service law to take any post required of us by the state.

Dead on time, at exactly eight o'clock, we were greeted by a civil servant in civilian clothes. His appearance was so boring that the civil service was about the only occupation I could imagine him in—everything about him was gray, from his receding hair to his shoes. He led us into a small hall with rows of desks, asking us to be seated in pairs. I chose one of the seats furthest back, hoping to avoid drawing too much attention to myself, but the civil servant marched up and down during his introduction, looking each of us sternly in the eye.

"You have been ordered here to do a great service to your Führer and fatherland by helping the Wehrmacht. The duration of your contract will be until the end of the war, or until such time as your services are no longer required," we were informed. "Although you are working for the Wehrmacht and therefore are officially members of the Wehrmacht, you are not soldiers in the true meaning of the word. At all times, you are subordinate to your military superiors, and you will at all times follow the orders of the superintendent secretary. The superintendent secretary is subordinate to the under-executive, who in turn is subordinate to the executive. The executive . . ."

By then, he had lost me. I wanted to start my training, not learn about the military hierarchy. I pictured myself surrounded by handsome officers with whom I could flirt, and a smile flickered across my face. "So, whom are you obliged to formally greet with the Hitler greeting, Fräulein . . . what was the name again?"

I stared at the instructor, still half dreaming, and replied quickly, "Öhlgart, Frau Öhlgart. The . . . officers?"

Perhaps because I put on an innocent expression and gave him a charming smile, he raised his voice only slightly as he corrected me: "As well as your fellow operators and all of your superiors."

He talked and talked, explaining the bureaucracy over and over until we were bored to death with it. We were subject to absolute secrecy, had to confirm this in writing, and were advised to "prove our worth" by our service to the army, to show that we were deserving of "trust and authority at all times, including when off duty."

The pay wasn't bad. I would earn 69 marks per month, plus meals, and 1 mark per day for clothing, as we were not given uniforms but only work aprons.

I began to examine the telex machines in front of us, as our instructor told us: "In case of any violation of the aforementioned duties, disciplinary action will be . . ." Interesting, I thought as I looked at the machine. What could this cylinder be for? ". . . financial penalty up to a sixth of your wages . . ." Remarkable! It was the strangest typewriter I had ever seen. The size of it alone was astonishing. ". . . a curfew of up to how many days? Fräulein Ölig, if I remember correctly?"

With a start, I realized he was talking to me. "Frau Öhlgart," I corrected him. "I'm sorry, I didn't hear the last sentence."

Innocently, I looked at him, and he sighed. "Up to seven days. We will get to the machine in a minute. Patience, my dear! You've got to be clear about your duties, and that goes for all of you. As helpers of the Wehrmacht, you have a great task before you. You serve your Führer and the fatherland. It is a responsibility that could decide the course of the war!" The civil servant shook his head and decided it was time to let us in on the secrets of the telex machine.

The incoming messages came through on thin paper strips, straight from the cylinder. Our role was to pick up these strips and cut them up so that each piece formed a word. These pieces were then glued to a sheet of paper until the result resembled a normal letter. Normal letters were typed into the machine by us. These would emerge at the other end as strips of words. To teach us to touch-type, a small plank was fixed over the keys so that we couldn't look at our fingers. I learned to type with a speed that surprised even myself, and soon I was the fastest on the whole course. Out of curiosity, I was interested in learning Morse code so that I would be able to take telegraph messages too, and because of my eagerness to learn and better behavior, I became one of those selected for this task.

I talked with the other women only during our break, when we ate our packed lunches and speculated about the posts we would take up when we'd completed our training. There were posts available abroad, in Poland, Russia, and France, promising good career opportunities and pay. Some of the women were really keen to seize these opportunities, to have new experiences and to escape bombed-out Hamburg. I wasn't tempted. I didn't want to leave my mother behind, nor did I see any advantages in working at the front or for the General Government in Poland.

When I got home in the late afternoons, my head would be spinning with letters, numbers, and regulations. Kuddel would fortify me with a schnapps and listen patiently to my news. One day, I told him, "We're going to have to swear an oath once we start at the Wehrmacht."

"You could always cross your fingers behind your back," he suggested, grinning, and I promptly planned to do so.

After six weeks' training, the time finally came. On April 1, I was to start my work at the Wehrmacht and had to report to Transport Command Hamburg-Altona. I was excited and woke up early, although there had been an air-raid warning during the night. I had even joined my mother and the lodgers in our own cellar to waste as little time as possible. Although most of us had grown used to the disrupted nights, you could tell that people were sleep-deprived by their edginess and the dark circles under their eyes. Maybe it was my young age, but it didn't seem to affect me so much, and getting a good night's sleep wasn't as important to me as it was to some.

I dressed myself smartly but unobtrusively, breakfasted on a piece of bread, and took the tram to the major railway station in the Altona area of the city. The Transport Command was housed in the Reich railway headquarters, a four-story brick building on my right as I walked out of the station. In front of it was a huge fountain of a mythological scene, the metal sculpture tarnished green; a bearded man fought with a horse while water sprayed from the mouths of various sea creatures. I resolved to ask someone about the fountain when I'd started work, but as I entered through the heavy wooden door, I forgot all about it at once.

In the corridor, soldiers stood or sat around. The doors to most of the offices were open, and everywhere people were busy. I pulled my letter out and marched into the nearest room, speaking to a uniformed man sitting at a desk. Startled, he looked up. "Ooh la la!" he exclaimed. "Oh, hang on! I know; you're to start as a telex operator. Hausdorf! Hausss-dorffff!" A sergeant entered the room. His uniform fitted so badly that he looked quite ridiculous in it. His oversize boots came up to his knees and prevented him from walking properly. "Please show the lady downstairs."

Hausdorf saluted, turned, and disappeared along the corridor without even looking at me. How rude! I thought, hurrying after him, down the stairs and into the basement. Down there were more offices with the telex machines that were now so familiar to me. At the tables sat women working busily. On my entrance—I had just caught up with the sergeant—they looked up and greeted me with "Heil Hitler!"

I nodded in return and gave them a friendly smile, whereupon the sergeant at my side almost had a fit. "Did they not tell you about the duty of using the Hitler greeting?" he shouted at me.

"Oh yes, of course. Heil Hitler!" I replied, like a good girl.

Hausdorf checked my letter and showed me to a place at a table. "Have you been sworn in yet?" he asked. I shook my head. He looked at his pocket watch and told me to come upstairs to take the oath in an hour's time. Until then, I was to organize a work apron and familiarize myself with the facilities—toilets, canteen, air-raid shelter. Hausdorf seemed to have a tremendous sense of self-importance. Although it was no doubt calculated to win him respect, his exaggerated air of efficiency only made him seem absurd as far as I was concerned.

After I'd got rid of him, I asked one of my colleagues where I could find my apron. She got up and led me to a locker in a nearby room, from where I could choose one that fit me. It didn't look smart at all. It was a mouse-gray color with a row of buttons down the front and a sewn-in belt. My fashion-trained eye was offended by the ugly cut. I decided straightaway that I would alter it to suit me better. After all, it was teeming with men down here. I couldn't possibly run around in such an unflattering item.

I took the oath with several other people, some women who were new, like me, and some new soldiers. First, we women had to stand in a row. In front of us, a high-ranking officer rose and told us to repeat his words with our right arms raised: "I swear I will be true and faithful to the Führer of the German Reich and people, Adolf Hitler, and fulfill my duty conscientiously and selflessly."

It wasn't possible to cross my fingers behind my back as Kuddel had suggested, but I didn't have any qualms about swearing an oath that I had no intention of keeping. I considered the oath meaningless and thought of myself as a stage actress playing a role.

The words the soldiers had to speak were weightier. They had to swear "this holy oath by God" that they would "obey the Führer of the German Reich and people, Adolf Hitler, commander in chief of the Wehrmacht, unconditionally," and that they would risk their lives for this oath at any time, as the brave soldiers they were. Of course, a soldier is expected to be prepared to die for his country. But this oath was all about "the Führer," so I watched with interest the expressions of the men as they spoke the words.

Aha, I thought, I knew it. One almost indiscernibly rolled his eyes; the second from the right even pulled a face, as far as it was possible without being obvious. I smiled. So, not even in the Wehrmacht was everyone captivated by Hitler. I felt less alone in the lion's den.

We, the "communications officers," were on duty for twelve hours, night or day, from 8 a.m. to 8 p.m., or vice versa. In between each shift, we had twenty-four or thirty-six hours' free time. Despite these long periods off duty, we would have struggled with the long shifts if we weren't able to rest at some point, so there was a side room with plank beds, where we were allowed to stretch out for one to two hours. Who went at what time, we decided among ourselves.

There was always a lot to do. We never sat around without work, and the machines were always rattling away. The messages were about transport convoys of all sorts—ammunition, soldiers, prisoners, Red Cross convoys. All major troop transports had to be announced within certain deadlines and the general head-quarters in the Knochenhauerstraße had to be informed about all movements.

Our breaks brought relief from the noise of the telex machines and the heat in our basement room. We were allowed to go to the canteen, where we got hot meals, freshly prepared by Polish prisoners. The food wasn't mouthwatering, but it was better than what we got at home. Here, they had all the main ingredients for a proper meal: meat, vegetables, and seasonings.

I quickly grew used to my daily life in the Wehrmacht. In our spartan room, we had six tables, each with two machines, where the women sat and worked. The letters that we glued from the strips of paper were placed in baskets next to the tables. Now and then, one of us would come around and collect the letters to take them upstairs to one of the officers. Occasionally, an officer came down to hand us a letter to type. This gave me an opportunity to flirt a little, a welcome diversion.

It wasn't long before I caught the eye of several officers. To my colleagues' envy, they usually came to my table first when they had something to send off. My refusal to greet the other women "properly" didn't help my popularity, either. My "Good morning" was seen as a violation of my duty. Anyone entering the room was met with a chorus of "Heil Hitler!" When the superintendent secretary threatened me with a disciplinary procedure, I turned it around. After that, I would give the Hitler greeting at every opportunity: "Heil Hitler! My basket's full!" Or, with glee: "Heil Hitler! I need the loo!" It wasn't particularly cautious, but at least I couldn't be accused of violating the "duty to greet."

My cheekiness was a thorn in Hausdorf's side. He tried his best to make my life a misery. Before the first week was over, he came up with the idea of testing me. I was to state in writing which Wehrmacht member had to wear which item of uniform, which rank individual officers had, and how I could tell. I looked at him incredulously. Surely that wasn't knowledge I was required to have? I was sure that he had no right to demand that I take such a test.

I shook my head and wrote down what I knew. A corporal, I might have recognized. Other than that, the military hierarchy was largely a mystery to me. Nevertheless, I wrote down whatever came into my head. A major was awarded an additional row of buttons and a stripe on the shoulder; I gave a general two stripes on his left shoulder and three on the right, not forgetting a little swastika on the collar and one on each cuff.

When he saw my answers, Hausdorf, already cursed with an extremely unattractive face, turned lobster red, enhancing his ugliness even further. "Is it not right, Herr Major General?" I asked uncertainly. "You won't . . . fire me, will you?" I knew that he didn't have the right to suspend me and watched his face closely.

"Completely useless! How you got this position, I will never know!" he thundered, incensed, crumpling my paper in his fists. "And I am neither a major nor a general!"

"But you'd love to be, wouldn't you?" I asked.

That was too much for him. Without another word, he stormed out the door, shaking with rage. Maybe I had gone too far, but I had to bite my lip not to laugh out loud. My colleagues went back to their typing; I hadn't noticed that they'd all been listening until the noise suddenly started up again.

It was then that I spotted an officer standing at the door—for how long, I wondered. Had he heard all of it? I returned to my work at once as if nothing had happened. The officer came over to my table and gave me a letter to type. "A bit more careful, if you please, otherwise they'll catch you out," he murmured. I looked up. At my desk stood a good-looking man in his late thirties whom I had not met before. His dark-blond hair fell over his suntanned forehead, his intelligent eyes sparkled, and as he stood up to his full height, I had to bend backwards because he was so tall. He gave me a friendly nod on the way out.

When I went to the canteen a couple of hours later, I scanned the room, full of hope, having deliberately taken my lunch break at the time when most officers from the upper floor ate. I was in luck. There he was, sitting near the door to the kitchen, talking to two other soldiers.

I got a portion of goulash with pasta and headed in the direction of the kitchen. He hadn't noticed me yet, so I put down my tray, returned to the food counter, and got a glass of water as well.

It worked. He raised his head and, seeing me sitting down at an empty table nearby, greeted me with a nod. Not long after the other two left the canteen, he got up and came toward my table.

"Captain Kunert, Karl Kunert," he introduced himself.

"Gretel Öhlgart, or just Öle."

We looked into each other's eyes and immediately took a liking to each other. I invited him with a gesture to take a seat.

"Hausdorf won't bother you for much longer," he told me. "His two weeks here are almost over. The day after tomorrow, he's got to report to the field transport and planning department. He's only in training and has to do the rounds."

"Oh, that's a pity!" I grinned. "I hope no one notices what an idiot he is—his career might be in danger."

Kunert smiled. "He won't have much chance if he carries on like that. They put great emphasis on employing experienced officers who can develop good working relationships with their civilian staff."

"The others are sort of all right," I admitted. "You quickly learn down there who's been wearing his uniform for a while and doesn't have anything to prove. Most seem educated and have manners, and don't feel the need to act like him."

"What do you think the Hausdorfs have to prove?" Kunert asked, interested.

"That they're somebodies. Yesterday, they were nobodies—teased at work and henpecked by their wives—then someone hands them a uniform and they think at once that they're Hitler in person, bullying people themselves and feeling great about it. Morons!"

Kunert didn't answer straightaway, thinking about my tirade. "You're not going to avoid those in life," he said. "They're on every corner, here as everywhere else. It's only annoying when they are the ones who win out in the end. That's why it might be a good idea to not always advertise one's point of view."

I avoided his gaze by stabbing my pasta. Of course, he was right. Especially here, it would have been cleverer to shut up.

His remark surely didn't refer only to my opinion on Hausdorf's qualities as an officer—but how could he know what other views I held? "I'll try to do better," I promised.

"Very well," he said. "Then I believe we'll see more of each other!"

"With pleasure," I answered happily, already looking forward to our next meeting.

I returned to my desk in high spirits. As I'd hoped, I spoke to Kunert regularly after that. If he had a letter for typing, he would come over to my desk and have a little chat.

"How come you look so much smarter than the other typists?" he asked one day. "I thought they issued you all with the same apron in the Transport Command?"

I laughed. "I suppose that's the tucks!" After a labor-intensive evening of sewing, my apron had become quite figure-hugging, looking tailor-made and accentuating my waist.

"May I invite you for a glass of wine at the end of your shift tonight?"

Of course I said yes, and we went to a harbor café, which was absolutely crammed; many people went out to try to forget about the war for a couple of hours in the evening. There was nowhere to sit, but we didn't care. Holding our glasses, we leaned against a wall at the back of the café while streams of people went to and fro. Amid the babble of voices, we were finally able to talk more freely.

"I think we're on the same side," Kunert started.

I sighed. "There's not many of us, it seems!"

"It may seem that way, but I don't think it's quite so few. It's not as if one can make it publicly known, and certainly not in the Wehrmacht."

"Sometimes I wish I could do something with the fact that I'm working there. At the moment, I'm helping rather than hindering the war effort."

Kunert cast down his eyes. "I know how you feel. In fact, though, you can use your knowledge. But first, you have to get ahold of the really interesting stuff. What you're typing at the moment is all petty bits and pieces. The really valuable information is being coded."

"Coded? Well, then I can't do anything at all, can I?"

"Not just yet. But as it happens, we're looking for staff to be trained on the encryption machine for these special messages. If you're interested, I'll suggest you, and then you can report to me what's going on."

I didn't hesitate for a second. "Why, of course I will! But whether they'll allow me to train is another question."

Kunert waved aside my doubts. "You're quick and you learn easily. If you're a little more cautious"—at this point, he looked me sternly in the eye—"then I'll recommend you on the grounds of good conduct, aptitude, and dexterity."

We raised our glasses and started to talk of more personal matters. "Were you born and bred in Hamburg?" he asked me.

"Not quite," I replied, "but I've lived here almost all my life. And you?"

"I grew up in Hamburg too, but I was only recently transferred here from the Suez Canal."

"That sounds interesting! What did you have to do there, then?"

He told me about his time there, and we got to talking about the climate, the country and the people. We had a great rapport. But a thought suddenly popped into my head. This had happened before—with Lutz! He too had been on the same side as me; he too had been interested in obtaining significant information through me.

"What's the matter?" Kunert asked me.

I shook my head, unwilling to talk about it. "I was married until recently, but it didn't work out," was all I said.

"I'm married as well. I even have a child," he said, without apparent enthusiasm.

I was astonished. I couldn't put my finger on it, but somehow he hadn't seemed like a married man to me. I looked at him curiously but saw he was reluctant to talk. He held his glass up to indicate that it was empty and asked me if I wanted more wine.

On the way home, I kept thinking of what he had said about the "really valuable information." I set my heart on training to use the encryption machine. I was dying to talk to Kuddel about the latest developments. Unfortunately, when I knocked on his door that night, I didn't get a reply. He must have been still at the university or have gone out. Disappointed, I made my way upstairs.

Hausdorf was soon replaced by another sergeant, a stocky man with ginger curls and thick glasses, who quickly proved to be more approachable than his predecessor. His name was Arnold Maier, and he often came over to my desk to ask how I was and to have a chat.

Maier's father had been mayor of Duisburg, but that hadn't helped him. He was a Jehovah's Witness, and he'd been imprisoned for his beliefs. Thankfully, Maier wasn't religious himself, otherwise I'd have wasted all my time on theological arguments. Instead, we talked about daily life and its hardships, about the food rations and the pitiful range of clothing available. When we were talking about this one day, Maier winked from behind his thick glasses, mumbled something about "ways and means," and disappeared.

During my next shift, I would learn what he had meant. To my astonishment, he gave me a whole ham. I was thrilled, taking it the same evening over to Monsignor Bram, who regarded it as a gift from heaven.

Not long afterward, Maier gave me another present—a generous piece of raw leather. I couldn't believe my luck; this meant shoes! Although I much preferred Kunert, I dutifully started to flirt with Maier, and before two weeks had passed, he was head over heels in love with me.

With Maier's presents to barter with, I had more choice than ever on the black market. He gave me cigarettes, which I could swap for anything: soap, delicacies, perfume—usually things that weren't officially available at all. I was able to use the long breaks between shifts for trading, and the market was flourishing.

What was more, Maier knew about my interest in working on the encryption machine and put in a good word for me. "The others aren't half as clever as you, anyway," he commented.

Kunert, whom I had nicknamed "Karchen," didn't seem too bothered about my fling with Maier. One day, as I was sitting with Karchen in the canteen, the mystery of his private life was solved. We were watching a handsome young officer at the next table.

"Not unattractive," I remarked.

"Indeed not!" he answered with a twinkle in his eye.

The penny dropped. "I . . . you . . . ? Pity, really!" was all I could say, sighing in defeat, and he laughed.

Occasionally, I went with Maier to a bar. Every now and then, we had a glass too many and I went home with him. What I wouldn't have considered doing if I'd been sober just happened—I slept with him. I didn't get carried away very often, but my judgment was colored by the situation we were in. Who could say that we would still be alive tomorrow? I let myself drift along and lived for the moment. For the time being, I had no one to be faithful to. I might as well do what I wanted.

Maier had fallen quite genuinely in love with me and asked me to marry him. He didn't irritate me, he was polite and steady, and always very busy organizing the transport trains coming from Holland carrying wounded soldiers. He would have made a nice-enough husband, but I didn't feel the same way about him as he did about me, and I wouldn't even consider his proposal in earnest. He had just separated from his wife and wasn't yet divorced, so I was able to decline without hurting his feelings too badly. He took it like a gentleman, continuing our relationship as if he'd never asked.

11

ENIGMA

One night, Maier came to my desk and said, "You can begin work on the encryption machine. During your next shift, they'll start to train you. Don't let me down! I told them you're by far the best candidate."

I was truly excited. My telexes hadn't been half as interesting (or potentially useful) as I'd imagined they would be. Now I was going to learn about things that really mattered. With a bit of luck, I'd be one of the first to hear news from the front. At the end of my night shift, I passed by Karchen's office to see if he was there so I could tell him my news. To my disappointment, his desk was empty, but as I turned to leave, I bumped into him as he charged into the room. "Karchen! It's happening! I'm going to start on the encryption machine!" I said breathlessly.

He took me by the shoulders and beamed. "Let me know how you get on. If there's anything interesting to type, let me know, will you?"

I nodded vigorously, beamed back at him, and made my way to the tram feeling wonderfully important and daring.

Apart from me, just one other woman was chosen to be trained in coding and decoding messages. She was called Ertrud Heimlich and was especially faithful to the Führer. We were led to a small back room, unfurnished but for a table with a strange oak box on it and two chairs in front of it. We took our seats and looked expectantly at the officer in charge.

"What you see in front of you is the encryption machine, which you will soon be able to operate in your sleep," he told us. "If you open it and fold back the lid . . . careful, gently . . . you will see the keys. Press the A. What can you see?"

"There's a letter lit up at the top, but it's a T!" Frau Heimlich answered.

"And if you press the A again?"

We did as he suggested. "Now it's the E that's lit up!"

In the box were three rows of letter keys, similar to a typewriter but without punctuation marks. Above the keys were, in the same order, three rows of letters that lit up. The letter that glowed was always different from the one pressed down. Confused, we raised our heads and looked at the instructor.

The keys were connected to electrical wires, we were told, running over a number of rotors. On their way through the machine, the typed letters lost their original meaning. The new letters that resulted followed a carefully selected and ever-changing code, which was to be entered beforehand. The sender and the recipient of a message had to enter the same code to make it work.

The main aim, of course, was to ensure that the enemy had not the slightest chance of guessing the code, so it had to be as complicated as possible. The rotors had to be turned into certain positions, the settings adjusted, and specific switch points—corresponding with letters and positioned at the front and the back of the machine—connected using leads. I was intrigued.

I nodded encouragingly to my colleague, but she only sat, her eyes wide, her hand to her mouth, murmuring, "I'll never be able to learn that!"

I almost felt sorry for her. I tried to calm her down, telling her, "Don't worry. That's what we're here for—to learn how to do it."

The officer gave us a piece of paper on which the letters "B-Z-M-R-T-N-G-I-E" were written, telling us to type them into the machine. Shrugging, I started straightaway, while Frau Heimlich took a note of the letters that were glowing at the top. The round keys were not easy to press down; I felt a slight resistance halfway down, and as every letter was typed, there was a kind of double clicking noise. *Ka-ding, ka-ding,* I pressed my coded text, Frau Heimlich scribbling away. "H-E-I-L-H-I-T-L-E-R" she read out, and I couldn't stop myself from rolling my eyes.

We received general operating instructions, which explained how to clean the machine, grease the cylinders, and change the bulbs. There was a handbook for the coding. The cipher was changed regularly, at midnight, and we were given it in a shortened form. With the help of the handbook, we were able to work out the code from the abbreviated version.

Over a few days, the machine became less and less mysterious to us. Four steps had to be gone through before messages could be encrypted or decoded. First, the order of the rotors had to be set: for example, I, III, II, or II, I, III. Then the letter rings had to be aligned with the rotors as determined by the code, which was numerical: 4 meant D, the fourth letter of the alphabet, 11 was K, and so forth. Third, the rotors themselves had to be positioned in accordance with the code. The last step was to connect the letters via the plugboard, D with O, for example, L with H, and so forth.

Our first attempt at encryption was done according to a detailed example in the manual. The cylinders were to be set at I, III, and II. The rings were to be set to 16, 11, and 13, so we adjusted them to P, K, and M. The start position was to be 01, 12, and 22—so we set the rotors at A, L, and V. The plugs had to be connected C to O, D to I, F to R, H to U, J to W, L to S, and T to X. Finally, we could start on our sample text.

"Ready?" I asked my colleague.

"Yes, go on. I might as well get used to it."

According to the book, the uncoded text had to be entered in a particular style. The message was: "Day 4.5, leaving time 17.55 hours, corps command VI, attack 5, 3 May. 45 hours with 3 and 10 div. enemy at Maisach. Gef. Stand: Milbertshofen North Exit." Our instructor reminded us that punctuation was to be entered as "x" and which data we had to type first. The transmission was to begin: "Corps command roman six x attack . . ." While Frau Heimlich typed, I wrote down the glowing letters.

To check that what we had done would come out correctly at the other end, we entered into the machine what I had noted down. "Lops commnad roean six x . . ." I snorted with laughter. Unfortunately, our instructor didn't find it quite so funny. "If you don't approach this task, which is vital to the war effort, with the requisite seriousness, Frau Öhlgart, you are in the wrong place here! I have been instructed to report on the suitability of the present assistants, and I would be delighted to subject you to a disciplinary procedure." Put firmly in my place, I choked back my annoyance, thinking of Maier and Kunert, who had supported me, and apologized.

I tried harder after that. We typed, coded, and decoded for hours on end. After a while, I didn't find it quite so difficult. If we were aware of having mistyped something, we had to type "mistake" and start again from the last "x." As we practiced, the coding key was changed constantly, and we practically dismantled the machines, cleaning, greasing, and checking bulbs and cables.

Soon we were ready to be let loose on real messages. Most of the time, we were still operating the telexes as before, but every now and then Frau Heimlich and I were called to send off or decode some special document that was subject to the highest secrecy.

Occasionally, Karchen came down to hand me a letter or pretend that he had something to be typed. He would chat for a bit—"Don't you look pretty today"—while I whispered to him whether something important had happened or not. Sometimes he would drop his pencil or something like that, giving me a chance to say a bit more, but mostly we arranged to go to the canteen at the same time. Every now and then, we went out for a beer after work to talk unobserved.

"I can't come down too often," he told me on one of these occasions. "It's too obvious. I think I'm already under suspicion to some degree." I knew from Lutz that the first law was not to ask any questions. What Karchen did with the information I gave him, I would never learn. That he passed it on, I could only guess—to whom and with what consequences, I didn't ask.

"Maybe I could type something wrong to create some chaos, and then we'd have stopped the whole system for a while?" I suggested.

"For heaven's sake, don't do that! They'll know immediately, and then you won't just get the sack! You're much more useful carrying on as you are, anyway, as long as you keep me up-to-date." I shrugged, resigned. "Don't worry," Karchen said, trying to cheer me up. "You're doing what you can, and that's more than you'll ever know."

When the air-raid alarm sounded while we were at the Transport Command, we went one floor further down, into the cellars. All the officers and employees would stream downstairs, but the prisoners of war, mostly Polish, who worked in the building were not allowed to join us. I was outraged that they were denied the relative safety of the cellars. "We can't leave them sitting on the stairs, can we?" I demanded of one officer.

"It's only Poles," came the answer, which left me fuming and feeling helpless. Deeply ashamed, I picked my way past them on the stairs to the cellar. I couldn't blame them for spitting at us. Not even Karchen had the power to do anything about it. As far as the Wehrmacht command were concerned, the prisoners' lives simply weren't worth saving. Every time the all-clear sounded, I sighed with relief that the building hadn't been hit. I couldn't have coped with the guilt if the Poles had been killed while we were left unscathed.

Before long, these prisoners made a serious attempt to disrupt the Wehrmacht. When I reported for my shift one night, I found the whole place in turmoil. We were badly understaffed, I realized. A lot of the usual faces were missing, and instead Gestapo officers were swarming around, notebooks in hand and asking strange questions.

I went downstairs and it wasn't long before an officer came down to interview me. "Heil Hitler! Name?" He wasn't exactly polite, but then, no one expected the Gestapo to have manners.

"Gretel Öhlgart."

"Where were you yesterday at midday?"

I looked uncomfortably at the officer, wondering how to hide the fact that I'd been involved with my black-market business. "At home," I lied. "I was sleeping to prepare for my night shift."

The officer looked me sternly in the eye. "Where at home?"

"Hochallee 67, Harvestehude." Oh, dear. Had someone seen me, or, worse, informed on me?

"We'll check that," murmured the man while he took his notes, turning around to speak to the only other telex operator in the office: "Heil Hitler! Name?"

When he went back upstairs I hurried toward my colleague. Normally there were about five of us down in the office. "What's happened?"

"Someone poisoned the food yesterday. It's hit a lot of us. Many people are in the hospital." I stared at her in disbelief. How could that have happened? The prisoners! Of course, it had to be them. But where had they got the poison from? No wonder the Gestapo were on the case. How lucky that it had been my day off!

We worked hard through the night, but it was unexpectedly quiet, as a lot of officers were off sick. When the other woman came back from her hour's sleep at two in the morning, it was my turn for a break. I climbed the stairs to go to the canteen. There was no hot food, only sandwiches. I got myself a cup of tea and had a look through the kitchen door. The usual hubbub had been replaced with a deathly silence. Not a single prisoner was to be seen. I felt uneasy when I thought of what they might be going through.

I didn't see Karchen or Maier as I left the building the next morning, tired to the bone. Only three women had come in to replace us, and we had discussed whether we should stay on. The ones who had come in had had terrible stomach cramps, they told me, and they knew about one telex operator who had died in the night. I was worried about Karchen, but I didn't have any way of contacting him, so all I could do was go home.

Some thirty-six hours later, I learned that he had escaped with bad cramps. "I was called away from my dinner to take a phone call," he told me. "I was really angry about it, because I was so hungry." Relieved, I thanked fate. Maier was all right too. On that day, he had had to report to the Netherlands, where his transports came from.

"What do you think will happen to the prisoners?" I asked Karchen.

He could only guess. "We lost a lot of people. Some high-ranking officers have died. I don't think they'll even get a fair trial. They will either be transported or condemned to death."

I had mixed feelings. If I had been in their situation, I would probably have tried to do something similar. For them, we were all in league. How could they know that even here, in the Wehrmacht, some were anti-fascists? Of course, even if they had gathered as much, they wouldn't necessarily be prepared to make any concessions. All that counted was to damage the war effort, even if it put them in mortal danger. I admired their courage, and regretted that I hadn't shown an occasional sign of complicity, to let them know that there was somebody on their side even here.

I went to see if Maier had come back from Holland and found a letter addressed to me on his desk. Judging by the handwriting, he'd written it in a hurry.

Dear Gretel,

They have transferred me to Holland to organize transport of
the wounded and their supplies. Don't worry, I won't forget you.
How could I? I wish you could be with me, as my wife. Maybe
you'll give it some more thought. I won't give up hope so easily.
In the meantime, I will do my best to speed up the divorce as
soon as I'm transferred back to Hamburg. Until then, we can
pretend to be married, my darling. The ring in the envelope is
for you. When you wear it, you are Frau Maier! You will hear
from me, I'll soon send word, and I'll send you something to
eat as often as I can.

With love,
Your Arnold

I pulled an opal ring out of the envelope. Was it stupid to pretend to be married again? I wondered as I looked at it. I tried it
on my ring finger, and it fit quite perfectly. If I turned the stone
around to the palm of my hand, it even looked like a wedding
ring. I didn't dwell much longer on whether to wear it or not, and
quickly got used to my new "wedding ring."
      A few days later, I received a telegram from Maier: "Red Cross
transport Wednesday stop ten thirty stop something for you stop
kiss A." How nice of him! Quite excited, I went to the station on
Wednesday to meet the train. First the wounded were unloaded,
some carried on stretchers and loaded into military vans to be
taken to the hospital, some walking with the aid of nurses. Some
of the soldiers looked in a bad way, wrapped in blood-soaked
bandages, with missing limbs or their heads completely swaddled
in dressings. I felt my hatred for Hitler rising in me. He had
burdened our men with all this. What else could they do but go
to war? Most had family at home and couldn't afford to disobey.
The children would be taken away, the wife tortured to reveal the

hiding place of the deserter. Sure, some had marched proudly and happily to the front, for Führer and fatherland, but who was still thinking that way?

Well, there was the Hitler Youth, of course. For about a decade, young people had heard nothing but propaganda, being taught to worship the Brownshirts. In their schoolbooks were caricatures of Jews with distorted faces and huge noses trying to outwit the true and good German people. In school, Germany's children learned that all "non-Aryans" were subhuman, and were instructed in how to recognize them by racial characteristics. Boys' toys were exact miniatures of German tanks and guns; they collected ammunition shells, banners, pictures of Hitler, Göring, and Himmler. At night, they marched in torchlight processions, roaring fascist songs, finding a sense of belonging in what was in reality the dream of a madman and his power-crazed henchmen. And here these young men were, lying on their stretchers, some of them not yet grown up, still believing in all of it. They must have lied about their age—or were children allowed to join up now?

Lost in my thoughts, I almost missed the voice calling, "Frau Mai-er!!" I rushed toward the soldier, who was straining his voice considerably shouting out "my" name. "Frau Maier?" he asked.

"That'll be me," I said calmly, looking expectantly at him.

"There you go. For you!" In front of me stood a pallet of eggs, and there weren't a dozen or two but hundreds.

I could barely believe it. "Eggs!"

"Yes, what else? Did you expect chocolate?" He shook his head impatiently and moved further along the platform.

Quickly I gathered my thoughts. If I didn't act quickly now, I could get myself into serious difficulties. "Can you keep an eye on my delivery, please? I'll be right back!" I called to the soldier as I passed him, without waiting for an answer. As I hurried along, I searched for a solution. In front of the station, I saw what I needed. A man was loading sacks onto a three-wheeled horse-drawn cart. It didn't look as if he would need all the space.

"Do you want to earn some eggs?" His eyes lit up. Eggs had become a rare delicacy. I knew he wouldn't decline the offer. "I need transport to Harvestehude." I explained. Without asking any questions, he loaded the eggs onto his cart, running to and fro. I didn't let him carry too many at a time. Altogether, I counted some 360 eggs. As I climbed onto the cart, I offered him 30 for taking me home. He was far too surprised about the situation to bargain.

My mother covered her face with her hands, despairing of me, as we brought the eggs into the kitchen. Before any unannounced guests or lodgers could discover more than was good for me, I threw some tea towels over the piles. After bidding my driver a friendly good-bye, I began to carry the eggs upstairs to my attic room. I slept until midday. I couldn't afford to rest any longer than that.

The afternoon I spent at the vegetable market, putting the word out here and there to people I trusted. On my way home, I knocked on certain doors before returning home. I put aside fifty eggs for the parsonage. That evening, I helped my mother to prepare pancakes, which we hadn't tasted in years. After I'd spread the word among my customers, it wasn't long before a stream of visitors started arriving at the door of my little room.

Not everyone paid with money. Some brought meat, jams and preserves of all sorts, books, fabric, and highly prized cigarettes. Some left the house with more than just eggs; what one person had brought along, another often needed. I tried to be fair and just, not taking advantage and charging normal prices. If someone didn't have much to swap I would give them the eggs for free. Sooner or later, that person would get ahold of some other rarity and let me share it.

I tried not to involve my mother too much in these dealings. She felt uncomfortable with the idea of doing such dangerous business with strangers. Black-market dealers were punished with severe prison sentences. If I was at work, she would ask people to come back later when I would be at home, keeping out of it.

I myself didn't dwell on the risk of being caught; I simply hadn't thought that possibility through. You had to do what you could to make sure you survived in these times, I thought to myself, and that was that.

With all the comings and goings, an air raid, and a trip to the parsonage, I didn't get a lot of sleep before I had to go back to work at eight the next morning. However, I was in much too high spirits to feel tired. I telegraphed Maier as soon as I could do it unobserved. "Breakfast wonderful stop lots of friends stop thousand thanks stop kiss G."

Naturally, he couldn't send food too frequently, but he did so often and with pleasure. My business flourished. I hardly knew where to put all the money I earned. Maier sent cigarettes, tinned meat, smoked ham, chocolate—always announced by telegraph and in huge quantities. Kunert knew about my activities by this time. He just asked me to be careful and make sure I dealt only with people I could trust.

"If it helps with your hobby," he told me one day, "you can actually take some food home from the kitchen, you know, for your mom, if you want. Here you go. You can fill this up. It even stays warm for a while." He gave me one of those metal boxes that I had seen the soldiers use for their meals. I was delighted and, from then on, after every mealtime I appeared in the kitchen, where the cook filled my container with a generous portion of hot food.

After a big delivery of cigarettes, I went to Willi Calsen, with whom I had done business before. "Have you got anything interesting?" I asked him.

He tapped the side of his nose and smirked. "Can you use black satin?"

"Sure! Anytime!" I answered. Fabric was extremely hard to come by, satin nonexistent. What he showed me exceeded my wildest dreams. In the back room of his house, he had three enormous bales of satin, which he happily gave me. "I can't get rid of them as easily as you. I'm sure you'll make a better job of it, being in the business."

I promised to give him a generous share of the profits, and we worked out a plan to transport the bales of fabric to the Hochallee without being too conspicuous. When the bombing raids had begun, we had been asked by the state to clear all wooden items, bookshelves, bed frames, and wall partitions from our lofts in order to minimize fire hazards. I hadn't bothered much about it—after all, I had to live in the attic. Willi, though, had cleared his loft like a good citizen, and so had a number of wooden planks in his cellar. We hid the bales between some of these and carried our load, apparently of wood, through the streets to my house.

The load was terribly heavy and extremely uncomfortable to carry upstairs, but the camouflage was effective. Not even Frau Gernot guessed anything. Only Mother declared herself at a loss as to what I wanted with wooden planks. As soon as everything was stowed in my room, I gave Willi a large amount of the money that I had stuffed in my pillow. We drank a cup of real coffee in the kitchen and chatted about our business. Willi told me about the parties he went to with his black-market "colleagues."

"It's such fun, really. You've got to go to one. They're extraordinary. If you want, I'll go with you. What about tonight?" Unfortunately, I had to work the night shift. "Fine, tomorrow night, then!" I went along. Somewhere in the St. Georg area, we turned down a side street, passed a big gate, and went through the backyard of a tall building toward a cellar. Willi hadn't been exaggerating. Even outside, the laughter and music were loud. "Always follow the noise," Willi called to me over his shoulder as we descended the stairs. Down in the cellar, there was a great atmosphere. Quite a crowd of people were there, some of the faces vaguely familiar. The air was thick with cigarette smoke, and everyone was talking and laughing. In a corner sat a young man with a guitar on his lap, playing old soldiers' songs, surrounded by young women who were singing along.

That night, I made many friends, sang Zarah Leander songs, and even danced. I couldn't remember when I'd gone home, but my head the next morning gave me some indication of the amount of alcohol I'd consumed.

After that, I went to many a black-market party, in venues all over the city, often in Hoheluft, sometimes in Altona, Uhlenhorst, or Eilbek. I heard about them at the vegetable market or through my visitors, most of whom I had gotten to know quite well. We forgot everything around us—the ruins, the danger of being bombed, the war. We were able to get ahold of all kinds of things, of course, and there would be red wine, white wine, beer, advocaat liqueur, bread, cheese, sausage, and cake. The partygoers would spend the night as if there was no tomorrow.

Sometimes I took Karchen along. We got on like a house afire, could talk about everything, and enjoyed each other's company. When we were drunk, we sometimes found ourselves lying in each other's arms and kissing wildly, but to my deep regret it never came to more. "Blast! You're no use for anything!" I would scowl, pushing him off, and we'd both laugh.

One evening in July, I was getting ready for a party when there was a knock on the door of my room. I was used to a constant stream of visitors, so I wasn't surprised to see a tall man in his thirties standing there when I opened it.

"Are you Gretel Öhlgart?" he asked. "Good evening! Louis Ferdinand, Prince of Prussia."

I looked him up and down—narrow face, noble features—indeed, you could have called his looks aristocratic. But what proof was that? "Sure, and I'm the Queen of Sheba!" I replied.

He smiled affably. "Whether you believe me or not, it's true. I'm told you have black satin?"

"Where did you get that idea from?"

"Friedrich Peters recommended you."

I nodded. Whoever Peters sent, I could trust. "How much do you want?"

"Twenty meters, if that's possible."

I pulled the bale out from under my bed and called my mother. She was far better than me in measuring fabric, and I would need her help anyway to unroll the bale. Mother wielded the yardstick skillfully while I chatted to my client.

"I didn't know we still had a Prince of Prussia," I admitted, still suspicious.

"You wouldn't, really. Our family moved to Utrecht when you were probably still in your nappies."

I had in fact been three or four years old when the Kaiser had gone into exile. Vague memories from my history lessons came back to me. "Was the Kaiser your father?" I asked.

Ferdinand shook his head. "I'm not that old. He was my grandfather."

Now I was impressed, in spite of myself. "Did you get on well with him?"

The prince told me a couple of anecdotes about life at Doorn House in the Netherlands, where the Kaiser had lived until his death the year before last. A sworn enemy of France, Wilhelm II had sent a telegram to Hitler in 1940 to congratulate him on the sacking of Paris.

Eventually, I was convinced that Ferdinand wasn't lying about who he was. He seemed modest and kind, so I ventured on to less-conventional topics. "Don't you sometimes regret the way things have turned out? You could have ruled the country yourself, couldn't you?"

Ferdinand nodded. "I would be Crown Prince if Max von Baden, the Chancellor, hadn't announced the abdication of the throne. Grandfather would never have abdicated of his own accord. The Republic was not such a bad idea, but the people were simply not ready for it then. We can see now what's become of it all. Not that I'd want to be in power, and certainly not during wartime. But some things would have turned out quite differently if I'd had a say. Maybe it would never have gone this far."

Another one! In what unexpected corners you could find enemies of the regime! I could have talked for hours on end, but Mother had finished measuring and I had to help her with cutting the material. Ferdinand paid me generously in cash and said good-bye.

Meanwhile, I had dressed half of Hamburg in black satin. Here I would recognize a skirt or a blouse with a bit of white lace, there a fashionable evening dress—all made from the bales under my bed. And now the Prince of Prussia was to be dressed in it!

The summer was hot, and in July the temperatures climbed even higher. I was in a whirl of partying and bartering, without much sleep. So far, life in wartime had been relatively easy to cope with for me; bombed-out houses, streets buried in rubble, and killed relatives I knew only as the fates of others. And yet I knew that I might be hit at any time, and if it happened, I wanted to have spent my last days in style and having fun.

I was far from the only one who thought like this. The cellars where I met with all the other partygoers were always full to the brim. Bottoms up! Who knew what tomorrow would bring? As we would soon learn, life in Hamburg as we knew it was indeed coming to an end.

12

FIRESTORM

The weather had been hot and dry for weeks, without a cloud in the sky, and July 24 was no exception, a beautiful summer's day. It was a Saturday, and I was sorry that I had a night shift to come. Although I had been out the night before, I would have loved to go to the vegetable market, as I'd heard that there would be get-togethers going on until late.

My only consolation was that Karchen would be on the same shift as me, which didn't happen very often. Resigned, I started work and looked forward to my break at midnight, when I would have a cup of coffee with Karchen. We'd been sitting in his office for about half an hour when we heard the air-raid siren.

There had been a lot of alarms lately, but instead of bombers all that came were reconnaissance airplanes, so we weren't too worried, although Karchen warned me, "They do say there could be a major attack, and that we should be careful."

A soldier who was going down the stairs close behind us interjected: "Oh, well, nobody takes that seriously. In the city, things are really happening. Hardly anyone is afraid of attacks. They've even camouflaged the Alster. They've drained it and disguised it as a built-up area!"

Karchen shook his head as we arrived in the cellar, saying, "The Tommies aren't stupid. They know exactly where the Alster is. Such cheap tricks won't stop them at all. And our lot know it, too. Think about all those emergency drills. Why else would they have prepared the city so thoroughly for a full-blown disaster?"

"Rubbish! The British are only interested in Berlin. They just use us for a flyover!"

At that moment, we began to feel shaking. The walls of the cellar were literally trembling, and Karchen repeated matter-of-factly, "They just use us for a flyover." I felt uneasy, as the raid lasted a long time. Two and a half hours; that was not a good sign.

When they finally gave the all-clear, I went back to my desk, full of foreboding. Almost immediately, I was called to the encryption machine and began to take damage reports, passing them on to headquarters in the Knochenhauerstraße. I felt increasingly sick with anxiety as I carried out my work.

Slowly, a picture of what had happened began to form. First, the British had jammed the radar by throwing tinfoil strips, wrapped in black paper so that they would be invisible in the darkness, out of their planes. Then they had bombed the city relentlessly. The whole northwest of Hamburg had been flattened, including large areas of Altona, where our offices were. A torrent of bad news came in: extensive fires in the harbor, in Wandsbek, Grindel, Eimsbüttel, Hoheluft . . . the worst hit was Neustadt around the Nikolaikirche.

At eight in the morning, I was allowed to leave at last, prepared for the horrendous sights that I would certainly see. On leaving the building, I wondered at first why it wasn't daylight yet, until I realized that the sun was blocked out by the smoke. I didn't even try to take the tram or the Underground; instead, I started walking toward home straightaway. I passed mere skeletons of buildings, only the façades intact, smoldering heaps of rubble, fires still burning. Often I had to negotiate piles of debris, and sometimes the street was completely blocked and I had to pick my way through the wreckage. What had been landmarks yesterday had been reduced to shapeless carcasses of buildings.

I didn't know how long it would take me to get home. I felt as if I had been walking for an eternity. Would our house still be standing? I tried to imagine how our street would look in ruins to prepare myself for the shock. What would I do first? Dig for survivors?

Finally, I turned into the Hochallee. There, our house! It was still there! The whole street was largely undamaged. I wiped the sweat from my forehead and ran up the stairs to the front door. I picked up the little porcelain pig that I had placed at the door as a good-luck charm to protect the house. "Well done!" I whispered to it before setting it back down.

"Mother?" I shouted as I went in the front door. I didn't have to search for long. She flew toward me and we held each other for a moment.

"Child, child," she murmured into my hair, "I've been so worried about you!" We went into the kitchen, where, to my surprise, Willi Calsen was sitting.

"Well, my dear, it looks as if we're to be real neighbors!"

I looked at my mother. "He's been bombed out and came straight to us. Of course we can put him up."

I nodded happily. We still had two rooms that we could use for accommodation. If it had been us who had been hit, Willi would have been just as helpful.

"Have you brought your things yet?" I asked him.

"Not much to bring, sadly. It's all gone, I'm afraid."

After some breakfast we went together to his house. Only parts of the façade and one side wall were left. In the rubble, we uncovered an armchair, creating thick clouds of dust. Every now and then, one of us would hold up a recognizable item: a faucet, the handle of a window. Willi sank down in the rubble and wiped his face. He looked at me with tired eyes. "And I always thought, it's not gonna hit me!"

I sat down next to him. "Stay at our house as long as you want. If you don't live there, they'll only give us some stranger. We'll have to take someone in anyway. And Mother's cooking isn't that bad!" Willi smiled.

At least he still had his parents, who lived in the country, if the worst came to the worst. But he had his business contacts here, and I knew he would want to try to keep up his black-market activities. He got up and brushed the dust off his trousers. Together, we carried the armchair—the only thing he had left worth salvaging—back to our house.

We had just managed to move the unwieldy piece of furniture into Willi's new room when the air-raid siren howled again. Willi looked at his pocket watch. It was twenty to three in the afternoon. This was very unusual. I could only remember one other attack in the middle of the day, last year in the summer; normally the alarms sounded at night—at the earliest between seven and eight o'clock, more often at midnight or in the small hours. In the middle of the day, the siren sounded strange and somehow more threatening.

We rushed down into the cellar. This time I didn't even consider waiting for Ilse or running over to the parsonage. As soon as we reached the bottom of the stairs, we heard the first bombs hit. "They want to finish us," Willi stated. No one contradicted him. After two and a half hours' anxious waiting, the all-clear was given. I hadn't slept a minute since I'd finished the strenuous night shift, and by this time I hardly cared about anything. All I wanted was my bed. I fell exhausted into a deep, dreamless sleep, still fully clothed.

The next morning, I got up at six and went down to the kitchen for breakfast. The evening issue of the *Hamburger Zeitung* was lying on the table. It reported the horrors of the last two attacks. The population was warned that they were allowed to leave the city only if they had a special permit; a mass exodus had to be preempted. Those made homeless were to be moved to Schleswig-Holstein by special transport. To raise morale, special rations were promised: an emergency ration card for three days, 50g of real coffee, 10 cigarettes, 125g of sweets, half a bottle of schnapps. I looked up as Kuddel entered the kitchen.

"Up already?" I asked. Kuddel had a tendency to sleep in.

"I wanted to talk to you before you head off to work."

I pushed a chair back, inviting him to join me. "Have a coffee first. We're to get special rations, so we can have a real one. What's up?"

Kuddel hesitated, which wasn't like him. He poured himself a cup of coffee and blurted out, "I'm going to get married."

"Married? You haven't even got a girlfriend, have you? Kuddel?"

"I wanted to tell you ages ago, but you're always busy. We don't have any time to talk these days. I've met a girl at the university, Rosie, and it's knocked me for a loop. You've got to meet her—you'd get on really well."

I was taken aback. There I was, thinking I knew Kuddel, and I didn't have any idea what was going on in his life. Nice friend I was! I'd been entirely caught up in my own worries and pleasures.

"That's amazing!" I said. "How long have you known each other? Are you sure you want to marry her?"

"We've known each other for more than a year now, but we only realized we loved each other two weeks ago. Now we can't imagine why we hesitated for so long. If we wait much longer, one of us could be gone, so we're going to marry quickly without any fuss."

"Boy, Kuddel! Have you at least got a photo?"

He pulled his wallet out of his jacket and handed me a crumpled picture. I saw a pretty face with intelligent dark eyes and curly hair, possibly red. "She's pretty!" I remarked. "And her parents have agreed?"

Kuddel rubbed his knee uncomfortably. "They've been transported."

Now I got it. "She's Jewish, isn't she? Then you're not really allowed to marry her."

Rosie was half Jewish, Kuddel told me. Her parents had been transported to a camp in the east—her mother, because she was Jewish, and her father because of "racial disgrace." Somehow, the parents had organized a different identity for their daughter, probably by buying ID papers, which would have cost a lot of money. Before the subterfuge was detected, she needed to marry an "Aryan," and Kuddel was more than prepared to help her. "We're good friends, I like her. It wasn't a complete lie what I told you earlier."

I had the greatest respect for his decision. That was something I could have done too, given the right circumstances: save someone by marriage. I hadn't thought of it before . . . I could ask Monsignor Bram if he knew of anyone I could help. But then I shied away from the very thought. Rubbish! Kuddel might do it—as lovely as it was of him, he at least knew the girl well and liked her. After my experience with Lutz, I had strong reservations about another marriage, even if it was purely one of convenience.

"I don't think I could do that," I admitted. "I can't imagine ever marrying again. No thanks! But I wish you all the best. May it become a real marriage, and you'll both be safe and happy in the end!"

"Let's have a schnapps to that one day. You'll learn to love her!"

Our good-byes were more heartfelt than usual that day, now that I knew Kuddel would be moving out sooner or later. Before long, the days would be over when we would burst into each other's rooms, day or night, to talk or listen to the BBC under the duvet. I didn't want to think about someone else living in his room. "Let's not lose touch," I begged him before leaving for work.

In the Transport Command, it was as busy as the night of my last shift. We had to type with flying fingers, and I had to decipher piles of messages without a moment's breathing space, until the air-raid siren sounded just after half past ten. We were squeezed together in the cellar for more than two hours before we could come back upstairs. My stomach rumbled and I went straight to the canteen. Karchen was nowhere to be seen, but some other officers I got on well with waved me over to their table, and I enjoyed their company.

". . . the electricity works, and in the Kuhwerder harbor they've sunk the *General Antigas,* where the marines are stationed. They know exactly what to hit. There won't be much of Hamburg left," I overheard someone saying as I sat down.

"Who? The British or the Americans?" I asked.

"The British at night and the Americans during the day, it seems. We get it from all sides. The antiaircraft guns can't do much about it; they're hit or miss. The bombers can't find all the important strategic targets in all that smoke they're creating. That's why there's a pause every now and then."

I looked uncertainly at the man who had spoken last. "Does that mean they're going to keep on coming? They can hardly destroy any more, can they?"

He looked at me with something like pity in his eyes. "That's not the end of it, love, mark my words—not by far. They won't give in until they've flattened the whole city."

How right he turned out to be! The next air raid came not long after midnight, getting me out of my bed at home. This time, I left the house to help Ilse and her children. With a blanket in one arm and little Helmut in the other, I ran to the Jungfrauenthal shelter, Ilse following behind with the baby on her hip and her little girl holding her hand, a bag over her shoulder and a milk bottle sticking out of her coat pocket. "If we survive this, I'm moving to the country," she groaned.

The alarm didn't last long. Some of the late arrivals told us that only a few bombs had fallen, that they must have been reconnaissance planes. "Do you think we should go back home?" Ilse asked.

I thought of the conversation of the officers at work and shook
my head. "To be honest, I would spend the next couple of days
in the bunker. Go and get something to eat, stretch your legs. I'll
watch the little ones; they're asleep anyway."

Ilse searched my face. "You know something, don't you?"

"I wish I did, but all I've heard is rumors. I haven't got a good
feeling, though—better to stay safe."

Ilse was relieved that for once the decision had been made
for her. She left the cellar and returned after three-quarters of
an hour with food and some games for the children, prepared
to spend a long time in the shelter. Reassured, I left her and
made my way back to the Hochallee. I had a day off and wasn't
expected back at work until 8 p.m.

To distract myself, I went to the vegetable market so I could get
some more food to take to the parsonage. I helped for about two
hours and got a bag full of broad beans, potatoes, and spinach. It
was an incredibly hot day. I was constantly wiping the sweat from
my forehead, and my blouse stuck to me. The atmosphere was
strange. Everyone seemed to expect another alarm at any minute,
and people scanned the sky as if to ascertain that no undetected
plane was about to drop its deadly freight without warning.

I took the majority of the vegetables to Monsignor Bram. If I
didn't do it too often or too conspicuously, no one could accuse
me of doing anything wrong by giving the local priest some
food, so I went in the middle of the day. Then, with my mother,
I made soup for us, Kuddel, and Willi from the leftovers. To
make sure that I warned them as best I could, I told them over
dinner about the conversation in the canteen at work, and before
heading off to Altona, I asked them to spend the night in the
cellar, even Kuddel.

Looking out of the tram window on my way to the Wehrmacht,
the atmosphere seemed strange. Although it was the evening, it
was still hot and sticky, and the streets would usually have been

busy. However, all was cloaked in a ghostly silence, like the calm before the storm. I saw a lot of people on their way to the bunkers, recognizable by the large bundles under their arms and the determination in their steps. The odd thing about it was that the air-raid sirens hadn't sounded, and still the whole of Hamburg seemed to be streaming into the bunkers. I shuddered.

I left the tram at Altona, so deep in thought that I even greeted my colleagues with a "Heil Hitler!" on entering the office. Work soon had me in its grip; messages were still coming through in great numbers, transports being announced and requested, news being sent to Wehrmacht headquarters. At twenty to midnight, the sirens howled. The impacts, making the walls shake, didn't come until later. The air was heavy with anxiety and fear, and it all felt different from previous raids. Nobody spoke. I didn't even talk to Karchen, who was sitting with a gloomy expression nearby. We just stared into space, resigning ourselves to fate. After about two hours, the enormous heat in the cellars grew until it was almost unbearable. Finally, the all-clear came. We had been lucky again. Without speaking but with a very bad feeling, I returned to my desk.

The machines rattled like never before. Hour after hour, ghastly messages poured in, talking about destroyed transports, stores, and telephone offices, the army provision office in Wandsbek, Barmbek station, the main station, the gas works at Grasbrook—it was endless. Karchen came down, his face distorted by worry. "The whole of Hamburg is burning. There's a firestorm raging. Everything is in flames: Wandsbek, Hamm, Hohenfelde, St. Georg, Eilbek, Horn, Hammerbrook, Rothenburgsort, Borgfelde. The fire engines can't do anything. It's an inferno out there!"

"Oh God!" was all I could say. My knees gave way. Karchen took me by the arm and led me upstairs to the canteen. He fetched me something to eat and two cups of coffee. I hadn't had anything to eat or drink for nine hours.

"Well, I didn't hear any mention of Harvestehude," he said, trying to cheer me up.

"Oh, Karchen, it's not just our own house, is it? What are all those people who've lost their homes to do? Is there going to be anything left of Hamburg?"

"Come on, now. You've never sounded as disheartened as this. It's not your way, Gretel. Those who've been bombed out are going to be evacuated, makeshift shelters are going to be built, and transports to the country organized. If you've had enough of this, you can go to the country yourself, you know. I'll help you if you want to get out of here."

It was tempting, I had to admit—to just pack my bags and escape the bombing and the chaos. It was up to them how they'd cope with their Wehrmacht transport stuff and the mountains of rubble. That's what had come of their "Heil Hitler!" I looked at Karchen, who was stirring his coffee, deep in thought. He wouldn't go, and nor would Mother. Somehow, I knew it wasn't really the solution for me either. I wouldn't have a moment's peace of mind if I left them all behind.

Vigorously, I shook my head. "Thanks, but I'm staying. Running away has never been my thing."

Karchen patted my arm. "There you go, almost yourself again! Shall I take you home when you finish?"

I accepted his offer gratefully, feeling extremely distressed at the thought of walking through the burned-out streets by myself.

About three hours later, we got ready to leave. My fingers hurt from all the typing; I hadn't had a chance to have my hour's nap. On leaving the building, we stepped out into darkness. The sky was largely covered in gray-black clouds of smoke with an unreal light behind them, orange-red as if reflecting what was happening on the ground. The sun wouldn't get through all day. We had known that not much of the city would be left, but we were still shocked by what we saw.

Everywhere, houses burned or smoldered, gutted. The streets, covered in bricks and debris, were deserted. A sickly sweet smell hovered in the air. Here and there, we saw twisted black beams, some in the rubble and some on the streets. Karchen inspected one of these, bending over it. Suddenly he slapped his hand over his mouth, retching, and turned away.

"What?" I shouted at him angrily, knowing that I didn't want to hear the answer.

"They're not beams. They're . . . they're . . . people."

I felt sick. All those black things lying around were charred bodies, almost unrecognizable as human. I clutched at Karchen's sleeve. "Oh my God! It must have been absolute hell."

As we carried on we passed more bodies. Some were still recognizable, some wore clothes; others, although close by the clothed ones, were naked. Not all of them had died in the flames; some of them must have choked or died from the extreme heat.

Karchen and I took each other by the hand, having finally picked our way to the Hochallee. I held my breath for the last 50 meters. As before, I tried to prepare myself for the shock by imagining our house as a pile of rubble. Again, I felt an enormous sense of relief at the sight of the house, still standing. Superstitiously, I swore to myself that if my mother had escaped unharmed, I would never deal on the black market again.

There she stood, sweeping the front steps in her finest dress, as if to show the world that she refused to be defeated. A glass skylight had been shattered and shards were lying everywhere. I leaped toward her, tore the broom from her hands, and threw myself into her arms. Karchen waited tactfully until I had calmed down before clearing his throat.

I wiped the tears from my eyes and distracted myself by looking for the little pig. There it was, among the shards of glass, in the small front garden of the house. Carefully, I picked it up. Its ears were broken off, the snout was a little damaged, and the tail was missing. I wiped it clean on my skirt and took it into the house. Kunert watched with interest, not saying a word.

During breakfast, we rubbed the soles of our feet, which had been burned on the hot pavements and rubble on the way home.

Our shoes had wooden soles rather than leather ones, because of
the rationing, but even these didn't offer much protection from
the heat. But to complain about sore feet, after what we had seen,
didn't occur to us. I didn't tell my mother about the awful sights
we'd witnessed—only that there wasn't much left of Hamburg.
She had joined us at the table but conversation didn't come easily. Too much was unsaid, and ugly images were burned into our
memories, impossible to chase away. "I think I'll be on my way
then," Karchen mumbled after a while.

"No, you're dead on your feet, Karchen!" I scolded him. "You
can sleep here. We've got enough space."

"Have you got a telephone?"

I had forgotten that he had a wife and child at home. Whatever the truth about his private life, after a night like this it was
imperative that he found out whether his family was all right and
let them know that he was safe. I showed him to the phone in
the corridor and left him alone.

Mother was not unimpressed by the handsome officer I had
brought home.

"Not for me, unfortunately." I tried to explain.

"Who knows? Maybe one day," she responded hopefully.

I let her believe it. What did it matter?

Karchen returned. "Everything all right?"

He nodded. "No one was harmed. But then they're not in the
city." His wife and child had gone to stay with an aunt in the
country when the first major attacks started.

Yawning, I showed Karchen to my room. We shared my bed,
both glad of the presence of the other.

After a fidgety sleep, I got up a few hours later. It was far
too hot, and I felt restless. Karchen didn't sleep much longer. In
the kitchen, my mother gave us some real coffee before Karchen
said good-bye.

"Thanks for not leaving me to walk on my own through that,"
I said.

He looked at me and then took me in his arms. "Take care, now. And don't show anyone your stock up there!"

I watched him walking down the street. Then I tried to help my mother to prepare a big pot of stew, but I felt twitchy. At last, a thought began to form in my head, giving me direction.

"Mother, I'm off to look for an emergency shelter for us, in case something does happen one day. We've been incredibly lucky so far. We mustn't assume it'll go on like that forever."

Mother stopped scraping the carrots. "I won't move from here!" she declared firmly.

Impatiently, I told her, "But what if the house is wrecked, I mean? We've got to have somewhere to go, just in case."

"Where do you intend to find a place, then? It's the same everywhere!"

But I didn't have to think for long. "I'll go to the Baltic Sea. Don't worry if I don't come home tonight. I'll have a look around and probably go straight to work tomorrow morning."

"You've got to do what you think is right, but I won't move out as long as there is as much as a wall left of our house."

I went upstairs, shaking my head at her stubbornness. I packed my bag, said farewell to Mother, placed the little pig back in its place on the stairs, and took off.

The whole of Hamburg seemed to be trying to get out. There were masses of people on the roads, their belongings on wooden carts, in baby carriages, and on bicycles. Often they had to heave their possessions over the piles of rubble or try to clear the way. They talked about collection points and food depots, where BDM girls and women's organizations handed out meals, and even sausage and chocolate. Soldiers and men in civilian clothes were already busy clearing the streets. Very few had any equipment—most worked with their bare hands—but the main roads were becoming more and more passable as the debris piled up on either side of the streets.

Clearance units, well-organized food supplies for the homeless—evidently, the city was prepared for this scenario. *The worst has happened; see how well we're looking after you. If you're bombed out, you'll get extra rations and accommodation with other citizens. In bad times, we all stick together; together we're strong. Never mind that you have no house; you'll get real coffee and cigarettes. And by the way, do give us your son as well. No, it's all right, he's not considered too young anymore. We need all hands on deck these days.* Enraged, I began to kick the remains of a wall. You've done this to us. Heil Hitler! Our beloved Führer! Into hell you've led us, you bastard. I hurt my shin and screamed, more in fury than in pain.

"Are you all right? Do you need a lift?"

I raised my head and saw a friendly face, blackened by soot, leaning out of the window of a truck. "Thank you," I said. "I'd love a lift."

I quickly climbed onto the back and looked for a place between the other passengers and their belongings, rubbing my leg. The driver dropped us off at a station, and after a long wait, I managed to secure myself a place on an overcrowded train to Lübeck. My anger had dissipated now. I focused on my project, trying to cling on to a semblance of normality, setting myself a goal.

Grömitz was out of the question; it would only remind me of Lutz. I decided on the seaside resort of Timmendorfer Strand, but soon changed my mind when I thought about the prices. Why not try somewhere smaller and less popular, like Niendorf? When I arrived, I walked straight to the shore to clear my head. The sea air was wonderful, the small strip of sand perfect. I removed my shoes and ran barefoot into the water. The sun was just setting on the horizon, gulls screeched, here and there was an old deck chair, over there some boats were moored. How peaceful! Slowly, I walked back up the beach and sat down in the still-warm sand until it got dark.

With a sigh, I went to look for accommodation. The houses were tidy, quite plain and simple. There were no thatched roofs or exposed beams like the cottages on Sylt. I imagined that rooms with a view of the sea would be more expensive, so I didn't even look at possibilities in the Strandstraße by the shore. Instead, I turned onto the next parallel road, and I liked the look of it.

A brick house with a veranda caught my eye. Without hesitation, I knocked at the door. After quite a while, it was opened by an unfriendly-looking elderly lady.

"Good evening," I beamed at her. "Do you rent out rooms?"

The woman cleared her throat and answered, "Not really, no, not anymore. I used to do that, but it's too much for me now."

I was undeterred. "You won't have much work with me, I promise. I come from Hamburg, and all I want is to get out of the city for a night or two, maybe put some stuff here for safekeeping, if that's possible. I'd pay a monthly rent, and you wouldn't even have to change the beds or make meals. The main thing is that I can come here if our house is bombed."

She thought for a moment. "Come on in then, lass. I've got a room with a door to the veranda."

The house smelled like a mixture of sausage, cabbage, and lavender. The furniture was simple and made of dark wood. The room she showed me had an old wardrobe, a washstand, and an ancient-looking bed with a chair next to it. No pictures hung on the walls; there was only a wooden cross above the bed.

"Perfect!" I smiled. What I liked most was the door to the veranda. I could already picture myself having breakfast out there. "If you don't mind, I'd like to stay tonight. I'll pay in advance and leave very early tomorrow morning."

The old lady nodded. Her face was marked by a long, hard life. She looked haggard, but she didn't stoop, and she looked directly into my eyes when speaking; she struck me as decent and honest.

"Can I still get something to eat in the village at this time?"

"You can try at the harbor." She was clearly not prepared to make any exceptions after I'd told her that I wouldn't need her to provide me with meals. That didn't matter to me anyway, as long as I had found a place to stay. I suggested that she think about how much to charge me while I was out. "Oh, and my name is Gretel Öhlgart."

"Minna Kirchler," she answered, and opened the door to let me out.

Fortified by a good portion of sole and potatoes, I returned to Frau Kirchler's house. She must have seen me coming, as she opened the door before I'd knocked. "Fifteen marks in advance for the month?" she asked without any preamble.

"That's fine," I replied. "I'll give it to you right now. I've got to get up at four tomorrow to make sure I get to work on time."

Frau Kirchler pocketed the money, but she didn't offer me a key. I told myself not to take it personally. After all, she didn't know me yet.

I hadn't slept so well in a very long time. I duly got up at four, in case the trains into Hamburg were delayed. There were no problems. I could get as far as Wandsbek by train, and then I went on to work by Underground and on foot. The city lay in ruins, still smoldering; clouds of dust and ash rose whenever a car passed. What a dramatic contrast to my break at the Baltic Sea! I decided to go back as soon as I could manage.

I got into the Transport Command about half an hour early— enough time to stop for a coffee in the canteen. Karchen wasn't in, but I saw a number of other soldiers and officers whom I knew well enough to chat to. Fortunately, none of the "Hitler brides," as I called my female colleagues, were to be seen. The men talked of nothing but the events of the firestorm night.

More and more horrific stories were told. A lot of people had been killed in their shelters, either through direct hits or by being buried alive. The "high bunkers," public shelters built aboveground, and which we had been assured were impact-proof, had not proved to be so safe after all. Many, believing themselves to be out of harm's way, had lost their lives when these were hit; others in the high bunkers died of the tremendous heat or of smoke inhalation.

In order to avoid choking to death, everybody had to get out of the damaged bunkers and cellars, which was impossible because of the sea of flames in the streets. Those who managed to get outside were incinerated immediately. It had been impossible to extinguish the flames; the firefighters were powerless and merely tried to save lives, often paying with their own.

The officers began to argue about the causes of the firestorm. They spoke of "accumulated heat in the city" and "cold masses of air above," of "the fire seeking oxygen," "the suction effect of the narrow streets," and other such technicalities. What did it matter now, the how and why? Surely the weather wasn't to blame. If anyone was, it was the Nazis and their warmongering. I didn't want to hear any more. I got up to make my way to my telex machine.

"Heil Hitler!" the women at the telex machines greeted me, as if to enrage me anew.

"Heil bomb terror!" I responded crossly. My colleagues looked meaningfully at each other, but I didn't care. I sat down at my machine feeling rebellious, so I typed a personal message to a supply officer at the Eastern Front, which was strictly forbidden.

"And how are you guys doing at the front?" I wrote. The answer came promptly: "All clear here stop heard of bombs stop huge favor stop mother in Altona stop tel 6344 stop still alive stop." That poor soul! Sitting there in a hole at the front, fighting for people and fatherland while his family might have gone up in flames. I stood up, climbed the stairs, and grabbed the phone on Karchen's desk. Quickly, I dialed the number. I was lucky. A shaky female voice answered with a hesitant, "Yes?"

"Your son just telegraphed me from the front. He's fine but he's ever so worried about you. Can I give him a message?"

"Oh my God! My boy! We survived, but we're going to friends in Pinneberg. We're not staying in the city. Please, would you be so kind as to tell him?" I assured her I would pass the message on straightaway and did so conscientiously.

After that, I continued to make contact with soldiers at the other end of the lines. At least one good thing would come out of my work here, I thought. All right, Karchen kept telling me how important the coded messages that he got from me were. But what did he do with them? Was I really doing anything to help?

The following night, there was another alarm. After the mass exodus and the many victims of the firestorm night, there weren't many people left in the city, but some quarters of Hamburg had not been hit too badly so far: Barmbek, Winterhude, Wilhelmsburg, Harburg, Bergedorf, and Blankenese still stood. Would they be destroyed as well? Harvestehude, where we lived, was not badly damaged either. Maybe it would be our turn next?

Full of foreboding, I decided to pop in at the parsonage during the next air raid. There the atmosphere was much better than in most places; no lamenting women, no screaming children and exasperated mothers, no blocked toilets either, as there had been in the high bunker at Heiligengeistfeld, where I had sought shelter once and never again. I would rather get hit by a bomb on an open road than expose myself once more to such an experience. The problem was the air-raid wardens, who made themselves feel important by catching people like me practicing "unlawful air-raid behavior." If we didn't seek shelter during an alarm, it was called "remaining in the open without permission," and penalties were imposed without discussion.

Monsignor Bram greeted me with his usual friendly nod while he talked to a young man who was standing next to him, before coming over to speak to me. "Nice to have you here with us. You haven't joined us for a while. How is your mother?" I hadn't spoken to him properly for a long time. I'd just dropped in to deliver my food parcels. I told him about my emergency accommodation in Niendorf, and he praised my foresight. I realized that he had no such place to go.

"What will you do if the church and your house are destroyed?" I asked.

Bram didn't seem concerned by the prospect. "The Lord will know my path," he said simply. The fascinating thing was that he believed it absolutely. His faith radiated from him. Trust in God—I wish I had that, I thought with a sigh.

Just after two in the morning, they gave the all-clear. I said good-bye to the couple with whom I had had an interesting conversation and went back home. The Oberstraße, the main road, was burning at the far end, but fate had once more spared us, if only just. The Harvestehuder Weg had suffered heavy hits, and in the east the night sky shone an unnatural gray-orange. Barmbek, I thought, maybe Uhlenhorst.

On my night shift, I heard where the city had been hit. Uhlenhorst and Winterhude had indeed been heavily affected; nothing much was left of Barmbek. Karstadt, the department store in the Mönckebergstraße, had been completely destroyed. The worst thing was that about 300 people had perished in the shelter beneath the store. On the last day of this doomed month of July, the *Hamburger Zeitung* printed an appeal by the city's governor, Karl Kaufmann. He spoke of a "catastrophe of an unheard-of extent," and asked us for our "relentless commitment" to cope with the "hardest challenge" that had been put before the people of our city.

The last major attack came on August 2, again during one of my night shifts. This time, a thunderstorm was raging above the city and it poured down with rain; the damage was nothing in comparison with the huge fires caused by the bombings in July. During the whole of August, we didn't hear the sirens, nor in September either. Hardly anything was left of Hamburg; the British and the Americans had succeeded in their intentions.

Slowly, order was restored. The streets were shoveled free, piece by piece, of debris; bodies were recovered; damaged water, energy, and gas supplies were repaired. For a time, we had to cook over a fire in the garden, but luckily we didn't have to pump water, as our pipe had stayed intact. Most had not been so fortunate.

Many found temporary homes in ruins and cellars; some, like us, had to take in bombed-out families.

When I came home after my shift one day in August, our house seemed to be bursting at the seams with a strange family. I couldn't tell how many children they had; I kept losing count. Mother told me that they'd just walked in without so much as saying hello. The house was assigned to the family as their new home, so in they marched, taking over our living room and leaving us no chance to escape the noise and chaos they brought with them.

I had no objections to taking in homeless people, but this family I did not like. Right down to the youngest child, they were rude and careless. They had no respect for our belongings, which they explained by declaring themselves to be communists. However, I had come across communists in the past, through my grandfather, and as far as I remembered, they had been nice, polite, idealistic individuals.

One day, when I came home from work, I found my mother upset and angry. "Gretel, they've emptied our stores from the cellar. They've taken almost all the preserves. And there are some clothes missing from the washing line—my best white blouse and even some of my knickers! What on earth can we do?" Mother wasn't easily troubled, but this had gone too far.

"We'll lock the cellar," I declared. We had spent hours preserving a load of pears so that we would have some fruit during the winter months. "If they'd asked us, we'd have given them something. Are you absolutely sure they didn't say anything to you about it?"

"Well, yes," Mother said. "'Everything belongs to everyone,' that's what they said when I asked them about it."

I couldn't understand such behavior. They hadn't helped us at all in preparing the food, neither by working for hours at the vegetable market nor by peeling or cooking the pears. "It's a disgrace!" I said. "We'll hide everything we need or value. And the washing we'll hang up in the kitchen from now on."

Of course, I had to be even more careful about my black-market dealings with these strangers in the house. I locked the door whenever I left my room.

I held a council of war with Willi, who lived in Kuddel's room now. "Get everything out of the house that you don't really need at the moment!" he advised me.

I thought of my room in Niendorf and agreed. "But I need a means of transport. I don't suppose you could get ahold of an automobile?" Willi promised to have a look around.

His connections were truly remarkable. Not long after our conversation, he knocked at my door. "Come and have a look," he said with a wink.

Excited, I dashed downstairs and tore the door open.

"That's . . . my car?" On the street was a boxy three-wheeler of undefined color.

"A Rollfix!" Willi declared proudly.

I looked at him uncertainly. Was he serious? I must be polite, I told myself. He must have put himself to a lot of trouble to get ahold of it. "But it's ancient!" I blurted out.

"About ten years old—one of the first ever built. It's a real Hamburger, comes from Wandsbek!"

For a brief moment, I remembered Fritz Müller's sleek, handsome BMW—I must have secretly hoped for something similar—but then reason won out. I needed something to get me from A to B, and here it was. For my purposes, it was more than enough; as long as the streets were free of debris, I'd have no trouble getting to the Baltic Sea in it.

"How much?"

Willi tilted his head to the side. "Fifty marks?"

"Deal!"

I drove my Rollfix to Niendorf regularly, sometimes even twice or three times a week, always after a night shift. More and more of our things moved up to Frau Kirchler's—feather duvets, linen, porcelain, clothes. If our house was ruined and we survived, we would at least have somewhere to stay and some of our valuables safe.

The sea did me good. I found an inner peace and calm that I couldn't achieve in the city. Minna Kirchler seemed to get used to me, too. She was almost friendly after a while. She kept up the no-nonsense North German manner, but seemed to genuinely like me. Over time, even my funny little car grew on me, and I nicknamed it my "Breakneck Emmi." Whenever I arrived back in Hamburg, I was shocked anew by the senseless destruction. Surely it couldn't go on much longer now. The war was bound to end soon.

The Nazis, however, were still far from ready to give in. The city got back on its feet bit by bit. The mail started to be delivered again, trains once more departed from the main station, buildings in danger of collapse were blown up. New ration cards were distributed, and I had to go to the authorities with my ID card and passport to collect them. Life went on. The cinema even began showing movies again.

One day at work, a letter arrived for me by field post, addressed to "Fräulein G., telex operator, Transport Command Hamburg-Altona." The envelope was strangely misshapen. When I opened it, a pine twig fell into my hands. Confused, I took the letter out of the envelope and read:

Dear G.,

I don't even know your name. Gertrud, maybe, or Greta? Whatever you are called, you've got your heart in the right place. Nobody can imagine what it means to get news from home when Hamburg is being flattened by bombs. I am so grateful that you passed our messages on to my mother and my comrade's wife and we know that they're well. I would love to send you something to express my thanks, but I haven't got

anything at all. Hang on, there's a branch knocking against
the window out there (we've barricaded ourselves in a derelict
house). I'll break it off and post it with the letter, as a sign
of my gratitude.

All best wishes,

Your devoted
Richard Jörns

I was so touched that I had to sit down. The pine twig I fastened to my telex machine, so as not to forget about my private
messages. Whenever I believed myself to be unobserved, I would
communicate with soldiers at the front and inquire after their
loved ones in Hamburg. Usually, I phoned them up, although
sometimes I would pop in and visit them in their homes. I heard
astonishing tales from these people, some sad, some wonderful,
and I duly telegraphed them to the front line.

For a long time, there were very few air raids; there was just
one in October and two in November. More and more refugees
returned to the cities to pick up where they had left off, going
back to the ruins of their houses. In the main square, a huge
gathering was held to honor the dead. I didn't go. Crowds in
front of waving swastikas sickened me.

One day, I was eating with Karchen in the canteen when a
high-ranking officer came in, surrounded by a swarm of Wehrmacht officials. "Have a look at this one, Karchen! Who is it?
Not bad-looking, is he?"

Kunert was taken aback by my ignorance. "You don't know who
he is? That's one of your highest superiors."

"Stauffenberg?" I asked, amazed. Kunert nodded.

Colonel Claus Schenk Graf von Stauffenberg. I had only heard
his name so far. The first thing I noticed about him was his
approachable but authoritative demeanor. His facial features were

finely chiseled and masculine, and his posture—straight but not stiff—demanded respect. Altogether, I liked his looks quite a lot, until he turned toward our table and I saw that he wore an eye patch.

He seemed to have a natural authority. He didn't raise his voice, but the officials around were falling over themselves to get his attention. "Seems to be a nice fellow," I commented.

Karchen nodded, watching Stauffenberg out of the corner of his eye. "More than just nice. He's also got his pretty little head and his heart on the right side of things."

Did I understand him correctly? Could it be that Stauffenberg, so close to Hitler himself, was not a true Nazi? I gasped, and Karchen shook his head as a warning not to say anything more. So I was right! But how did Karchen know about it? Suddenly, I felt very small, unimportant and uninformed. But at the same time, I took heart. If such high-ranking officers were on the right side of things, there might be a chance after all to rid ourselves of the fascists.

By this time, the black market had become a lifesaver. Rations were shorter than ever, and we could barely have survived on what we were given alone. Connections counted more than all the money in the world. We were glad we were sharing our house with Willi, because he was able to get us extra food. Not even Frau Gernot complained or asked where it came from; hunger affects hypocrites like everyone else.

What Frau Gernot did not know, nor the family of thieves, either, was the extent of his resourcefulness. My own bartering carried on as well, if a lot more secretively. The need was greater than ever. Sometimes I asked myself whether the others in the house wondered about the stream of visitors, but I had made a habit of boasting about my many friends and acquaintances to preempt suspicion. About three or four times a week, I took a delivery to Monsignor Bram.

Of course, lining up was still a daily necessity. We still needed all the food we could get, and besides, it had to look as if that was our only source of supplies. I took turns with my mother and Willi. Life revolved completely around getting enough to eat. Above it all, the constant danger of further attacks hung like the sword of Damocles. In December, another major air raid came, but our luck held out, and the house and our lives were spared.

The Nazis didn't have much influence among the general populace anymore. Whatever they might tell us now, most of us were clear that we were reaping what we had sowed. The only ones who still believed in the Führer were those who had made a career through the National Socialist institutions, and the youngsters who had been indoctrinated all their lives into fascist ideology. No one else believed what Hitler said now. In his 1944 New Year's speech, he shrieked that we would "rebuild our cities, more beautiful than they have ever been before," and that out of the ruins would "blossom a new German age of magnificent cities." I definitely wasn't the only one who switched the wireless off.

13

THE STAUFFENBERG PLOT

1944: British and American troops land in France. Finland and Romania withdraw from the war. Rommel commits suicide. American troops occupy Aachen.

Hamburg issues 400 air-raid warnings and 182 bomber alerts and is the target of 39 bomb attacks, many of which target large areas of the city. Almost 8,000 people are killed or wounded; nobody records damage to property anymore.

Since 1938, there have been numerous serious plots from within Germany aiming to overthrow the fascist government, and there have been various attempts on Hitler's life, by high-ranking army officers, by a group of political philosophers known as the Kreisau Circle, and by individual citizens. For many unfortunate reasons, none of these attempts has succeeded.

I started to go to black-market parties again. They became wilder and fiercer than ever, and I too behaved as if I had only hours left to live. When it all got to be too much, I'd drive up to Niendorf to soothe my soul.

In the new year, the air-raid sirens continued to sound. It went on and on. By now, the habits of wartime life had become so entrenched that I found it hard to imagine that things would ever change. I worked, ran down into the shelters, dealt in food and cigarettes, drove to the Baltic Sea, and partied endlessly.

At the Wehrmacht, we got together for a glass of wine every now and then. Sometimes, when I was on night shift, Karchen would come down and ask if I fancied a break. He'd take me to one of the offices where a couple of soldiers and officers would be standing around a desk, glasses in their hands and the air thick with smoke. No one, of course, was about to admit that he had acquired the wine on the black market at a high price, so the pretense would be that the bottle had been discovered in the furthest corner of a cellar.

The Hitler brides were never invited, which I was pleased about. If they weren't wanted, it could only mean that I was surrounded by anti-Nazis. Again, I mused on the fact that the rank in the Wehrmacht seemed to be no sure indicator of loyalty to Hitler, as these little get-togethers showed; some high-ranking officers could be heard making quite a few subversive comments. Usually, I was the only woman present, but that had never bothered me much. I flirted outrageously and had a great time.

On July 20, I experienced the strangest night shift of my career. I hadn't been at work for long when Frau Heimlich and I were called to the encryption machine. A message from the Wehrmacht headquarters in Knochenhauerstraße had come in. We adjusted the rotors, rings, settings, and plugs to the current code, took the long ciphered letter, and typed it in. Frau Heimlich sat at the machine while I wrote down the letters that lit up.

"A mysterious clique of unscrupulous party leaders had tried to assert power for "selfish reasons," the machine told us, to my bafflement. "In this hour of extreme danger, the Reich govern-ment has declared a military state of emergency for the upkeep of law and order." I glanced at Frau Heimlich, but she was too busy typing the scrambled letters to notice their meaning.

What followed were details of which commanders had executive power and the instruction that the Wehrmacht and every single authority and government department was from this moment subject to these commanders. "Every resistance to the military executive is to be broken ruthlessly. In this hour of extreme danger for the fatherland, the obedience of the Wehrmacht and the upkeep of the fullest discipline is the highest priority." My eyes widened. "The German soldier is faced with a historic task. It will depend on his actions and attitude whether Germany will be saved." The letter was signed by the commander in chief of the Wehrmacht, although the usual signatory, Wilhelm Keitel, had been replaced by Erwin von Witzleben, and it was authorized by von Stauffenberg.

What on earth had happened? Was there a plot against Hitler? That would be . . . I didn't dare even to think the thing through. Karchen! I had to tell Karchen! I leaped to the telephone. Hopefully he was on duty tonight. With trembling fingers, I dialed his number. Thank God, he picked up. "Karchen! Something's happened! Quick, come down!" I cried, my voice choked with emotion. He must have flown downstairs, he arrived so quickly. He tore the letter out of my hand and read. I studied his face.

His eyes showed not even a hint of surprise but rather a glow of satisfaction. I didn't understand. Before I was able to bombard him with questions, an officer shot into the room with another letter for Frau Heimlich to type into the encryption machine. Karchen stood behind me, reading along:

> By the executive power given to me by the commander in chief
> of the Wehrmacht, the most important buildings and facilities
> of the Wehrmacht communications network (including radio
> facilities) are to be secured according to military procedure.

The forces deployed are to be assigned in such strength that
unauthorized operations and sabotage are prevented. Essential
technical facilities for communications are to be staffed with
officers . . .

Arrests. To be dismissed and taken into specially secured
solitary confinement without delay are: every mayor, governor,
minister, police commissioner, SS and police leader, Gestapo
leader . . . The concentration camps are to be restaffed at
once, the camp commanders are to be arrested, the guards
to be disarmed and detained . . . The offices of the Gestapo
and the SD are to be restaffed . . . Arbitrary acts and revenge
must not be tolerated while implementing executive power.
The population must understand that the arbitrary methods
of the previous rulers are at an end.

This was authorized again by Stauffenberg, and signed in the
name of General Fromm.

Silently, I handed the letter to Kunert, and he, Frau Heimlich,
and I went back up to the telex room. The choice of words—"the
arbitrary methods of the previous rulers"—said enough. The Nazis
were about to be overthrown. What could have happened?

"The Führer is dead!" Karchen announced, not only to me but
to the whole room. He squeezed my shoulder briefly and rushed
upstairs, the letters in his hand.

We didn't react. The other women carried on with their work
as if Karchen had said that it was raining outside. They couldn't
have heard him, or perhaps I had understood it all wrong. Mysti-
fied, I arranged the pile of papers on my table and got to work.

Then the next coded message arrived: "[Operation] Valkyrie [a
military contingency plan in case of any major uprising or threat to
state security] 2nd step for W.Kdo. I-XIII, XVII, XVIII, XX, XXL
. . ." Weapons, equipment, and vehicles were to be transported
to "AHA Stab Ib" immediately. All that was too technical for me.
I didn't understand it. But it sounded terribly urgent and serious.

As I went back up to the main office, I wondered if it could really be that Hitler was dead. It hadn't been mentioned in any of the communications, but that was what Kunert had said, I was certain of it. Where could he have got this unbelievable idea from?

Then, as I sat down in front of my telex, it hit me like lightning. It was a putsch, a *coup d'état*, and Karchen was somewhere right in the thick of it. That was why he hadn't been surprised! Now everything would be reorganized, the whole system would be turned upside down, we would be able to breathe again, the war would end. The governor, the police chiefs, the leaders of the Gestapo and the Wehrmacht were about to be arrested. Slowly, an incredible feeling of joy rose up in me.

I stood up and shouted out, "Hitler is dead! Hitler is dead!" Ecstatic, I turned to my colleagues. My outburst had put an end to the unnatural quiet, and the others all assembled around Frau Heimlich's desk to try to find out what she knew. They were all shouting at once. One woman sobbed at the top of her voice, moaning, "The Führer! It can't be true! It's simply impossible!" She was taken into the arms of her coworkers, who themselves seemed to be on the verge of nervous collapse.

"Heil Hitler! Ha ha!" I muttered to myself, wondering whether anyone upstairs still had a bottle of champagne.

Karchen was racing around the upstairs offices. The telephones didn't stop ringing for a second. I found him and handed him a copy of the most recent communication, which he skimmed while shouting into the phone: "Are you absolutely sure—100 percent? Shouldn't we simply—Sir! Yes, sir!"

He sank onto the edge of the desk, loosening his collar. The expression on his face was far from promising. My smile froze. "There's been an announcement on the radio," he said. "The Führer is alive. The orders you just passed to me have been declared invalid."

"What do you mean, the Führer is alive?" I whispered. "I've already practically been dancing around my office. You told me Hitler was dead and—"

Karchen, whom I had never known to be impatient, interrupted me. "How should I know what's going on? Go back downstairs. You've got work to do!"

I turned and left.

"Gretel!" he called.

I knew he was right. I didn't really mind him having a go at me. He was obviously under tremendous stress. At the top of the stairs, I heard Frau Heimlich calling for me. "Coming!" I shouted, and within seconds I was back at the encryption machine ready to decode the next message. "The communiqué given over the radio is incorrect. The Führer is dead. The procedures ordered are to be carried out with haste. The commander of the Ersatzheer [Reserve Army] and the commander in chief of the homeland war zone Stab/Nr. 5000/44 geh.+ . . ." More military terminology. But, basically, it was true, then!

This time, I got up silently and took the message upstairs. I watched Karchen as he read. He ran his hand through his hair, bit his lip, and jumped up as if he had suddenly made a decision. At that moment, the telephone rang again. Karchen hesitated. Almost apologetically, he said, "That's not the outside line. I'm not getting direct orders from the command." I looked at him, surprised. He seemed to know what would happen. The conversation was short, his answers monosyllabic. He put down the receiver and looked at me without seeing me. "The order is invalid," he said.

I went back to the machine. The next message read:

The Führer has appointed Reichsführer-SS Himmler commander of the Ersatzheer and bestowed on him authority over the members of the Ersatzheer. Orders are to be taken solely if issued by the Reichsführer-SS and myself. Any orders issued by Fromm, von Witzleben or Höpner are invalid.

The Chief OKW Keitel, Generalfeldmarschall

It was Frau Heimlich who was in high spirits now. She tore the message from my hands and took it upstairs herself. I went back up to the telex office. Frau Heimlich was away a long time. When she returned, she called excitedly, "The Führer is alive! A miracle has happened. He is unharmed. They tried to kill him, but they failed. I've just heard him on the wireless!"

Again my colleagues flew into each other's arms, this time in tears of joy. "It was fate! The Lord has protected our Führer. The German Reich is not lost!" They shot me poisonous looks, which I ignored. Stupid women! Why couldn't I have kept my mouth shut? I hoped there wouldn't be serious consequences to my open delight at the Führer's supposed demise. It was easy to imagine the Hitler brides informing on me out of spite.

With half an ear, I listened to Frau Heimlich's report of the Führer's speech. "You should have heard him! It was only a tiny clique of ambitious, ruthless, criminal, and stupid officers, he said. They plotted against him and planted a bomb that exploded just two meters away from our Führer. Imagine that! How close! And you'll never believe who was responsible: Stauffenberg!"

A murmur went through the women. "Stauffenberg? Impossible!"

Triumphant about her superior knowledge, Frau Heimlich continued: "And the Führer escaped. He has only a few grazes, bruises, and minor burns. He sees it as a sign of providence, because there have been many attempts on his life, none successful. That's what he said. And that the traitors are going to pay for what they did, and that he will continue his work. How good it was to hear his voice, I tell you! You didn't know what to believe in the end, did you?"

Suddenly I felt terribly tired. It was past 1 a.m. I decided to have a coffee and lie down for a moment. The canteen was full. Swarms of soldiers and officers came and went. The place was only usually so busy during the day. I couldn't see Karchen and hoped he was all right. I fetched a cup of coffee and drank it without sitting down. As I left the canteen, I bumped into Karchen.

"Gretel! I'm sorry if I—"

"It's okay. You'd better tell me what to do now."

"What can we do?" he whispered. "Whatever happened, happened. The best of our people will disappear. All those even remotely connected with it will—" He broke off as a soldier approached us.

"What exactly did happen then?" I asked in a subdued voice once the man had passed.

Karchen gave me a look. "Not here," he said.

It was driving me half crazy not having a clue what was going on, and he could see it. He gave me a friendly punch on the arm and went to the officers' table, where heated arguments were going on.

I was about to go for a rest when Frau Heimlich stuck her head around the corner. "Here you are! Do hurry, will you? I can't do the messages on my own, can I?" Resigned, I followed her to receive the next communication.

> To all departments who received orders from the specified generals. The attempted putsch of the renegade generals has been ruthlessly crushed. Every single ringleader shot dead. Orders of the generals von Witzleben, Höpner, Beck and Olbricht are not to be followed. I have resumed authority, having been temporarily detained by force.
>
> Signed,
>
> General Fromm

So, several generals had tried to depose Hitler, not just Stauffenberg on his own. I would never have thought it possible. That was where all the official-sounding military orders had come from—high up the ranks. Who else had joined them? Had the generals mentioned in the letter been among the ringleaders who had already been shot dead? And what about Stauffenberg, who had authorized the first instructions?

I asked Frau Heimlich whether I should take Fromm's letter upstairs, but she didn't trust me to come straight back. To annoy her, I took my break, although I was far too wound up to sleep. However, my eyes must have closed after a while, because the next woman who came to lie down had to shake me to wake me up.

In the small hours of the morning, one of hundreds of messages came from Himmler personally, addressed to all. He denied Fromm's authority and made it clear that for the time being we were to disregard any orders that were not from him: "According to the Führer's orders, I have taken over command of the Ersatzheer. Only my orders are to be followed. Operation Valkyrie is aborted with immediate effect."

There was an incredible amount of work to do. The telex machines rattled without cease. Everyone was confused about what had really happened, and not all the departments had received all the messages. Often, we couldn't transmit our messages at all, as the lines were constantly busy, and we had to try time and time again.

At last, my shift drew to an end. I was completely exhausted when I stepped into the light outside. Fresh air! How good it felt. I decided there and then to recover in Niendorf after a couple of hours' sleep at home. I bought a newspaper on my way home. As I couldn't see the *Fremdenblatt*, my usual paper, I took the *Hamburger Anzeiger*, skimming the headlines: "The People's Answer: Long Live the Führer!"; "Rigorous Crackdown on Conspirators"; "The Smashed Plot"; "The Führer Stayed with Us!"

Walking slowly, I read on. Hitler's speech on the wireless was printed alongside an overblown report on the night's events:

> For some hours, a shadow has unsettled the clear front of the fighting Reich: a plot tried to extinguish the life of the Führer.

It has been crushed, and the Führer is standing unharmed as before at the head of the people and their Wehrmacht.

I almost bumped into a street lamp, the metal distorted by the fires, and decided it was best to stand still and read.

Some of the ringleaders have taken their own lives after the failure of their attempt; some have been shot by battalions of the army. One of the dead is the plotter Oberst Graf von Stauffenberg . . . The remaining culprits will have to account for their involvement.

That would mean more searches of people's homes, more spying, more accusations against innocent people—as if there wasn't enough of all that already. Everything would be treated as suspicious, and measures against alleged conspirators and even sympathizers would be executed with the utmost brutality. They would search for every single person who was in any way connected with the "crime." "There must be no mercy!" said the paper.

My mother rushed toward me as I entered the house. "You'll never believe what happened last night! There's been an attempt on the Führer's life. He survived by a miracle!"

Worn out, I put down my paper and my Wehrmacht apron. "I know, I know. Here!" I pushed the paper toward her and she read the report, her eyes wide.

Willi strolled in and leaned casually on the door frame. "Did you hear?"

I nodded. "I've had quite a night. Message after message. He's dead; he's not dead. First we were ready to celebrate and—"

"Gretel!" my mother said, alarmed by my frankness.

"It would have been too good to be true. Just think, Mother! We can't win the war anyway. Everyone knows that."

"Frau Gernot! How nice to see you!" Willi shouted, warning me. Angrily, I rolled my eyes to the ceiling. You couldn't speak your mind even in your own house! I stared crossly at the door, where Willi received Frau Gernot with exaggerated friendliness. "Would you like to take a look at the papers?" he asked.

She let her heavy body slump onto a kitchen chair. "Thank God nothing happened. Dodged death at the last minute, he did! It wasn't to be. He was sent to us from on high, as we knew all along! This'll give a boost to our soldiers who are fighting so bravely at the front, and to the whole people as well." Triumphantly, she gazed around the room, leaving her eyes on me for a long while.

"It won't do any good now. The British and the Americans are already in France," I muttered under my breath, ignoring Willi's warning looks.

"Oh, no, our boys will stop them. We don't need to worry at all. The Führer is going to lead us to the final victory, and whoever doubts that is a traitor to the German people."

I opened my mouth, but Willi was quicker. "How about a cup of coffee, Frau Gernot? Have you had breakfast yet?" In his consternation, he thumped a mug down on the table, almost breaking it in the process, so that Mother pushed him aside and took over.

"You go to bed, child," she told me. "You look exhausted." Willi waited for me to follow my mother's orders before going about his business. I got up and patted his arm as I passed him. Willi was a nice fellow, the way he looked after me. Stupid cow. It was Frau Gernot's sort who had got us into this trouble, not just the leaders.

I took my little wireless and pulled the duvet over my head to listen to the BBC, but it wasn't the right time for the news. Instead, there were poems and songs, and I switched the radio off again, rolling over to sleep.

Around midday, I got up again, as I still wanted to go to Niendorf. When I stepped into the kitchen, my mother and Frau Gernot were listening to speeches by Göring and the Admiral Dönitz on the lunchtime news. I didn't want to hear it. For me, the ones responsible for the plot were heroes. Unimpressed by

the speeches, I made myself a slice of bread and jam and headed
off. As I walked out the door, Frau Gernot called after me, "You
can't go away today! There's a loyalty parade at . . ."

Despite searching feverishly through the papers over the next
few days, I learned as good as nothing about the whole affair.
It was remarkable how much was written about the attempt on
Hitler's life without saying anything about the actual course of
events and their planning. Already the very next day, a Saturday,
the papers reported that the putsch had been "effortlessly nipped
in the bud . . . without spilling a single drop of blood apart from
that of the traitors." I didn't see any names I recognized in the list
of the plotters, as much as I searched. Their fate was not described
in detail, either. The Reich boasted about having "freed front and
homeland from saboteurs," called for the people to be vigilant,
and went on and on about how cowardly and power-mad the
plotters had been, how the Führer had received telegrams from
well-wishers all over Europe, and how disappointed the enemy
was that events had turned out the way they did. With glee, it
was declared that "the case is closed."

Eventually, we learned more through leaflets dropped by the
Allies. They gave us long lists of the names and ranks of the
conspirators, contradicting the Nazis' claim that the perpetra-
tors had been a tiny minority. There were many familiar names
of senior figures: Stauffenberg, Witzleben, Oster, Canaris, von
Tresckow—all high in the Wehrmacht command. I was deeply
impressed that resistance had been organized from so high up.

Of course, I had already realized that men in high positions
were not all true supporters of Hitler. But that they would go so
far as to attempt to kill him and overthrow the entire government,
earned these men the highest respect from me. In my naiveté, I had
assumed that resistance in my country consisted almost entirely of
small acts of sabotage and defiance, the only means available to
the ordinary people. Whoever dared to help the persecuted—like
Monsignor Bram—put themselves in mortal danger.

The list of executions, imprisonments, and suicides linked to the arrests was endless, Karchen told me. What must the families of those involved be going through? At the beginning, I felt enormously worried about the ones who were caught; but then I heard of more and more giving themselves up voluntarily. "How can they do that? Have they gone crazy? They should be glad to have got away!" I ranted to Karchen.

He shook his head. "They've arrested Stauffenberg's whole family, even his children. 'Clan arrest' they call that; they fancy the whole lineage to be 'rotten.' And the wives and children of those who don't turn themselves in will be targeted."

"But that's awful! They haven't got anything to do with it!"

Kunert sighed. "Not usually. But that's how they find those they want. There's another reason why they give themselves up. When they are standing in court and it's being reported, they can finally speak out publicly about what they think about Nazi rule. You should follow the court cases on the wireless and the newsreel at the movies. It's amazing what's going on."

I did as I was told and went to the cinema to watch the newsreel. With gritted teeth, I listened to the fanfares, the bell ringing, and the hysterical voice of the commentator. What enraged me most was the presiding judge, who constantly interrupted the accused and shouted at them. My respect for the conspirators grew even greater. Many literally gave up their lives to tell the truth to the public. Obviously, everyone involved knew that they would die, but none of the conspirators gave the impression that they regretted their participation in the putsch. Many even encouraged the people of Germany to follow their example—hopefully with more luck.

Suddenly, in about mid-August, the court reports stopped altogether. Perhaps Hitler had realized that the condemned were, in spite of losing their lives, winning the propaganda battle. What was no longer reported in the German newsreels and on the wireless, we now learned about from the BBC.

A new wave of arrests swept the country; hundreds if not thousands of people were detained, often without any apparent reason. At this point, we had to be more careful than ever when talking among ourselves. It was rumored that even for such small sins as not using the Nazi salute, not displaying a picture of Hitler on your living room wall, or not owning a swastika flag, you would be regarded as suspicious. I was sure my colleagues were up to no good. Maybe I should have taken Karchen's advice about discretion more to heart.

He came downstairs less often now and made it clear to me that I shouldn't try to see him too frequently either. "They've got their eye on me," he whispered to me one day in the canteen, passing my table with a plate of stew, heading for a different table. Worried, I stared after him. How deeply had he been involved? I recalled again that he had shown no sign of surprise when the first message had been decoded on July 20, and how he had spoken of Hitler's death before it had been announced.

A week later, I realized that that comment in the canteen was the last I'd heard from him. The next time I passed his office, a stranger was sitting at Karchen's desk.

"I'd like to speak to Hauptmann Kunert," I said, feeling nervous and looking apprehensively at him.

"What's it about?" he asked, without lifting his head from his papers.

"It's personal," I replied evasively, and he looked up, suddenly interested.

"Kunert was taken to the town hall last night to be interrogated. He had been under suspicion for some time. How are you personally connected to the man?"

The town hall—the central office of the Gestapo in Hamburg. I felt hot and cold at once. Don't say anything wrong now, I told myself.

I ran my hand through my hair and over my hips and answered with pretended coyness, "Well, just . . . personally!"

The new captain laughed spitefully and looked me up and down in an insolent way. "I have orders to take over Kunert's duties," he said. "I'm more than happy to extend that to all areas."

Defiantly, I answered, "I've got to get back to work." How rude! But it had worked. He hadn't smelled a rat and believed our relationship to be purely private. Back at my desk, I put my head in my hands. If Karchen was at the town hall, I couldn't help him. The only thing to do now was to pray, like Bram.

Later that August, the Allies distributed a new set of flyers with the following encouraging words:

> You now know that open war has been declared between the Army and the Party. The generals demand an immediate truce with the Allies, but the Party insists on prolonging the war, delaying the end by a few more months. For the first time since 1933, the German people have the opportunity to decide independently and autonomously . . . Don't forget that Himmler is afraid of you, because he needs you. Through united, disciplined actions in factories and workshops, in mines, railways and offices, you can paralyze the machinery of war.

If only that were true! United, disciplined actions . . . It wasn't quite so easy; you couldn't even open your mouth to speak without fear. Even picking up such flyers was extremely dangerous. For years, we had been lectured by the newspapers to take enemy flyers immediately to the nearest police station. If you didn't do this, you'd be helping the enemy, they said. And these days there could be serious consequences. Himmler must have realized how dangerous the situation could become if such leaflets were widely distributed. Now, you had to face prison if you were caught with enemy propaganda, and you might receive the death penalty even for so small an act of defiance.

Most people didn't seem to care much about this threat, however. All you had to do was look around carefully before stooping and stuffing the leaflet into a large bag or the pocket of your coat. I even heard that some mothers hid larger amounts of flyers beneath their babies in their carriages, so that they would be able to pass them on to others.

Since the tightened controls and mass arrests had begun, I had become a bit more careful myself. Before, I might have given Karchen a leaflet to circulate among fellow sympathizers, but since his arrest I burned them in the oven at home immediately after reading them. Willi was the only one to whom I spoke of them or showed them to, and he in turn showed those he picked up to me.

It was through these leaflets that we found out how far the Allies had advanced. In November, they flattened Aachen, having asked the population to surrender in vain. By now, with the war unwinnable, even to those who had once supported Hitler, everything must have looked like senseless bloodshed. "Is this what the Führer wanted?" asked one of the flyers provocatively, ending with the assertion that the Party and the SS were the real enemies of the German people.

No one doubted the end of the war was near, but the government wouldn't give up. At the end of November, the Allies dropped an official-looking announcement over Hamburg. These leaflets set out what would happen when they advanced into Germany, telling us that a military government was to be installed in the occupied areas. All members of the Nazi Party and the SS would be removed from positions of power. The civilian population was to carry on as normal.

At the Transport Command, I learned of illustrated flyers showing the German soldiers how well they would be treated when they were Allied POWs. Some officers expressed their anger about the "impertinence and lies" of these leaflets, but I thought it was a brilliant idea to combat the fears the soldiers would feel about being captured. They knew as well as we did that the war was only being prolonged unnecessarily by this time. Many of them must be asking why they were still risking their lives when they had no hope of changing the outcome anymore. Maybe it was fear of the treatment they would receive from the Allied forces that prevented them from surrendering. Could it really be loyalty to the Führer?

Opinion was divided. I still went to the occasional office party, and there I met some diehards who still believed the war could be won. Since Karchen's arrest, I didn't enjoy these parties nearly as much. I thought about him all the time. However, I still went sometimes. Some of the officers I found quite nice, and I always discovered some new piece of information when I listened to their discussions.

"Won't be long now. It's only a matter of time. The Allies have broken through and pushed our army back. We've long lost Paris."

"That doesn't mean anything. The Führer will lead us to victory, you'll see!"

"You don't really believe that? No one can stop them now. We've had to evacuate the whole Atlantic coast already!"

"Once we use the secret weapon—"

"Fairy tales! Secret weapon—what utter rubbish!"

"It does exist, to be sure! Just think of the V-rockets to England. There you see the genius of the Führer. They're in for a shock, I tell you."

Secret weapon or no secret weapon, the ruined landscape of my hometown alone seemed proof enough to me that the Allies were going to win. Now the air raids came largely during the day or in the early evenings. Harburg was the worst-hit district. Not that the bombs could do much more damage now. Public life had suffered immensely. We couldn't go to the cinema or the theater anymore; sporting events like the annual Christmas soccer games were all that was on offer. Those who felt like celebrating would have to do so in private—and those who were involved in the black market had the means to do so.

On New Year's Eve, I made no firm plans. I left the house with a mental list of addresses that I intended to visit to see what was going on. By now, I knew such a lot of cellars where regular parties were held that I was confident of finding a good place to see in the new year. I wanted to find the loudest and the wildest party.

The next morning, I could remember about three cellars and several long walks between venues, but not the rest of the night. It must have been great, though, because I woke up in a half-derelict attic room with a hellish headache and a strange man. Quietly, I collected my things and tiptoed out of the house.

That night, when I toasted the new year with my mother, it was with certainty that we would finally see the end of the war before its end. As much as we longed for it, our hopes were mixed with doubts and insecurities. What would the Allies do to us when they marched in? One thing was certain: Those in civilian clothes would be better off than those in uniform. But would they leave us women alone?

While the Nazis called up the youngest and the oldest for the Volkssturm, the so-called "people's militia" conscripted in a last-ditch attempt to repel the Allies, more and more soldiers deserted the front to escape the pointless death they would inevitably face. The Party distributed leaflets ordering the populace to denounce the "pitiful traitors" and to refuse to shelter them under any circumstances. They were called cowards, scoundrels, shirkers—but my outrage was directed toward the leadership, who seemed to be prepared to fight to the last man standing, and never mind the cost.

"We will never capitulate!" declared one leaflet in February. There were tips on what to do if the Allies arrived: "If the enemy asks the way, direct him to the cemeteries, where thousands of men, women and children lie who have been murdered by that very same enemy." I stared at the flyer, which a BDM girl had pushed into my hand. Who had started the war, after all? We were warned not to help the Allies in any conceivable way. We were to mark down the names of those who did so and thereby committed "treason against the German people." "We'll come again!" said the leaflet. "Long live the Führer!"

I shook my head and continued on my way to work. How long would I still have to work for the Wehrmacht? There was no talk of dismissals; we had our hands full. There were transports going in all directions, carrying wounded, medicines, food, troops. We ran from one room into the next, and the rattling of the telex machines didn't stop for a minute. The keys were practically hot to the touch—*rat-tat-tat* around the clock.

Occasionally, I joined the officers, sitting on the edge of a desk with a glass of wine in my hand, listening to the conversation.

"We shouldn't have attacked the British air bases. That was the end of the Luftwaffe. Now it makes no sense to carry on fighting."

"What's become of Guderian's lobbying for peace?"

"Nothing! They won't give in. Now they're deploying all remaining troops to Hungary."

"Why Hungary?"

"Because of the oil."

"But the Red Army is already there, and in the west it's the British and the Americans!"

"That doesn't mean anything. They haven't got us yet, just you wait! And anyway, the Führer is building tank traps all along the coast."

"He'd better be quick about it, then," I commented. "That's like fighting a forest fire by spitting." The others laughed at that and I felt encouraged. Mockingly, I turned to the bust of Hitler that stood on the shelf. "Hang on, we don't want you listening to all this," I told the bust. I folded a hat out of a sheet of paper, put it on the Führer's head, and turned the bust around so that it was staring at the wall. The officers laughed even more and gave me another drink. We had a great time, and for the first time in a long while, I felt happy and relaxed.

Cheered up, I left for home the next morning. Maybe it really wouldn't last much longer now. What would the end of the war be like? By this time, I couldn't even imagine a life without bombs, the black market, and being on my guard all the time. It was as if the war had always existed. The prospect of peace was almost bewildering. My head was spinning with the thought of it as I climbed into bed, and I fell asleep in an instant.

14

THE CAMP

My rest wasn't to last long. A loud hammering woke me up. It was as if somebody was trying to break down the front door. I heard loud voices and my mother's anxious voice on the stairs. "But you can't . . . Wait! Gretel!" The door was flung open and two men stomped in.

"Frau Öhlgart?"

"That's me."

"Gestapo. Come with us."

Shit, was all I thought. Somehow I had always known that it would happen one day. So this was it. With pretended calm, I picked up my clothes.

"May I get dressed first, please?"

The eyes of the officer next to me narrowed to small slits. "Depends on how quick you are. Go on, hurry up!" He made no move to turn around.

Angrily, I crouched down behind my bed, piling the duvet into a heap to give me some privacy, and got dressed as quickly as I could. I wasn't going to give them the satisfaction of watching me. Oafs! My anger helped to calm my nerves.

Mother stood behind the officers wringing her hands. "What will I do? Child," she cried.

"It's obviously a misunderstanding," I said coolly, partly to calm my mother down, and partly for the benefit of the men. In my heart, though, I knew that wasn't the case. This time I wouldn't get away with it. I felt sure of it.

I was pushed into the back of a black car, and we drove off before they had even shut the door. During the journey, I feverishly racked my brain as to what had caught me out. Was it the black market? My joy at the premature announcement of Hitler's death? Surely it wasn't my joke with the bust last night? Or had they caught Dr. Manes and made him give up the names of those who had hidden him?

The journey was all too short. Before long, we passed the music hall; we were nearly there. The car stopped directly in front of the town hall. "Out with you!" I was ordered. I looked up at the imposing four-story building, with its huge arched entrance and a bell tower on its domed roof. I shuddered. Up until Karchen had been taken, I had always hurried by the building, trying not to think too hard about the poor people who had been dragged here. Since then, it had only frightened me more.

The two officers grabbed me by the elbows and pushed me upstairs and along a corridor, shouting at me. Finally, we reached a door, one of the officers knocked, and we stepped in. The room was big and empty; there was only a desk in the far corner. An attractive man sat at the desk, staring at me with piercing steel-blue eyes.

"Sit here!" one of the officers hissed, shoving me into the chair in front of the desk. I threw him a look full of hatred, lifted my chin up, and turned toward the man behind the desk, ready for battle.

The Gestapo men planted themselves behind my chair, but were waved off by the other officer. "I'll manage her on my own," he told them.

I knew it wasn't worth even trying my usual methods of getting around authority figures—flirting, charming them, looking innocent. That kind of thing wouldn't do me any good here.

"Öhlgart, Gretel?"

I nodded.

"Telex operator at Transport Command Hamburg-Altona?"

"Yes."

"I want to know names from you. If you give me names, nothing will happen to you," he said, giving me a sharp look. He turned the desk lamp so that it was shining directly in my eyes. I blinked so much that my eyes watered. I could no longer see my interrogator, and I turned my head to the side.

"How do you know Stauffenberg?"

"He was my commanding officer. I've only seen him once, in the canteen. I've never even spoken to him."

"Who was he with in the canteen?"

"With the other officers."

"Who?"

"I don't remember."

"I'm not sure that I've made myself clear. You want to get out of here, don't you?"

I nodded.

"Names are what I want. Names!"

Helplessly, I shrugged.

"Who was Stauffenberg with in the canteen? Who talked to him?"

"I really don't know any more. The officers all came in as a group, and, out of curiosity, I only paid attention to Stauffenberg, because I'd never seen him before."

The officer changed his tone. "You will tell me now who you know! Witzleben!"

Astonished, I looked toward him, but the bright light forced me to turn my head back. "I've read the name once in a telex, or typed it," I said, truthfully.

"Generaloberst Höpner?"

"I don't know him."

"Stieff?"

"I don't know!"

"Fellgiebel?"

"I don't know him either!"

By now his voice had risen to a hoarse cry. "Oberst Jäger?"

"I don't know!"

"Von Oertzen?"

"I don't know!"

"Kleist-Schmenzin?"

"I don't know!"

"Von Hassel?"

"I don't know any of them!"

Suddenly, his voice was in my ear. He must have got up and stepped over to me. "You're not doing yourself any favors carrying on like that," he hissed. "The sooner you confess, the quicker we'll get this over with. Schulenburg?"

The list of names seemed to be endless. If one of them sounded familiar, I knew it must only have been from a telex that I had sent or received, so I was able to tell the truth.

"Whom did you work with at Transport Command?"

I tried not to change my expression as I answered: "No one in particular. I've only been working there for—"

He started to ask about my colleagues. "What did Peters do? Who did he spend time with?"

"I don't know. I just brought him a message now and then."

"Whom did Kunert speak to when he was in the canteen?"

"I don't know. Could I possibly have a sip of—"

Of course I couldn't have a sip of water.

The interrogation went on and on. I started to sweat in the bright light of the lamp. My eyes hurt and my mouth was completely dried out. And yet I was aware that I had no real reason to complain, not given the stories that went around about the town hall. They said that barbaric methods of torture were employed in interrogations here; luckily, perhaps, I had never been willing to listen to any details.

Behind me, the door opened and I hoped that this meant the end of my questioning. No such luck. Whoever came in exchanged places with the attractive officer. The new voice was yet hoarser, presumably from a great deal of shouting, I surmised, as he roared at me, "We want to hear names! Who did you speak to at Transport Command?"

I gave the same answers as before. Again, he went through all the officers. Did I know this one? Did that one do anything out of the ordinary? "I don't know!" was all I would say.

Hours had gone by, and I'd still not been allowed a glass of water, was still sitting on the uncomfortable chair, and still had the bright light shining in my face. By this time, I was sitting with my eyes shut. I was asked the same questions over and over again. The first officer had returned. He'd had a nice break, I supposed, but I was too exhausted even to think of a smart remark, and would have kept my mouth shut in any case.

At this point, he seemed to try to get through to me using a different approach. Instead of asking about the Wehrmacht officers whose names I'd heard repeatedly until now, he said, "You are truly useless, it seems. Couldn't even keep your husband for long, could you? Good old Lutz."

Startled, I looked up, regretting it immediately because of the light.

"Where's he now, then, our Lutz?"

"I don't know."

"Shall I tell you something? I don't believe a word you're saying. Of course you know where he is. He's just the same as you and all your riffraff friends—a traitor. And where's this Jewish dog, Manes?"

"I don't know what you're talking about," I said defiantly.

"Right. You don't know him either. He was your family doctor for twenty years, and you don't know him!"

What they knew! Quickly, I backtracked. "I did know him, but that was a long time ago. He wasn't allowed to practice any longer, so I haven't seen him for years," I lied.

"Where is he? That's what I want to know!" shouted the officer.

This time I could truthfully reply with my usual "I don't know."

Then he started from the beginning again, asking about Stauffenberg and all the officers. I was shattered. It seemed as if it would never end. Eventually, though, he yelled, "Hartig!" and the door flew open. "Take her out. We're not getting anywhere with her. Get out! Go and give her a nice little number!"

It was a moment before I grasped that the interrogation was over. No torture. They hadn't so much as slapped me. I could hardly believe my luck. A Gestapo interrogation and I had left the room unharmed. Was it possible? Maybe I had a guardian angel after all, or God on my side. Maybe I should go to Monsignor Bram and convert, I thought in my confusion, stumbling as I was pushed along in an attempt to make me speed up.

"I need the loo," I told Hartig.

"You can wait," he barked back, but then changed his mind and pointed to a door. I dashed in, and he stood guard at the door.

I felt much better when I came out. I had washed my face and hands, and drunk so much from the tap that my stomach ached. Hartig shouted something incomprehensible into an office, upon which another man appeared. They ushered me along the corridor. I didn't know what would happen next. Would I be released?

"This way! Quickly!" Hartig bawled. We hurried downstairs, not outside, as I'd hoped, but into the basement. Suddenly, I felt panicky. The last words of the interrogator came back to me: "Give her a nice little number!" What were they going to do? Would they rape me?

I tried to stay calm. I was determined not to show any sign of weakness now. We entered a bleak room. There was a table in the center and shelves with tools on them lining the walls. Was I to be tortured now? The second man picked up a device that looked like some kind of stamp. He grabbed my right arm and motioned to Hartig, who gripped my left arm firmly by the wrist and elbow. He turned my forearm to face inside up on the table. I felt a sharp pain as the device was pressed into my skin.

It had happened so quickly. It hurt, admittedly, but torture it wasn't, I told myself. After a minute, they released me. Numbly, I stared at my arm. I saw a six-figured number in blue-black ink. I realized what the "nice little number" was: a tattoo. The numbers were difficult to make out. They kept blurring with blood, despite my attempts to wipe them clear with my other hand. One . . . three . . . zero . . . eight, or was it another three?

"Come on, we don't have all day." I was taken upstairs and pushed into a room that reminded me of a doctor's waiting room, in which there were several silent and nervous-looking women.

"Out, all of you! This way! Go, go, go!" They ordered us out of the main entrance to a kind of wooden van and shoved us inside. The door was shut with a bang and we drove off.

I didn't bother to try to look through the slits between the planks; what did it matter now whether I knew where we were going? A kind of apathy came over me. I couldn't even say what the other women were like or how long the journey took, whether the others spoke to each other or not. It was as if I was enveloped in a thick fog. Perhaps I had battened down the hatches to pre-empt fear or hysteria; perhaps it was just that I was completely exhausted. In any case, I was in an almost catatonic state.

The next thing I was aware of was lying on a plank bed. I swung back the woolen blanket and sat up, but I banged my head as I did so. Looking up, I saw that it was a bunk bed. Swearing, I stood up and looked around. There was no one in the room. All I could see was a lot of bunk beds.

Curious, I looked into the next room. There were washbasins, a shower, and a toilet, which I used gratefully, although there was no paper. I ran some water over my hair and face and went back through, passing the beds and a table. There were some lockers near the entrance. I stepped outside and saw a group of women, some standing, some sitting on the ground. I approached the girl sitting nearest to me, who had a friendly, freckled face.

"Slept enough, have you?" she asked me.

I nodded. "Where are we?"

"A reception camp. For criminals!" she grinned.

A reception camp? Was that the same as a concentration camp? Probably not. From the rumors I'd heard about the concentration camps, I would have imagined much worse than this: guards with dogs, maltreated prisoners with shaved heads. I had often seen prisoners from the camps forced to work on the clear-up operations in the ruins of Hamburg. They wore ragged, dirty, gray-and-blue-striped shirts and trousers, but here the women were all wearing civilian clothing.

"Don't worry," said the freckled girl. "It's all peace and quiet here. They leave us well alone. We're just hoping that it's all over soon." I sat down next to her and let my gaze wander. Everywhere, I saw women sitting and standing around in small groups. Some chatted, but most just stared silently into space. The yard was filled with prefabricated huts at regular distances from one another. The ground was unpaved. A few guards watched us from a perimeter fence topped with barbed wire.

"Have you been here long?" I asked the girl.

"Three weeks. The longest weeks of my life!"

"Is this a labor camp?"

She shook her head. "We don't have to do anything. To be honest, it's deadly boring. All we can do is wait until the whole farce is finished."

"And why are you here?"

She laughed. "I listened to the enemy on the wireless, and our block warden denounced me as a traitor to the people." Was that really all? I looked at her skeptically, but she didn't seem to care what I thought. "And you?" she asked.

"They didn't say. The black market, maybe. Or a stupid remark I made at work."

She showed no surprise. "What's that there?" she asked, looking at my tattoo. I stretched out my arm to show her. "That's strange," she said. "No one else has got a number here. Did you come from a different camp?"

I shook my head. "Straight from the town hall. That's where they did this to me."

Now it was her turn to be skeptical. After all, for all she knew, I could have been a real criminal. Then again, what did that mean in this day and age?

The freckled girl must have been thinking the same thing; she tilted her head to one side a little, shrugged her shoulders, and carried on talking to me. "I'm Inge," she told me.

"Gretel," I answered. We fell silent. I rubbed my arms. It had turned cold under the cloudy March sky. Soon it would be evening.

"Why aren't you sitting with the others?" I asked after a while.

Inge sighed. "Sometimes you don't feel like company."

I had to make do with that explanation. Maybe it was a hint. "I'll go and say hello to the others," I suggested good-naturedly and stood up, brushing the dirt off my skirt. Inge's eyes followed me as I approached the next hut.

About a dozen women sat on the ground. Most of them looked quite neat, considering the circumstances: clothes in not too bad a state, hair tidily brushed. It occurred to me that I had nothing with me: no comb, no toothbrush, no soap—not even anything to barter with. The others might be prepared to help me out, so forming alliances was crucial. How did you introduce yourself in a camp? How do you do? I decided merely to nod in greeting; my gesture was answered with a few barely raised hands.

One of the faces looked familiar, but I couldn't put my finger on it. Those slanted eyes, the coarse dark-blonde hair . . . I could see a glimmer of recognition in her eyes, too. "Five mettwurst sausages and a smoked ham!" she exclaimed suddenly. The others turned to look at her in astonishment.

"Sixty fags and a gas lighter, but without the fuel," I shot back, and we both laughed.

"Gretel Öhlgart!"

"Anna Schäfer!"

We shook hands. I didn't have to ask why Anna was here. The others had similarly insignificant reasons for being detained. Careless remarks, listening to the enemy on the wireless, picking up an Allied leaflet—it was absurd. One had been accused of black-market dealings, although she'd done nothing; her only fault had been not to use all of her ration allocation. We fell into conversation, but it all had an unreal quality. There was a sluggishness about the women, in conversation as in move- ment, similar to that induced by a stifling hot summer's day. The lethargy seemed to result from weeks of hanging around. Here, with nothing to do, the days dragged.

Finally, a haggard middle-aged woman stood up, saying, "Time for supper." We followed her example and walked slowly toward the mess. From the outside, the building looked exactly like the other huts, but inside it was a canteen, though without tables or even chairs. We lined up at the food counter. Many women were in front of us and still more streamed in to take their places behind us.

Nobody pushed. There was a certain discipline that was abided by, and I wondered how the hierarchy was structured in this place. "Is she someone special?" I asked the woman behind me, pointing at the haggard one who had got up first and led us to the food hut.

"Lotte. She's the eldest. If you've got a problem, you can talk to her. But watch out—she might want to know more about you than you'd like to give away."

I was grateful for her advice. It wasn't unlikely that they had spies among us, and offering confidences could well backfire.

We had chicory coffee and crumbly black bread with syrup— only one slice each. I hadn't eaten all day and my stomach was rumbling audibly, but there was no more. I looked around. At the other side of the room, a door led into the kitchen. Occasionally, I caught a glimpse of the cook—a man, which I was pleased about. In fact, all the guards and kitchen staff were male. That was promising. I felt my usual initiative returning.

Before I attempted anything, however, I wanted to get to know more about life in the camp. I watched the other women, how they gathered up the last crumbs of bread with their fingertips. Their eyes were hungry. I chewed each bite of my little portion for a long time, making the most of it. When the last morsel was eaten, the last drop of chicory coffee drained from the cup, there was nothing left but water, with which I tried to fill myself up.

About five women went to the kitchen to wash up. The rest of us dispersed slowly. Conversation became a bit livelier now, and there was even some laughter. I followed Anna outside. We stretched our legs and then joined a small group sitting on the ground. Anna collected a few little stones and started to play a game with five of them. One of the stones was tossed into the air, and the others had to be picked up, first one at a time, then two, and so on, before she caught the thrown stone again, all with one hand. Anna explained the rules: "When you've got them all in your hand at the end, you throw them in the air and let them fall onto the back of your hand, push them again in the air, and what you then catch is your final score."

When it got dark, Lotte went back to the hut in which I had woken up, and a few other women followed her. As Anna and I could hardly see our stones any longer, we followed them. Anna's bed was in a different hut, so we bade each other a friendly good-night.

In my hut, I looked out for Inge. She nodded to me before going to line up for the shower. "Could you lend me your soap maybe?" I asked when she came back with wet hair.

She hesitated. "You don't get ahold of much in here," she evaded.

I understood. Very well. Water would clean me well enough. I went to the washroom and scrubbed myself and my underwear, which I hung on my bed to dry. I wasn't tired, as I had slept in the afternoon, but I felt damp and cold, so I wrapped myself in the blanket and sat on my bed.

Some women lay down to sleep, while others talked. I watched them absentmindedly, thinking back on the events of the day. I had so many questions. How long would I have to stay here? Would we be transported somewhere else? What was my mother doing right now? Was Karchen in a camp like this, or was he in one of those I had heard such terrible stories about? I hoped he was at least still alive. I recalled what Dr. Manes had said about the camps he had been in. He hadn't told me much, but I gathered that they were cruel and inhumane. It seemed that I had been lucky. It looked as if the worst I would experience would be the leaden boredom of a place where a game with five stones was the highlight of the day.

Over the next few days, I learned that the meager meals were in fact the real highlights of each day. The food wasn't even bad; there was just far too little of it. We were always thinking and talking about the meals we'd have once we were free again. The cook tried to conjure something decent from the ingredients he was given, and we had prawn soup, rutabaga with potatoes, pea soup—but never more than a ladleful each. We were bitterly hungry.

One morning, when a cold rain kept us huddled together inside the huts, I decided to visit the cook. I strolled over to the mess and went to lean in the kitchen doorway. The cook was moving between the huge pots when he noticed I was standing there. "Hello, there," he said. "Nothing to do?" I shook my head. We took it in turns to help in the kitchen, but it was far too early for the shift, and I hadn't even helped at all yet.

"What did you do, then, that put you in here?" the cook asked, not unkindly.

"Oh, well," I said vaguely, "nothing, really."

"Do you want a coffee?"

"Have you got real stuff?"

"I do!"

To my delight, he poured me a cup of proper coffee from a flask. I savored every sip, holding each one in my mouth for as long as possible.

The chef invited me to sit down and I took a seat on a stool. Then I asked him straight out, "Can't you give us a bit more tonight?"

He looked me up and down. "Quite possibly. But then I would want something in return!" His gaze lingered on my breasts. Ordinarily, I would have been furious, but these weren't normal circumstances. After all, it wasn't out of greed that we wanted more to eat. Some of us were already weak and unsteady on our feet; malnutrition was taking its toll, although none of us had been imprisoned for more than two months.

Quickly, I weighed up how much my self-respect would suffer if I got involved with him. By God, he certainly wasn't attractive—it was obvious that he kept all the extra portions we needed for himself. He was quite fat, with a big belly and jowly cheeks; his dark hair was combed back with some oily substance. I could have wished for a more pleasant partner. But if it was for the good of us all? It's not as if my lovers have always been beauty contestants, I thought, remembering Fritz Müller. I raised my head and answered his look with a steady gaze.

He motioned to me to follow him and went through the back door of the kitchen, which led to his living quarters. The room was quite homey: pictures on the wall, a wireless on a shelf, everything tidy and in good condition. The bed was properly made and didn't look grubby. I took a deep breath and undressed.

It wasn't long until I could put my clothes back on. "You can call me Albert," the chef told me, holding the door for me as I left. I hesitated and looked him in the eye. "Don't worry," he said. "I keep my promises." That was what I had wanted to hear. I left and marched back to my hut and straight under the shower.

"Don't think too much," I told myself, standing under the cold water until I shivered.

When we went for dinner that night, I was very anxious. Albert doled out the food himself. When he saw me, he winked, in a good mood. To my great relief, I saw that the portions were considerably bigger than usual, for all of us. The guards didn't seem to notice, but the women couldn't believe their eyes. Incredulously, they stared at their plates. I couldn't help grinning. My eyes met Inge's and she mouthed, "I saw you go in."

I was worried she would despise me and searched her face for a sign of her feelings. All I could see in her expression was respect. The atmosphere during the meal was great, almost happy. Everyone chatted, stories were told, and I marveled at how much hunger could change a person.

Inge pulled me aside when we were outside again. "That was very honorable of you!" I felt a bit embarrassed. It wouldn't have occurred to me to call my behavior honorable—at least not in the ordinary sense of the word. "I mean that you didn't just get something out of it for yourself." Nudging my arm, she said, "If you need soap again, just let me know!"

There were two times when it was practical to see Albert: early in the morning or late at night. If I went over there both times, he'd give me something special: cigarettes, a small nail file, a pencil and paper. It was all wonderful stuff to barter with. "Put in a good word for me once this is over," he begged me one day. I looked at him thoughtfully. He wouldn't have chosen to work here. If he'd been a cruel man, he could have forced me and the others to sleep with him. But that wasn't his way, and nor was it that of the other guards at our camp in my experience. The staff were all in their fifties, seemed friendly, and on the whole kept themselves to themselves. They knew, as we did, that once the Allies arrived, they would be under suspicion. Quite often, they would say to us, "Don't look so closely at my face."

Maybe Inge told the others what she knew, or perhaps the atmosphere improved simply because we had more to eat. In any case, we began to share and swap much more: here a piece of bread for a bit of soap, there a toothbrush for a comb, or a needle might be passed around, with which we could sew ourselves an extra pair of knickers from our petticoat. Our underwear was usually still damp from the daily wash the next morning, which surely wasn't healthy.

I was very troubled when I got my period. I didn't know what to do. Lotte, in whom I confided, gave me some towels, and I was too relieved to inspect their state too closely. If there had been no provision for this, it really would have been too primitive, I thought. Little did I know what other women in other camps had to go through. To my relief, Albert put up with a week of celibacy without cutting back the rations, while I enjoyed the break.

15

THE END OF THE WAR

1945: Five million refugees from the eastern provinces stream into western Germany. Dresden is destroyed by bombs. Cologne is occupied by American forces, Danzig, Königsberg, and Vienna by the Russians. The Ruhrgebiet, the industrial heart of Germany, capitulates. Berlin is surrounded. Hitler and Goebbels commit suicide. On May 7, the commander of the Wehrmacht signs unconditional surrender documents in Reims, France.

Hamburg issues 278 public air-raid warnings and 142 alarms, and is the target of 27 air raids, leaving about 2,500 people dead or wounded. Approximately 100,000 refugees and returning former residents stream into the city. Four out of five of all buildings have been damaged or completely destroyed. On May 3, 1945, the city is handed over to the British forces.

The days dragged on, turning into weeks; the weather got no warmer. Cut off from any information about developments on the front line, we couldn't do anything but wait for an end to appear. Bombs still fell. When the air-raid sirens sounded, we went into a specially reinforced building that was referred to as a bunker, although I couldn't imagine that it would withstand a direct hit. Most of the attacks happened early in the morning or late at night, between two and nine days apart. Once, I was still at Albert's when the alarm began, and it shook him out of his usual calm.

"God, what if they realize I've been with you! They lock us up just for talking to you lot any more than is absolutely necessary."

I calmed him down. "It's all right. I won't go to the bunker. I'll stay here until it's over. They don't count us."

Grateful, he blew me a kiss and rushed out of the hut to the shelter. As soon as Albert was gone, I went over to his wireless and searched for the BBC. I would have enough time when the all-clear sounded to tune back to his normal station before he returned. Impatiently, I listened to the music. It was ten to midnight. I would have to wait until one o'clock before it was time for the midnight news in England. Unfortunately, the all-clear came after only twenty-five minutes. Disappointed and frustrated, I tuned the receiver back to Albert's wavelength. It was driving me crazy not having any news from outside. If only Albert would dare to give me his radio. But he had refused once before. "I'd get in so much trouble," he'd said. "I really can't do that."

Soon the weather began to get warmer. It was about mid-April. I had lost all sense of time. The days dragged by monotonously. Then, one day, Lotte said something out of the blue that made us all stop in our tracks: "The guards! I can't see any guards!" Surprised, we looked along the perimeter fence, and indeed, not a single guard was to be seen. Unbelieving, we stood up. The rest of the women had noticed as well and came over to us. We stood together in a big group and discussed what this could mean. Suddenly, one of us broke free of the group and marched bravely toward the gate. We held our breath.

None of us knew whether it was locked. It had never occurred to us to try to flee when the guards were there. They would have been forced to shoot us. Why would we risk that when we all anticipated the end of the war? The woman rattled the gate and, to our surprise, it opened. It was a strange feeling to stare at the open gate. Nobody spoke. All of a sudden, three guards came out of a building where they must have been having a meeting. The woman at the gate gave a start and we all froze with fear.

They came toward us without raising their weapons. "Go!" the first one said. We thought we'd misunderstood him. No one moved. "Off you go! Run! It's over!" A murmur went through the group. Anna stepped first toward the gate, and together with the woman who had opened it, she marched through it without looking back.

Then we were all running. Quick, before we lost our chance! We crowded by the gate, but nobody pushed or elbowed others out of the way. In a flash, we were on the other side of the fence. I looked back one last time. There stood Albert in front of his kitchen hut. He lifted his hand and I answered his farewell with a brief wave. Then I turned and ran in the direction in which I guessed the city lay.

We didn't all agree on which was the way home, so we spread out in several small groups. Around us were forests, and some women fled straight into the shelter of the trees. Others, me included, stayed by the road, in the firm belief that no one would stop us now. "Does this mean the war is over?" I asked excitedly. "Soon we'll know what's going on. Girls, I can't believe it. We're free!" We ran down the road until a pickup truck almost knocked us down.

"And where are you going?" shouted the driver out of the window.

"To Hamburg!" we screamed in one voice.

"Look, it's our vegetable man!" my neighbor said, nudging me. True enough, this was the man who brought daily deliveries of vegetables to Albert. We had seen him often. He must have recognized us too, as he asked, "You're from the camp, aren't you?"

For a moment, my heart sank to my stomach. What if he denounced us as escapees? But he didn't seem to think of that.

"Have they finally let you go?" he asked. "Well, it's about time! The Tommies are at the door! Hop on, and I'll take you to Hamburg!"

It was wonderful to be traveling back into town on the rickety old truck. I felt so emotional I thought I'd burst, stretching out my arms and letting my hair fly in the wind. The others must have felt the same, but here and there I could see worry on their faces. How long it had been since we'd seen our friends and relatives! Nobody knew how they had fared, whether they were still alive or not, whether the houses we had been living in were still standing, what life would be like.

Lost in thought, I let my eyes stray over the lovely landscape. How much sky we could see! Far away, I could see a stand of trees, and I marveled at the different shades of green as if I had never seen them before. Here dark, there light green, sometimes with a tinge of blue, then again almost yellow, and among these the near black of the pine trees. Old thatched cottages nestled underneath, their terra-cotta-red bricks and dark-brown beams an attractive contrast to the fresh green of the trees.

Our truck clattered past orchards; blossoms shimmered on the branches in the sunshine, the fields of long grass divided by rickety fences. I breathed in deeply and bent my head back to watch the clouds racing by. The other women had gone quiet too, all caught up in their own thoughts.

As we reached the outskirts of the city, the streets became more and more familiar, although some were quite changed by further bombing. Our faces grew more serious as we passed the yawning ruins of bombed-out buildings, the skyline ominous and fragmented. Everywhere were huge heaps of rubble—stone, concrete, charred beams. Bricks spilled from doorways; faded, scorched shop signs and advertisements bore witness to a long-gone era. Single trees stood among the ruins like black carcasses. It was a terrible picture of destruction. In spite of this, people walked to and fro, going about their daily business, having grown used to this unreal landscape of ruins. We, who had not seen it for so long, were shocked.

The vegetable man stopped and let us off one after the other, wherever we asked to be dropped. After the first of us had knocked on the driver's cabin as we neared her home, he had offered to take us all to our doors. Whenever one of us climbed down and said good-bye, our spirits rose again. We were on our way home! For so long, we had dreamed about this, and now the moment had come. How many weeks had I been away? Six? Seven? Finally, we reached the Rothenbaumchaussee. "Left here!" I shouted to the driver. "Werderstraße and then right! Stop! I'm home! I'm home!" The house was still standing. Would Mother be at home? Waving and crying, I said good-bye to the others, gave the delighted driver a kiss on the cheek, and dashed up the stairs to the front door.

I saw that a little way down the road, in the middle of the street, there was a huge bomb crater directly in front of the church. I hoped that Bram and those he was hiding were safe and that Mother had been in the cellar when it happened. She didn't always take the alarms seriously anymore. My heart was in my mouth.

"Mother!" I shouted as I walked through the door. Where was she? The kitchen was empty. I ran out into the garden. There was some washing hanging up to dry, but no one was there. Back in the house, I raced upstairs to my room and pushed the door open. There she stood, bent over my bed. She turned and dropped the pillow she was just about to cover. "Child!"

We hugged each other for ages. "I've made your bed freshly every day and aired the room," she told me. "I knew you'd be back!" Tears were running down her face, and my cheeks were wet too. "Come down into the kitchen! Where have you been all this time?" The whole afternoon, we sat at the table and talked about what had happened to us. Apart from Albert, I told her about everything. "Ilse was often here and always asked after you," Mother told me. I was touched that my neighbor had been so worried about me, and I planned to go and see her later.

"And how's Kuddel?" I asked her then. "And Willi?"

"All is well with Kuddel. His wife is expecting her first child."

"And?"

"And what?"

"And Willi?"

Mother sighed. "They came and got him."

"Willi as well!" I exclaimed, rigid on my chair. "Did they say why?"

"They've insulted him. You know, said that he doesn't like women and all that . . ."

I suddenly understood. Of course! Once, not long after I was divorced from Lutz, he had asked me if I would marry him so that he'd be "safe." Back then, I had shaken my head vigorously. I didn't really know what he meant and I had no intention of getting married again, not even to him. Now I understood why it had been so important to him, and I regretted my refusal bitterly.

After my mother had conjured the best meal I had ever eaten out of what little she had, I went next door to see Ilse. Her daughter opened the door, a pretty little girl of primary-school age. Ilse came out of the kitchen, a tea towel in her hand. "Öle!" she exclaimed. "I thought I'd never see you again!" Spontaneously, she embraced me, and I was very touched by her affection. We sat together for a long time and I noticed that I had a lot of funny stories to tell about my life in the camp; I didn't mention the unpleasant things. It might have been because Ilse's children were playing around us, or maybe it was just that her apolitical attitude steered our conversation away from more serious matters.

Ilse was neither for nor against the Nazis. Because of her husband's position in the army, she was addressed as "Frau Hauptmann," but status was of no importance to her. She and her husband had grown apart and had been sleeping in separate rooms long before he was sent home from the front as an invalid. He seemed happy to let her do as she pleased, and she had plenty to keep her busy and her mind off politics with five children to look after and various affairs to conduct. She lived life to the full but always prioritized her family's welfare over everything else.

In her position, I would probably have approached many things differently, I thought as I watched her with the little ones. I had no responsibilities, but those who had children couldn't afford to draw any attention to themselves. Many of the women in the camp had had children, and I would never forget their worry about what the authorities might have done with them. The best that could be hoped was that they'd put the children in an orphanage, where they would be raised as true German National Socialists who would be embarrassed about their traitor mother for the rest of their days.

Ilse had kept only the youngest two of her five children at home, the girl who had opened the door for me and little Helmut, who I had so often carried to the air-raid shelter at night. The three elder boys had been sent to the country to escape the bombs, and Ilse worried constantly about their welfare. "And now they've taken the eldest away," she told me. "They've recruited him into the Volkssturm. Sometimes I go and see him in Wandsbek. That's where his barracks are."

"But that's outrageous!" I said, infuriated. "He's just fourteen years old. And he's got asthma!"

Ilse shrugged her shoulders. "That doesn't matter now. They need every man, even if he isn't yet a man."

I felt sorry for her. It really wasn't easy bringing up children in these times. I hadn't always understood that, I thought, reflecting ruefully on the day I'd told Ilse to listen to the BBC so she'd know what was really happening. "For God's sake, Öle," she'd said. "What if they catch you? They'll lock you up." I had been so annoyed by her answer that I responded angrily that she should hang her Mother's Cross around her neck and go for a walk to calm down. Ilse, however, never objected to my opinions, and therefore I didn't say anything about her having the occasional Nazi as a lover.

"And now," she was saying, with a cheeky glint in her eye, "the English and the Americans are coming . . ." I had to laugh. We made plans to try to watch the arrival of the Allies together.

My next visit was to the parsonage. With uncertain steps, I approached the house. The bomb crater was frighteningly close. It was a deep hole in the middle of the street, so wide that I had to be careful not to fall in as I passed it. My mother had told me that it had happened recently. "Please, God, let nothing have happened to him." A muttered prayer came to my lips despite my lack of faith.

The house was badly damaged. The roof had fallen in, and burn marks were clearly visible. With my hands clenched, my fingernails digging into my palms, I went up the steps and entered the parsonage. What would I do if Monsignor Bram had been hit? Would the people he was hiding still be in the cellar? Would I be able to look after them? And what if someone caught me? I was carrying a bag of food into a ruined house. It was just a few tins that I had found in my room, some cabbage and a few soft carrots from our kitchen. But after my experience in the camp I was not as carefree as before.

I quickly thought of a believable excuse. Monsignor Bram was frequently anxious about his parishioners, trying to help where he could. He had asked me to bring him some vegetables whenever I'd been helping at the market so that he could pass them on to the most needy. That sounded plausible enough.

Before I could search the damaged rooms for a sign of life, Bram came through a doorway toward me. "Gretel!" he said, stretching out his arms to welcome me. He took my hands into his own and looked me in the eye. I felt deeply moved as I looked at his rosy, friendly face. "You are all right, thank God! I thought of you every day in prayer, my child. We have also been lucky here that nobody was hurt. The Lord has watched over us." That answered my unasked question, and I felt an enormous sense of relief.

After a few days in Hamburg, I picked up my old habits. As I wasn't working for the Wehrmacht any longer, I had plenty of time on my hands, which initially I spent largely at the vegetable market to get hold of produce for bartering. Miraculously, the Gestapo hadn't searched my room, so I found the money in my pillow untouched. Soon, I was up to my neck in black-market deals again, although I conducted my business even more carefully than before.

On May 2, 1945, I went down to the kitchen to get some breakfast before heading off to the market. Something wasn't right. Mother was sitting silently at the table with Frau Gernot, and it was as if something invisible was hanging in the air.

Before I could ask what was going on, I realized what was so unusual. Frau Gernot, who would usually have been tossing out cutting, know-it-all comments and boasting about her loyalty to the Führer, sat crestfallen in her seat, with red-rimmed eyes. There was no sobbing and no conversation. Frau Gernot just stared straight through me. "Mother?" I said questioningly.

Without speaking, my mother pushed the *Hamburger Zeitung* toward me. "The Führer is fallen," it said in huge letters. I gaped at the headline without believing a word. No, I wouldn't fall for it again. He's dead; he's not dead. Celebrate, rejoice, only to be crushed by tremendous disappointment when it turned out it was a hoax.

Abruptly, I turned to the stove and put the kettle on. But as I turned again and saw the pathetic bundle that had once been the battleax Gernot, curiosity got ahold of me despite myself. I grabbed the paper and began to read, slowly sinking into a chair. Nobody said a word.

After the soldier's death of the Führer was announced to the nation yesterday evening on the wireless, Großadmiral Dönitz spoke to the German people and gave the day's order to the Wehrmacht. He said: "The Führer Adolf Hitler has fallen this afternoon for Germany, at his command post in the Reich's

Chancellery, fighting to the last breath against Bolshevism . . .
In deepest mourning and awe, the German people bow down
. . . At the end of his fight and his undaunted, upright life
was a hero's death in the capital city of the German Reich.
His life was lived in service to Germany . . . The Führer has
declared me to be his successor.

I looked up and my mother nodded to me. She was holding Frau
Gernot's hand. The old woman was obviously completely in shock.
"Karl Kaufmann has made a speech declaring Hamburg an open
city," Mother said. "He said that nobody should shoot at the Allies
and then nobody will be hurt. The English are taking everything over
now. 'May the Lord protect our people and the Reich,' is what he said.
And Uncle Baldrian spoke too, telling us that British troops were
already marching into Hamburg." Incredulous, I looked at her. "Uncle
Baldrian" was the nickname of Georg Ahrens, the deputy of Karl
Kaufmann, Hamburg's governor.

At last, it dawned on me: This was really it! The war had ended.
It was finished, over. The Allies were marching in. For years, we
had been waiting for this moment! I swallowed. In spite of my joy,
I suddenly felt a lump in my throat. What would happen now?

Frau Gernot still hadn't said a word, which was probably for
the best. In my mother's eyes, I could see confusion and worry.
I hesitated, not sure what to do next. It felt wrong to carry on
as if nothing had happened. I couldn't possibly go and deal with
vegetables right now. The atmosphere in the house was strange,
unreal. I was dying to talk to Karchen, or at least Willi, about the
events, and I missed them more than ever. Keeping myself busy
by helping my mother didn't make me feel any less restless either.
Maybe I should take a break and go to Niendorf for a while.

The Rollfix hadn't been confiscated, to my surprise, but it
had become next to impossible to find fuel. However, my connections proved successful even there. On May 3, I drove to
my refuge by the sea, where Frau Kirchler actually expressed

something like relief about my return. "I thought you'd been hit," she grumbled, hurrying to find something to do so I wouldn't see that she was happy.

I decided to go for a long walk to blow the cobwebs away. I was looking forward to watching the waves again. But when I arrived at the beach, I was pulled up short by what I saw. All over the sand lay strange dark heaps that I had never seen there before. With a sense of foreboding, I went closer. What now? What was the meaning of this?

As I approached, the strange dark heaps developed into long-ish, twisted figures. An image shot through my head, a sight that I had never been able to forget: the bodies that I had thought were charred beams lying in the street as I walked home with Karchen the day after the firestorm. I knew at once that these were corpses. The whole beach was covered in dead bodies. They wore prisoners' uniforms. Their starved bodies were bloated and looked terribly disfigured. My eyes began to swim and the beach spun around me. Don't fall now, I groaned to myself, turning on my heel and running as fast as I could back to Frau Kirchler.

"Don't go to the beach!" I shouted frantically at her. "It's dreadful! It's covered with—with bodies."

Frau Kirchler stared at me, shocked. "Sit down!" she ordered, before asking me what exactly I had seen. Breathless, I told her, holding on to the edge of the table so hard that my knuckles were white. Frau Kirchler got up, patted me on the shoulder, and left the house with the words: "I'll go and report it."

After a short while, she came back and told me that she had informed the police. She made me a cup of coffee, and, against my better judgment, I soon found myself back at the beach to see what would happen. That was where I saw British soldiers for the first time. They had organized big carts and were watching over German prisoners of war who were collecting the bodies and loading them onto the carts. I saw a wrecked ship on the horizon, leaning steeply to one side and billowing clouds of smoke into the sky.

I couldn't say how long I sat in the sand watching the men carrying out their atrocious task. Much later, I returned to Frau Kirchler's. She had cooked for me, quite against tradition. "It won't help them now if you don't eat," was all she said. Grateful, I ate what she put in front of me without registering what it was.

Frau Kirchler had kept her ears open when she went to the village to shop for the meal. "The Nazis had loaded the prisoners onto ships, the *Cap Arcona* and the *Thielbek*, but the ships were bombed by the Allies. It seems they thought the ships were carrying soldiers, not prisoners." I stared down at my plate. "The Allies are there, on the beach. Just a day or two more and the prisoners would have been free. Now they're all dead." We fell into a dismayed silence.

I couldn't stop thinking about the dead prisoners on my way back to Hamburg the next day. It was unbelievable that they had met such a fate. What gave me the right to survive when so many others had not? Of course, it didn't make any sense to feel guilty about something I couldn't have prevented. But I was sunk in brooding the whole way home.

I went straight into the kitchen and put the kettle on the stove, wondering if I'd ever be able to forget what I'd seen. The only person who always cheered me up was Ilse, I thought. Then I remembered—hadn't we planned to witness the Allies marching in? I jumped up and ran out of the house just as the kettle began to whistle.

"There you are!" beamed Ilse as she opened the door, as if we had arranged to meet at this very moment. Her husband was at home, as usual, so she could leave the children with him. Without saying good-bye, she raced out of the house with me in tow. She had put on her makeup very carefully and wore a pretty dress that didn't leave much to the imagination. I looked down at my own clothes. My skirt was crumpled from the journey from Niendorf and my blouse was slightly stained, but what did it matter? Infected by Ilse's enthusiasm, I ran after her.

We went to the Rothenbaumchaussee, where crowds of people had installed themselves on either side of the road. The atmosphere was tense. Everyone was excited, and faces showed mixed emotions. Uncertainty, worry, and nervousness were blended with anticipation and relief. "Thank God it's not the Russians who are coming!" I heard people saying over and over. That had been our greatest fear. The Nazis' propaganda had told us that they would show no mercy, as little as the Germans had shown toward them.

I studied the faces in the crowd. How many of these people standing here had been real Nazis? Surely, at the beginning, most of them had been. It had all looked so good on the surface: order, jobs, restored national pride. Everything had seemed so well organized and had run so smoothly—at least as long as you supported the government and didn't say anything against them. Suddenly, I thought of my grandfather, who had raged against them so early on, being begged by all sides to shut up. It was a good thing that he hadn't lived to see Hamburg in ruins.

Finally, the moment came. Late afternoon had become evening when we heard the noises of the engines. They rolled up in a long train of military vehicles and tanks. At the front, in the very first car, was Kaufmann, making it clear that he had indeed handed the city over to the British. The people around us appeared to be calmed by his presence. Ilse and I didn't look at him for long; we were far more interested in the soldiers.

"Don't they look good?" I whispered to Ilse. They made an immaculate impression, heads held high and dressed very smartly, their faces not unfriendly, without any sign of arrogance but with an air of victorious determination.

"We'll soon have our hands full!" my friend answered with a wide smile, winking at a particularly handsome soldier who blew her a kiss. She elbowed me in the ribs, and we burst out laughing.

When we went home much later, we felt excited and inspired. We noticed smoke coming from many chimneys, and I wondered how many books and pictures were being burned all over

Hamburg at that moment. Frau Gernot's fire will probably warm the whole house up, I thought. She was absolutely devastated; her world had collapsed. You could almost have felt sorry for her sort, if their merciless dedication to the authorities hadn't been the ruin and even the death of so many innocent people.

We were just washing up after dinner when there was a knock on the door downstairs. Outside stood a handsome British officer, tall and in an immaculate uniform, with three crowns on the epaulettes. He was probably someone quite high in rank, maybe a major. Behind him stood a private. "Good evening," he said. "We're looking for suitable quarters for our officers. I'd like to have a look at your house, please."

For a moment, I stood as if frozen to the spot until some of the English I'd learned in school came back to me. "Of course, erm, *hier. Ich meine* . . . this way, please." I realized that he was asking our permission only as a formality; he could have walked in and looked around without an invitation. Our house, officers' quarters? Would that mean we'd be thrown out if he found it suitable? Maybe it would just be Frau Gernot and the self-righteous, thieving family in our living room who would have to find somewhere else to go, I mused, while Mother and I would live in a house full of good-looking British officers . . . Ilse would die of envy!

Unfortunately, this was not to be. The tall Englishman talked briefly with his comrade, turned back to me, and said farewell without further explanation. "Good-bye!" I called after him, somewhat disappointed, and watched as they went to the next house.

As it turned out, the next day they moved into the villa across the street. It was bigger than our house and had once belonged to Jewish owners, before they disappeared without a trace and a repulsive Nazi family moved in. I didn't bother to hide behind the curtains as I watched their hasty departure. Everyone gets what they deserve in the end, I thought, without sympathy.

On May 8, the newspapers and the radio announced Germany's surrender. The headline of the Allied newsletter was: "Peace.

Dönitz capitulates." So now it was official. The Nazis could no longer dream of the final victory. "The day of victory over Europe is here," I read.

> In accordance with the arrangements of the three superpowers, the end of the war in Europe will be officially announced over the radio today at 3 p.m. The news of the unconditional surrender of all German armed forces to the Allied powers has already been announced via Radio Flensburg to the German people.

Following Dönitz's orders, the commander in chief of the Wehrmacht had ordered the cessation of battle. "Five years, eight months and five days after it started, the war in Europe has now reached its end." Five years and eight months. No wonder I had become so used to the war. The implications of peace were unbelievable. No more air raids; no more going to sleep half-dressed to be ready to run to the shelter at night; no more fearing that our house had been hit whenever I was away from home; no more constant wondering about whether I'd still be around tomorrow.

How long would Hamburg need to get back on its feet? Most of the city lay in ruins. Would it ever be the same as it had been before the war? Would all the criminals be called to account? And what about the Frau Gernots? I had so many questions circling in my head. Again, I wished I could have talked to Karchen or Kuddel about it, but I didn't know where Kuddel was. All I knew was that he and his pregnant wife had been bombed out and had made a shelter for themselves somewhere in the ruins. If he was lucky, he would be assigned to a room in one of the few remaining houses, but usually people who already had children were given priority. And Karchen . . . would I ever see him again? I could only hope that he was still alive.

16

AFTER THE WAR

In Hamburg alone, countless meters of rubble have to be disposed of. The "de-Nazification" of Germany will require years of investigations; while the senior figures are put on trial, all those who had been civil servants have to find new jobs, reporting to committees and filling out questionnaires. Organized looting becomes a problem, and British military courts punish looting and possession of weapons with the death penalty.

In August 1946, the first British women and children come to Germany to join their men. Two and a half million refugees from the east of Germany stream into the British-occupied zone alone.

The worldwide food shortage affects Germany acutely. In 1947, the official daily number of calories per person is under 1,560, but unofficial reports speak of only 850 to 1,000 calories per day. More and more Germans show symptoms of malnutrition.

The Allied-occupied zones develop into East and West Germany; Berlin is blockaded; the Iron Curtain goes up. In 1949, the first central-government election takes place in West Germany. In October 1949, the German Democratic

*Republic (GDR) is established. In 1951, the Western Allies
declare the state of war with Germany officially ended. The
USSR acknowledges the sovereignty of the GDR in 1954.
The Western Allies acknowledge the sovereignty of the
Federal Republic of Germany in 1955.*

W e soon learned that while the British officers were making
themselves at home in the grand houses of Harvestehude,
the rank-and-file soldiers were to take quarters in Kellinghusenstraße, about three Underground stations to the north of us. Ilse
and I were excited about the possibilities, but first I had more
pressing issues to think about. It was high time I found work
again. So, one morning, I marched off into town to try my luck.

Before I set out, I chose my outfit carefully. After all, as a sales
assistant you represented the shop, and in fashion your appearance
mattered even more. However, it wasn't easy to stay clean and
smart as I walked through the city. I kept having to climb over
heaps of rubble, although most streets were by now comparatively
well cleared. Suddenly, I realized that the ruined buildings were
now something normal and familiar to me. How sad that I didn't
find the destruction depressing anymore—that it was simply a fact
of life. Here and there a tree, having survived as if by a miracle,
showed green shoots. On one corner, I heard a thrush in the
branches of one of these trees singing for all it was worth. It
made me think of all those mornings when I had stepped out of
a bunker after the bombings. Often, birdsong had reminded me
of the fact that life carried on, despite all the chaos.

The few shops that still stood had barely anything for sale.
I introduced myself at one, but the pitiful display gave me a
hint of how fruitless my search for a job was likely to be. There
weren't many people who could have afforded to buy clothes even
if they had been available. Many children ran around barefoot

or in shoes that didn't fit or were falling apart. Their trousers or dresses were often too small or far too big, the tears patched up if they were lucky.

After three hours, I returned home without success. "Well?" my mother asked.

Shrugging, I told her of my vain attempts. "There simply isn't anything!"

"Now, chin up! We'll manage somehow," she said.

I nodded and resigned myself to the situation.

Ilse, meanwhile, had made first contact with the British. She told me about her new friend Bert, a high-ranking officer who was quite smitten with her. "You wouldn't believe what he does for me," she told me. "He's with the provisions depot. I couldn't have chosen any better. He can get anything, whether it's food or soap or cigarettes. You've got to meet him."

"What does he look like?" Ilse took on a beatific expression and I had to laugh. "That good?"

She grinned. "Well, not exactly. He's got curly dark hair and he's a bit sturdy—but he's got some good qualities, I'll tell you!"

"And where do you meet him? In his quarters?"

"Of course not. They'd all get wind of it if I did. It's not permitted, private contact with a German. No, he comes to me, to my house."

"Your house?" I asked incredulous.

She laughed again. "It's like in the olden days when I still lived with my parents. He comes in through the window. He waits in the front garden until the coast is clear."

We both knew that her husband would find out about it sooner or later, whatever the arrangement between them was, but neither of us said anything about that. "What about the children?" I asked. "Won't they notice?"

"Now that there are no more air raids, they sleep like logs at night. And school has started again, in the room above the church, so I get a break now and then even if it's not whole days yet.

There's talk that the British will be giving out food in schools soon. That'll be a great help for a lot of people."

I thought of all the children who'd been indoctrinated by the Hitler Youth or the BDM. "What will they teach now? Surely racial science won't be on the curriculum anymore?"

Ilse didn't quite know herself what was going on in the schools. "They hardly have any books, as the history and geography texts were full of stuff they're not allowed to learn any longer. Even the math books had to go . . ." Before we started getting into politics, Ilse quickly brought me back to more important matters. "We could go to the cinema one day," she suggested. "They're showing films again." I was delighted. Finally, I could forget the world around me once more, deeply involved in a film. How wonderful! We planned to go the next evening.

Most British soldiers didn't seem too concerned about the orders not to go out with German women. Ilse took me along to small private parties where the soldiers had a great time with the women of Hamburg, parties that always took place behind closed and innocent-looking doors. They reminded me of the black-market parties, with all the secrecy, and alcohol was similarly plentiful.

Whiskey and cigarettes were passed around freely, and we didn't hesitate to take up the offer. I had a marvelous time. The more I drank the better my English was, and it wasn't long before I too found someone I liked. He was tall as a tree, a private, and had the longest eyelashes I had ever seen on a man. I met him at a party where he was walking around offering chocolate. "Chocolate!" I exclaimed, taking a piece and letting it melt on my tongue. I hadn't tasted anything so wonderful since Herr Mengel's praline shells. I almost felt sick.

The tall soldier laughed, pleased by my reaction. "Richard Deane," he introduced himself. "My friends call me Dixie." While Ilse disappeared with her Bert into the next room for a while, I made friends with Dixie. I liked him straightaway, and he seemed to feel the same. "If you want," he told me, "I can get you lots more chocolate—and cigarettes or whiskey. We get fifty cigarettes a week and loads of whiskey, and on top of that we can buy some more, tax-free." I thought of my black-market connections and beamed.

Ilse came back, her face red and her eyes shining. "We've got to go," she said. "It's almost curfew. It's twenty to eleven already— we'll never get back in five minutes!"

I waved off her concerns. "We'll sneak through the gardens. Don't worry. They won't catch us."

By the time we left, dawn was breaking. We crept through back courts and gardens toward home. Ilse and I enjoyed it, running through the darkness, on forbidden territory, like children.

Dixie Deane became a good friend. He provided me with all the things he'd promised he would, and my black-market business flourished once again. I had chocolate, whiskey, coffee, and—particularly sought-after—soap. Best of all were the cigarettes. Even cigarette butts were of value. We saw children picking them off the streets when they weren't playing war in the ruins.

During one particularly long evening in a cellar apartment at the Gänsemarkt, I got so tipsy that Dixie, worried about me, insisted on taking me home. Surprised and reassured, I took him up on his offer, realizing that finding my own way home would indeed be a problem for me in the state I was in.

"Where did you say you lived?" he asked.

"Hoch-al-lee," I told him speaking slowly so as not to slur my words. He understood, apparently familiar with the address.

How we got to Harvestehude, I couldn't remember later, only that when we got there, we walked three times around the block before sinking exhausted onto a front-garden wall. As hard as I tried, I couldn't remember how to get to our street from where we were. It was driving me crazy. Each time I thought we'd turned the right corner, unfamiliar façades stared down at me, swaying in the night breeze, or so it seemed to me.

My companion bore the situation with calm and patience. By now, he knew that he wouldn't be staying overnight at my place, but nonetheless we had a great time sitting on our wall until one of my neighbors came by. "Öle? What are you doing here? It's past curfew, don't you know?" He directed us to my house, and what seemed like no time later, I was torn from sleep by my tormenting alarm clock, with a hellish headache and huge gaps in my memory.

As he now knew where I lived, Dixie Deane soon popped by frequently. Sometimes he came on his own, occasionally with friends, and once in a while we had a party in my little attic room. Not everyone was prepared to sneak through the back gardens like Ilse and me, so the guests would usually stay overnight in my little room under the roof after one of these get-togethers.

As we crowded into the bathroom and kitchen the next morning, I would catch a disapproving look from my mother. It was time to find my own place, I thought, but the way things were, that wouldn't be easy. Mother would have to put up with my lifestyle for a while longer. "Child, you really go too far sometimes!" she would say to me. "You'll be thirty-one soon, and still you don't behave like a lady. Just look at how others are living while you're enjoying yourself as if there's no tomorrow. Most people are starving."

She was right, of course. Life wasn't easy for the people of Hamburg. While the British military government was reorganizing the city, bringing back law and order, streams of refugees were arriving and Hamburgers were returning from evacuation. Mother and I were incredibly fortunate to still be living in our own more or less unscathed house. Not many citizens were so lucky. Many had to make their homes in the ruins of the few remaining buildings, moving into the ground floor of an otherwise-ruined building, or living in the cellar of a house where that was the only inhabitable place. The shanty houses people constructed among the ruins often looked uncomfortable, and some rather dangerous, but anything was better than nothing.

Those who had nowhere at all to call home moved into the abandoned shelters, having to share with many others. I shuddered at the thought of living in those shapeless, windowless places. The meter-thick walls that had once offered protection now made prisoners out of their inhabitants; any attempt to knock a window through was doomed.

It wasn't only those who had been bombed out who were homeless. It turned out that my hope of sharing our house with British officers had been very naive. The Nazi family from across the road had not been alone. Wherever the officers moved in, the occupants were expelled. If you were lucky, you could find accommodation in your loft or your cellar, if they were still intact. Suddenly, for many, the privilege of owning a lovely villa spared by the bombing meant nothing anymore, at least in the short term.

We were issued with ration cards once again, this time by the British authorities. I had to prove that I was working to get my full entitlement. Mother employed me officially as housemaid, which wasn't a lie as such, as I did indeed help her on a daily basis. On the rations alone, however, we could barely have gotten by, so I thanked the Lord for my black-market connections. Thanks to Dixie Deane and other soldiers, I had a constant supply of goods for bartering; at least we wouldn't have to starve like so many others.

I'd have loved to go out properly with Dixie, for a meal or to a concert, but he reminded me that it was strictly prohibited for the soldiers to fraternize with Germans. We weren't even allowed to go to the cinema or to a concert at the same time as the British. Even the radio orchestra played the same music twice: once on Sunday afternoon for the British, and the same program again for the Germans on Monday evening. "What utter rubbish!" complained Dixie. "How are we supposed to live with you when we can't talk to you at all?"

My Rollfix had finally been confiscated, but in any case fuel was very strictly rationed, and my trips to Niendorf wouldn't have justified a permit. What was more, we weren't allowed to use private transport on the weekends, and that would have been the only time I would have needed the car. So, sadly, I had to say farewell to my Breakneck Emmi, but at peak times the trams ran, and I could get the train to the Baltic Sea, after all.

The people of Hamburg developed an enormous zeal for rebuilding their houses. On my way to the shops, I would see women on almost every street pulling from the rubble all sorts of materials that could be used in some way, stacking them carefully into neat piles. Nobody could get ahold of new materials. If you wanted bricks, you had to search for them in the debris and knock the mortar off them.

There were hardly any men around apart from the British soldiers who patrolled the streets in their vehicles. Most German men were dead, wounded, missing, or prisoners of war. I hadn't lost anyone but Karchen and Kuddel, and I was aware of being very lucky. So, in a funny way, I minded even more when Dixie told me one day that he had been posted back to England.

"Come with me," he begged. "You'll like England."

But my feelings for him were not as deep as that. "You're a good friend, Dixie, but let's leave it there," I answered, promising to write.

The British understood that we were in dire need of housing, and they delivered strange constructions made of corrugated iron. They looked like tunnels cut in half and were called *Nissenhütten*. These Nissen huts were set up in rows at the sides of the streets, with heaps of rubble and debris behind them. Often I wondered what they were like inside; they didn't look particularly warm or cozy, but for many families one of these huts was their new home.

Coming home on a cold, gray January evening, I met Ilse waiting in front of our house. "Listen, Öle," she said, "if you thought you were getting away without a big party, you were mistaken. Tomorrow evening, be prepared for visitors, and don't try to get out of it!"

I had hoped to quietly ignore my thirty-first birthday. I didn't particularly want to let everyone know that I wasn't as young as I behaved. "Do I have to?" I grumbled.

"Well, what do you think? You don't usually let an opportunity to celebrate pass you by! Don't worry your pretty little head. I'll get some people together."

I gave in. Maybe it would be too sad to sit down for dinner at the kitchen table with my mother on my birthday as if it were any other night.

The following evening, I took care getting myself ready. You never knew who you might meet. And anyway, they'd all be staring at me, trying to gauge whether I looked my age. I put on my best gray satin dress and made a bit more of an effort than usual, just in case. Who would Ilse bring along? Surely soldiers! Still, it was a pity that Dixie wasn't around anymore.

Footsteps and laughter on the stairs interrupted my thoughts. The door was flung open and in came Ilse with a bunch of British men. Each of them carried a bottle under his arm, and one caught my attention immediately. He had lovely blue-green eyes, brown wavy hair, and was very tall. Wasn't he . . . of course! The officer who had come to our house in May to inspect it for potential quarters. Did he remember me? "Happy birthday!" he said with a smile and gave me a friendly kiss on the cheek. I was starting to like the idea of having a birthday party.

Soon it got loud and lively. Since my gramophone had been stolen, we had to sing if we wanted music, and so we did, more and more noisily as the evening went on, even dancing in the confined space of my room. We kept falling over, which made us laugh even more. Some of the songs we sang Ilse and I knew from the wireless; others we learned from "the boys." The handsome tall Englishman, Patrick, impressed me with his courtesy and his understated sense of humor, and we looked more and more frequently at each other throughout the night.

At dawn, when everyone had gone, I got ready for bed, tired and happy, still humming the songs that we had been singing. I couldn't find my nightdress, which was very annoying because it was my best—pink, sheer, and beautifully made. I was sure that I'd left it on the bed. But why get irritated over a missing nightie after such a successful party? I must make sure to thank Ilse in the morning.

Two days later, in the evening, there was a knock on our door. I flew down the stairs and opened it, to find myself looking straight into a huge bunch of roses. Carefully, I pushed the flowers aside to see who had brought them. My heart leaped. Patrick!

"Do you feel like going for a beer?" he asked in English. Briefly, I thought of the ban on fraternization between Allied soldiers and Germans. Did it not apply to officers? Or had they relaxed the rules now? Whatever the case, I felt sure he wouldn't have asked if he'd had any concerns about it, so, beaming, I agreed, unable to hide my excitement. How lucky that I hadn't made any arrangements for this evening! For once, I'd planned to have an early night.

"Just a minute," I said. "I'll go and get changed."

But Patrick shook his head. "You look great. Let's go."

I quickly put the flowers in some water and we took the tram into town.

"And how does it feel to be thirty-one?" he demanded to know.

"Incredibly old!" I retorted. "I've already booked a place in the old folks' home. I'm moving in on Monday."

By this time, my English had improved a good deal, and I could communicate quite easily, although I didn't know half as many words as I needed and didn't always understand everything. If I got stuck, Patrick helped me to find the right word; if I made mistakes, he laughed in a friendly way and told me without patronizing me how to express myself better.

When we finally sat down with a beer and a wine in a bar by the canal, we got the chance to talk properly. "Don't you mind

going out with a German woman, after we've been your enemy
for so long?" I asked.

Patrick seemed unperturbed. "I could ask the same. You're going
out with an Allied soldier and we've destroyed your whole city."

"That's different. After all, I was never loyal to Hitler. But you
had no way of knowing that."

Patrick looked at me, his head tilted to one side. "I do believe
that I'd have spotted it if you'd been a Nazi. As far as I can
gather, you'd have been much more likely to have caused trouble,
or maybe you were even politically active."

I felt honored. So I seemed as if I'd had nothing to do with the
government. Thank God! "I wasn't a hero," I responded. "There are
others who were. And politically I couldn't do anything, although
I would have loved to. Somehow I never got the chance. I only
wished I could do something."

From across the table, Patrick took my hands, pushing the
sleeve of my blouse up so that the tattooed number was visible.
I watched him, unsure whether I should pull my arm back. "And
what's that then?" he asked.

"They did that in the town hall, but I don't know to this day
why. The others in the camp I was in didn't have numbers."

"So you were in a camp?"

"Only for a few weeks, right at the very end. When you came,
they let us go."

"And what camp was that?"

"I think it was a satellite of Neuengamme. A reception camp,
that was what they called it."

Patrick nodded. "Did you have to do forced labor?"

"No. We just waited around, bored to tears. But we didn't
complain after what we'd heard of other camps."

"So you knew about the concentration camps?"

"Well, you'd hear rumors. We could see the prisoners often
enough, clearing the rubble and so on. And a friend who escaped,
our family doctor, told me how awfully he was treated as a prisoner.

They'd been transported in cattle wagons, like animals, without water. And then they killed them."

Patrick nodded. His eyes had darkened. "I know. It's all true, I'm sorry to say. But I don't think you can imagine on what scale it happened."

He started to talk about Bergen-Belsen. He had been among those who had liberated the camp. Human skeletons, barely alive, walked among thousands of corpses in various stages of decay. The stench had been appalling, the sight horrific.

"Everywhere there was excrement and dirt. And in these conditions, these emaciated people. They seemed barely aware of what was happening. They didn't show any relief that we had come. Many were in a state of apathy. Sometimes you could hardly tell who was dead and who was still living. We had to hold our hands in front of our mouths. Some of us were sick, and many shrank back from the horror of it. I was sick. The evacuation took four weeks. We didn't know where to start. Typhus was rampant. We made the SS men collect the bodies and bury them. The prisoners who were still alive had to be deloused and washed. The Red Cross and German nurses did that. When the survivors were clean, they had to be dusted with DDT to fight the lice."

Silently, I listened to him. The survivors could not all be saved. They died in their thousands, of typhus, starvation, and exhaustion, in the barracks and hospitals to which they were evacuated.

"But surely you gave them food straightaway?" I asked Patrick.

"Yes, but it wasn't that simple. When you have been starved for months, or years even—and I mean really starved—then you can't eat a normal portion of food right away. Your digestive system can't cope with it. At first, we fed them ordinary food, and they were doubled over in pain. Some died as a result."

"What did you do with the SS officers?" I asked.

"They were imprisoned in Celle. There will be a lot of trials. I don't want to think about how many escaped."

We sat without talking for a while, looking at the people coming and going in the bar. How many of them knew about the situation in the camps? How many had taken part in the dreadful horrors perpetrated there? How many offenders would be dealt with and how many escape punishment? I remembered the guards at the camp I had been in saying, "Don't look so closely at my face."

Patrick stroked the number on my arm. "We'll get rid of that, at the military hospital. Or do you want to keep it?"

"Of course not," I answered. His hands were so soft.

As he took me home that night, I knew already that I wasn't prepared to give this man up easily. I hesitated to admit to myself that I had fallen in love. In the past, there had never been a happy ending when I had fallen head over heels in love; surely it was better to suppress any feelings right from the start. Determined, I lifted my chin. No, this time, I wouldn't have my heart broken; I would enjoy a nice friendship, maybe more, but without any deeper emotions. But as he said good-bye, giving me only a peck on the cheek, all my resolutions melted away.

We hadn't arranged another date, and the whole of the next day I was on tenterhooks. At the same time, I was in such a good mood that my mother got suspicious.

"Right! Out with it! What's his name?"

"Who?" I asked innocently.

Mother rolled her eyes. "I suppose I'll hear about it soon enough if it's serious."

Ilse came around in the evening and wanted to take me out to a party, but I hesitated. "What's the matter with you?" she asked. "This isn't like you!" I told her about Patrick and she realized that I intended to stay at home for him, just in case he came by. She told me off. "You're not going to stop going out because of a man? What will he think of you if you're cooped up at home waiting for him to call? How boring you'll be!" She was genuinely cross. "If you really want to impress him, then play hard to get."

I let her persuade me. She was probably right. We schemed during our evening out to take him to one of our parties when he asked me out the next time. Hopefully there would be a next time!

I needn't have worried. The next morning, I found a message from Patrick pinned to our front door. Did I feel like going to a concert? He'd come over in the evening. The day dragged on. Finally, late afternoon came and Ilse appeared. We'd planned to go out again, and now we just had to talk Patrick into coming along.

When he knocked on the door at eight, I was determined to make our plans sound great. But what if he wasn't in the mood? "Patrick," I said as I opened the door, "my friend's just popped over. We're thinking of going to a party. Are you in?"

"Okay!" he said simply, and I was relieved it had been so easy.

The evening was good fun. Ilse knew the host, Roswitha. I had met her a couple of times before. She had a pretty face and a full figure, and she was very nice but also very loud and fiery. When she was introduced to Patrick, she was clearly very taken with him and was so charming and flirtatious that we all started to tease her. Ilse gave me a nudge when Patrick got up to get us all a drink. "Keep him, he's a good one," she murmured, with a hint of seriousness, before we started to taunt Roswitha again, who by now was deliberately exaggerating. At that moment, she pushed her skirt up a bit more to show her knees and turned so that Patrick would literally stumble over her on his way back to the table.

"They're nice, your friends. It's quite a laugh to party with your crowd," he commented as he walked me home that night. I was happy that he had enjoyed the evening, and wondered whether our friendship might develop into more. In front of our house, he kissed me good-night again, ever so lightly, holding my shoulders for a moment, before saying good-bye.

"Shall we go to a concert tomorrow?" he asked.

Of course, he'd wanted us to go to a concert! "You didn't have tickets, did you?"

"Never mind about that!"

"But it's so difficult to get ahold of tickets! You must have had to be in line half the day."

Patrick tapped his nose and smiled. "Let that be my problem. See you tomorrow."

Suppress any feelings! No deeper emotions! Who was I kidding? I had fallen in love, totally, completely. I'd get hurt again, wouldn't I? He would be called away, like Dixie Deane or Wolfgang, the American at Sylt. He'd be here one day, gone the next. I wondered what his faults would be. So far, he had made an almost frighteningly good impression. Surely he wasn't perfect. He had to have his flaws. I had met enough men to be certain about that. But brooding on it wouldn't help me, and all I wanted for now was to be with him.

We went to the concert and we went to the cinema, we went to parties with friends, sat in harbor cafés and bars. Almost every day we met, got on extraordinarily well, and drank enormous amounts of alcohol. I told him about Lydia; he told me about Dunkirk, the battle of El Alamein, Salerno and Burma.

Dunkirk was the most impressive story I had ever heard. "We were sure we'd had it. Suddenly, there were hundreds or maybe thousands of boats on the sea, coming to fetch us. I thought I was hallucinating. Little boats with civilians in them, fishing boats and the like—anything just about seaworthy. They'd come all the way from England to rescue us. We tied our shoes around our necks, held our papers in our mouths, and swam out to them. I was picked up by a fishing boat and taken home." He told me that the British public celebrated this act of solidarity as if it had been not a military defeat but the greatest success ever.

"But it was," I commented. "Just imagine! A little fishing boat could easily have sunk. They're not built to cross the Channel, are they?" Patrick agreed. For him, this had been one of the best moments of the war.

"And you were in Egypt as well?" I asked. "When Rommel was defeated? Right there in the desert?"

Patrick nodded. "Right there in the desert. We tend to complain about the bad weather in England, but as soon as it gets hot we take it all back. And hot it was—you can't imagine! The sand gets everywhere; you can't get rid of it. And the flies! They crawl into every opening of your body. It's unbearable! But when Montgomery took over, he gave us tents, at least, and some things definitely got better, especially our morale."

I had heard about Montgomery. After all, it was he who had beaten Rommel, which had been unthinkable up to that point.

"It wasn't easy," Patrick said. "Rommel was something of a genius at his job, I've got to admit. He was just a few days' march away from Cairo; our troops had already burned their documents and fled the city. But he was no match for Monty. He knew how to organize a battle! Before El Alamein, he simulated an attack using everything we had. He planned it down to the last detail, with tanks made of cardboard, false railway tracks—he even laid an imaginary fuel pipe. He took two months to prepare for the attack, and Churchill was getting impatient, but he told Churchill we had to do it properly or not at all, and Churchill had to let him get on with it. Monty wasn't one for compromising, arrogant as he was, but all the boys were on his side."

Patrick's eyes shone as he told me about El Alamein. It had been the first decisive victory for the British, and they had gained strength and pride from it. I wanted to know how Patrick worked his way up to become lieutenant. "Did you do any heroic things or do you just gain promotion if you're there for longer?"

He shook his head. "I went to the officers' school in Sandhurst. You would have loved the buildings there, very old, with huge rooms. The dining room alone was like a church, with stained-glass windows and paintings on the walls."

How differently he and I had spent the war years! As much as we told each other about our experiences, it was almost impossible for us to imagine how the other had lived from day to day. "In one respect, it's easier for you than for us," I mused during one of our conversations. "At least you can celebrate your fallen comrades as heroes. Our soldiers were fighting for the wrong side, even those who didn't want to join in." I told him about the problems you faced if you didn't greet people with the Hitler salute or if you dared to inquire after someone who had disappeared.

Patrick understood quite well. "You lived under a dictatorship. You didn't have a choice. You shouldn't have let him get into power, that was the mistake. Some say the Treaty of Versailles was really responsible, that without it Hitler wouldn't have stood a chance. But I feel I can at least show some respect to the German soldiers I've come across. I have more of a problem with the Japanese, considering how they treated our boys." He shook himself, as if trying to get rid of the memory.

"In Burma?" I asked sympathetically. Patrick nodded. He had been dropped as a parachutist behind enemy lines, as all the passes had been blocked and the British troops were marooned. I hadn't heard much about the war in Malaysia and Singapore, so I had no idea how hard the British had fought for Burma.

"I think you've seen and lived through much worse than me," I told him. "The night of the firestorm was as much as I could bear. And Kristallnacht, when I was searching for Lydia."

"Your Jewish friend?"

I nodded gloomily. "I don't think I'll ever see her again."

We sat lost in our own thoughts for a while. Then Patrick suddenly said, "Come on! After all, the war's over now. Reason enough to celebrate!" He poured us each a glass of whiskey, which burned my throat, and suggested that we got drunk.

When I got home, swaying heavily, I declared to my mother that I intended to marry Patrick.

"That one?" she asked, aghast. "But he's constantly drunk!"

"Yes," I slurred, "but when he isn't, he's really lovely!"

17

FINDING KARCHEN

Weeks became months, and a year passed. One evening, when I was peeling potatoes, I received a phone call from the British Military Hospital in Wandsbek.

"Frau Öhlgart?"

"That's me," I answered, my voice shaking with fear. "Has something happened?"

"I don't know if you can help us, but we've got a strange case here. It's about a German officer who was a Russian prisoner of war. I don't suppose the name 'Karchen' means anything to you?"

Karchen! I almost broke the receiver I squeezed it so hard. "Of course! I'm coming! Where is he?"

I raced to the hospital, went to reception, and was led onto a ward. The soldiers' wounds were terrible. Some had their eyes or their whole head bandaged, some were in plaster practically from head to toe, some were in wheelchairs. They played cards or lay on their beds, apparently barely conscious.

A nurse led me to Karchen's bed. There he was, his head turned away from me. "Karchen," I called gently. "Oh my! Karchen!"

He turned to face me. "Gretel," he muttered simply. "There you are!"

How terrible he looked! His beautiful face had at least not been shot to pieces, but he had clearly suffered. Deep lines were engraved on his forehead and around his mouth; his skin looked leathery and was stretched over his prominent cheekbones; his unwashed hair was streaked with gray.

Carefully, I sat down on the bed and took his hand. "God, I'm so glad to see you again! What happened to you? Suddenly you were gone from your office and instead some slimy Hitler fan was sitting there. All I heard was that you'd been taken to the town hall."

Karchen groaned. "Don't remind me of it." He held his hands to his stomach. Fearfully, I pulled his blanket back. There was a thick bandage wrapped around his middle, soaked in blood. Before I could ask what had happened, two British military officials entered the room and came straight over to us.

"Are you Frau Öhlgart?"

I nodded.

"Thank you for coming. Would you please follow us to the office?"

I looked questioningly at Karchen, who closed his eyes and vaguely shook his head. Shrugging, I followed the officials to an office at the end of the corridor. One offered me a chair with a wave of his hand. It was in front of a desk covered in papers, behind which the two men sat down.

"Hauptmann Kunert was found with a stab wound which is . . . very serious," one of the officials began.

Worried, I asked if it was life-threatening.

"The doctor thinks he'll pull through. But that's not our concern. We have to clarify what this is about. A stab wound is not a normal war-related injury, and in any case, it's a fresh wound. The suspicion has arisen that Hauptmann Kunert fell victim to an act of revenge, which in turn could mean that he has committed war crimes."

My jaw dropped. "Kunert? A war criminal?"

The British watched me with interest. "Due to his high rank, it is possible that one of his victims recognized him in spite of his civilian clothes and retaliated for atrocities committed by him."

"That's outrageous! Kunert was no Nazi at all—quite the opposite. He was involved in the Stauffenberg Plot."

Now it was the officers' turn to stare at me. "Do you have any evidence of this?"

"Not really, of course not, but during the night, as the messages came through about the attack—I worked for the Wehrmacht, a telex machine operator—that was when I realized that he'd known about it all along. He wasn't at all surprised like the rest of us. Anyway, he'd always made it clear what side he was on, even long before that July. I can vouch for that."

They questioned me in detail about my work, about Kunert's activities as far as they were known to me, and about the night of July 20, 1944. The officers were friendly and patient; they made notes on my statements and offered me cigarettes, water, and a cup of tea, which I gratefully accepted. The final question was whether I had any idea why he might have been stabbed or who would have wished him harm, but I was at a loss myself. "I could ask him," I offered. "Maybe he'll tell me."

Karchen was still lying in the same position as when I left him, his eyes closed. Again, I sat down on the bed and took his hand.

"You must have gone through quite something," I said gently. "And now the British even think you were one of the Nazis."

Reluctantly, he opened his eyes, looking so very tired. "Oh, well," he said. "Let them think what they want. What does it matter?"

"It matters a hell of a lot," I said angrily. "How can you lie here, so indifferent, after all you've done? You risked your life to do something against Hitler. Do you think I didn't realize?"

Now he smiled despite himself. "Oh, Gretel! You're still the same. You'll never change! Somehow I knew nothing had happened to you. How did you find me?"

"They telephoned me, at home. You kept saying 'Karchen' when you were delirious, and my name, so they found me. I almost fell over myself trying to get here as quickly as possible! But now tell me, how did it happen, your wound? Who was it?"

"It was my lover."

"Are you seeing someone . . . I mean . . . a boyfriend?"

Karchen nodded and, for a brief moment, the familiar sparkle showed in his eyes. "Not just the one, to be quite honest."

There. The story was easily explained. Karchen had been caught by his lover having taken home another man after a night of drinking. His boyfriend was beside himself and, seething with jealousy, had reached out for the nearest weapon—a kitchen knife. Blind with rage, he had attacked Karchen.

"Please let me tell the British," I begged, and he shrugged. I got up and returned to the office, where one of the two officers was sitting at the desk, typing. I knocked and he looked up. I quickly told him what I'd heard from Karchen. He noted down that this was a private matter rather than a concern for the military. "Well, that seems plausible enough," he said. "We'll check your report and if it's all confirmed, Hauptmann Kunert is free to go as soon as he has recovered."

Relieved, I went home after one more check on Karchen. He had already gone back to sleep. I planned to look in on him regularly.

When I got home, my mother told me that Patrick had been at the house asking after me, but I didn't mind having missed him as I usually would have. I was too happy to know Karchen was alive and back in Hamburg.

As I had missed Patrick anyway, I resolved to have a peaceful evening at home. I tidied up my room while listening to the BBC, but they were broadcasting a play that didn't interest me much. Just as I was wondering whether I should go to bed early for once, I heard a knock on the door of my room. Surprised,

I opened it to find a small blond boy with unkempt hair and a desperate expression on his face.

"Helmut! What are you doing here?"

"Can you come quickly, please? Mommy . . . my mom doesn't feel well, I think. I don't know . . . Can you come, please?" He burst into tears, and I didn't hesitate for a minute. We ran down the stairs and over to Ilse's house.

Helmut led me into her bedroom. She was on her bed, quietly whimpering and doubled over, in a pool of blood. "Oh shit! Ilse! Ilse? Can you hear me?" Nothing. I lifted her head, which felt hot, shaking her slightly, calling her name again and again, but she kept muttering confusing things, whimpering and groaning. "Cellar" was all I understood, occasionally a name, Ludwig or something like that. I didn't waste much time trying to understand what she was saying. I dashed to her telephone and asked to be put through to the hospital. "Please come as quickly as you can. My friend has lost an awful lot of blood. I don't know what it is, but it looks like a miscarriage."

I put a cold compress on Ilse's forehead. I couldn't think what else to do. They came faster than I'd expected, and within minutes the two nurses had put her on a stretcher and carried her out of the house and into the ambulance. I stayed back with Helmut, who clung to my hand as if his life depended on it. As in earlier days in the shelter, knowing I had to comfort him helped me to stay calm.

"It's all right. It'll all be fine. They'll make her better in the hospital, and tomorrow we'll go and see her. And I'll introduce you to my friend Patrick, who's an English officer and really nice. But now you've got to go back to bed. Or are you hungry?"

Where on earth were Ilse's husband and the other children? They were almost always in the apartment somewhere when I came to visit. Why today of all days was the place empty? I made a sandwich for Helmut and gave him some milk before I tucked him into bed. I promised to stay the night if the others didn't come back. He fell asleep almost immediately, still squeezing my hand. Gently, I stroked his unruly hair. Then I went to Ilse's room to change the sheets and clean up.

The next morning, I took Helmut to school before going home. Helmut had come straight up the stairs to my door, and since I'd been out all night, Mother had come to the wrong conclusion about what I'd been up to. But when I explained what had happened, she promised to help me look after Helmut. After school, I took him back to our house to feed him before taking him to the hospital as I'd promised.

Ilse looked much better, although she had dark circles under her eyes. She took her son in her arms. She looked at me and said, "I'm sorry. I've been so stupid." I asked if she felt a bit better. "I'm dead tired," she said, "but I think I'll be fine. Do you understand, though, why I did it? I couldn't have had another one . . ."

I understood. "Where did you get it done?"

She pointed to the boy and shook her head.

"And where are all the others?"

"They've gone to my sister's in Altes Land. I said I needed a few days' peace and quiet. How could I have known that it would go so wrong?"

"Shall I call someone to fetch them?"

"No, please don't. Would you mind looking after Helmut until I'm out? They're coming back at the weekend. By then, I'll be back on my feet."

I sighed and gave in. The easiest way was if the little one lived with us for the time being.

"Don't you dare do anything like that again," I warned Ilse on my way out.

"Hang on, just a minute!"

I turned around.

"There's something else . . ." She hesitated.

"What? Out with it! Come on!"

Ilse evaded my eyes. "I've . . . helped someone."

"Yes, and?"

"Well, he's . . . in our cellar."

Unsure what she meant, I tried to make eye contact with her. "So that's what it was! You said something about the cellar last night. You've hidden someone?"

Ilse squirmed a little, obviously uncomfortable. "He's a cousin. Ludwig. One day he came to us, begging for my help. He had quite a good position during the war, and now they're after him—"

I got angry. "Ilse! You've hidden a Nazi? I can't believe it! And then you fed him with things your English lover gave you?"

"What should I have done? He's family. I couldn't let him down. Please?" She pleaded.

"Well, I won't help him, if that's what you mean. But I won't denounce him either. Calm down. He can pack his stuff and run for it."

Ilse sighed, making her anxiety about it clear, but I didn't care. I grabbed Helmut's hand and marched determinedly out of the room. I'd planned to look in on Karchen, but as the British Military Hospital was miles away and I was determined to deal with the Nazi in the cellar, I headed straight for home and, having dropped Helmut off at my mother's, stormed over to Ilse's house.

The cellar was locked, and I searched for the key for some time before I found it in the kitchen on a hook. At last, I unlocked the cellar door and descended the steep steps. Where on earth was the light switch? Frustrated, I went back upstairs, feeling for the walls so I didn't trip. Ah, there it was. I switched on the light, a sad little bulb illuminating the pantry, revealing nothing but empty shelves.

Determinedly, I pushed open the door to the coal bunker. "Ha!" I heard a deep voice, sounding startled. "Ilse! About time! Where have you been? Do you want to let me rot down here?"

"Your time down here is over!" I shouted at him before I could even see his face. I heard him moving and felt for the cellar light switch, which, luckily, I found straightaway. In front of me was a partition all the way up to the ceiling. Through the gaps between the planks, I could make out movement. It wasn't until that moment that it occurred to me how naive I was, trying to confront a Nazi soldier alone, without a weapon or any way of defending myself.

Quickly, I put my doubts aside and summoned all my courage. I still couldn't see him, but I did know his name. "Ludwig," I called, "listen, I won't give you away, but I want you to go, and I mean now, this minute." Silence. I scanned the cellar for a sign of him: rough, blackened walls, the floor covered in coal dust, here and there a lump of charcoal, an old potato sack by the wall, a holey bucket in the corner.

Then, on the other side of the partition, I saw the shape of a man coming around the corner with a stick in his hand. Don't get nervous, I told myself, wishing I could have asked Patrick to come with me. I took a deep breath. "You can put the stick down," I called out. "I'm on my own. I told you, I won't give you away. Just go!"

"Oh, yes? And who's to say that you're honest and the Tommies aren't waiting for me up there? How did you even know I was here?"

"I'm Ilse's friend. She's in the hospital, and if I don't call her within the hour, she'll call the military police and send them here."

As the lie flowed from me as if by divine inspiration, I had a chance to examine the man before me. He was tall and wore ill-fitting civilian clothes. The light was too poor for me to make out his face clearly. He still held his stick fast and was limping toward me. "It's not over yet. That's what you think, but you'll see!" he hissed, pushing me aside and climbing the stairs.

Hastily, I followed him before he got any ideas about locking me in the cellar. Keeping my distance, I watched him go into the kitchen, where he filled a glass twice with water, drinking it down in one go. He opened the bread bin and the larder, took what he could find, stuffed his pockets with the food, and turned to the door. Without a word, he left the house, unable to move his leg properly, as if his knee was stiff. I watched him through the curtain until he was out of sight and breathed out the lungful of air that I felt I had been holding in for the last half-hour.

When I had put Helmut to bed in the evening, I wished I could talk the last few days over with Patrick. I wondered whether to go and call for him. Until now, I had only seen him when he came to call on me. But maybe he thought it was my turn to make contact. He didn't live far away, just a few streets further on in a block of apartments in Kellinghusenstraße.

Mother told me she'd look in on Helmut to make sure he was sleeping all right, so I was free to go. I was in high spirits as I walked the short distance. Kellinghusenstraße was by no means pretty—the buildings were simple brick-built blocks of apartments—but it was clearly well suited to army quarters. Only the senior officers had commandeered villas and luxury apartments for their billets.

I started to become nervous. What if I got him into trouble? He had once said that I could come and visit him, since, as a lieutenant, he was able to do as he wished, and he'd told me the number of his apartment, but I was still slightly concerned. "Oh, well," I told myself as I walked along the corridor, "the worst they can do is throw me out!"

Finally, I reached the right door. Should I surprise him? No, better not. He always knocked at our door, so I'd knock too. "Just a minute!" I heard from inside. Eventually, he opened the door, dressed only in a pair of trousers, his chest bare. "What's . . . Gretel!" The smile on my face froze as I glanced into the room. I found myself looking straight into the eyes of a pretty brunette who was sitting up in bed and holding the duvet over her breasts.

I saw red. Without thinking, I pushed Patrick aside, stomped into his room, and positioned myself in front of his bed. "What do you think you're doing here? Out! Go on, quick! This is *my* man!"

I hadn't been so furious in a long time. It was as if a dam had burst. I turned on my heel, grabbed some items of clothes that I vaguely identified as feminine, and stormed to the door. Bra, blouse, skirt, stockings—I threw everything into the corridor, came back, found her shoes, flung them out the door as well, and then turned to the woman in the bed, who had been watching me, speechless. "I said OUT!"

Pulling back the duvet, I took her elbow and pushed her naked as she was out of the room. Everything had happened within seconds. Patrick hadn't had a chance to react. He went as if to call something to the woman or go after her, but I had slammed the door shut the second she stepped outside. Wild with rage, I stared at him.

"Hang on, hang on!" he said, trying to calm me down.

"Hang on *what?*" I raved. "What kind of idiot do you think I am? This is how seriously you take our relationship? You jump into bed with any old hussy while going out with me? You bastard! And I thought—" While I was shouting myself hoarse, I was tearing the bedding off the still-warm bed; I had thrown the duvet to the floor and was just slamming the pillow down when something stopped me. My eyes fell on something pink. But wasn't that . . . "My nightie!"

Completely wrong-footed, I stared at Patrick who had been watching me with a mixture of bewilderment and embarrassment. "I . . . well . . ." he stumbled, and then shrugged his shoulders helplessly.

"My best nightie! No wonder I couldn't find it. But why . . ." Suddenly, I felt really touched; my tantrum was forgotten in an instant.

"I wanted to return it to you." Patrick had found his tongue again. "I just wanted to keep something of yours, and the best thing I could find on that night was this."

He looked so innocently at me that I could barely believe how furious I'd been a moment ago. "And out of longing for me, you're doing it with that . . . that . . ."

He gently took me in his arms, and his eyes confirmed what he said: "Sorry. Gretel, I'm so sorry."

I gave up. Patrick told me that he had not wanted to seduce me because he really "meant it" with me.

"Nice way of showing it!" I sulked, but I had already started to forgive him. The woman had disappeared without a fight, which lent his words credit, and as the ultimate proof of his feelings for me, I was still clutching my nightie. "And what are you planning to do next time you want to sleep with a woman?" I asked him directly.

"I think I'll know who to turn to," he murmured softly into my neck. "And anyway, I've always wondered how you'd look when you were actually wearing that nightie."

Dawn was already approaching when I left the block of apartments to go home and take Helmut to school. I didn't talk much that day. There were too many things I had to digest. Not that I had much time to think or be alone, however. I had Helmut to deal with, my mother to help, and a short visit to Ilse and one to Karchen to make. All the while I was quietly hoping that Patrick would show up that evening.

When there was a knock on the door at half past eight, I knew it was him before I opened it. I pulled him into the house and upstairs to my room. I was glad that I'd thought to put Helmut to sleep downstairs on my mother's chaise longue.

I found it difficult to stick to Ilse's advice to play hard to get, although I knew there was some wisdom in it. I knew I mustn't turn my life upside down for a man, even if I wanted to spend every minute with him. At least I knew that he was no saint, and in the end I felt more relieved about that than I had been angry about the woman in his bed.

Meanwhile, as I grew more and more attached to Patrick, Hamburg recovered only slowly from the consequences of the war. The rebuilding of the city went on steadily, but the once-beautiful streets would be marred by the rubble and the ugly skeletons of buildings, not to mention the unsightly corrugated-iron tunnels of the Nissen huts, for years to come.

When autumn came and it grew colder, supplies started to become a problem. Coal was scarce, and electricity was so strictly rationed that it became impossible to make a meal on the electric stove. Mother and I built a fire in the garden using some big stones that I had collected from the bomb crater on our street. We would put our old preserving pan on the hot stones and cook a huge stew for us and our lodgers, so we didn't have to line up at the soup kitchen like most people. At first, I found it exciting and enjoyable to cook on an open fire in the garden, but doing so on a daily basis in rain and ever-lower temperatures I found increasingly hard.

Firewood became our most valuable possession. Many a chair fell victim to the flames, especially as autumn turned to winter. It grew colder and colder, although maybe it seemed so much worse than usual because we had no heating. I thought uneasily of those who had no home. Would they survive this winter? Would they make it through the war only to starve or freeze to death now?

On a particularly gloomy day, Ilse came over, with Helmut holding her hand, to discuss the situation with me. "Have you heard the forecast?" she began.

"Do you mean about the hard winter?"

Ilse nodded. "We've got to do something, and quickly. If this goes on, we won't get any more coal, and then we've had it."

"And what exactly do you have in mind?" I asked doubtfully. "Do you want us to scavenge from the coal trains like the others?"

Ilse shook her head. "I've heard something, through Bert. You know the British have their wives and children here now?"

"So?"

"They're being looked after quite well. Don't think they're as badly off as we are!"

"I know. Patrick's been working on logistics and supplies for the families lately. They're determined to make sure they're as comfortable as possible, he says. But the women don't feel too happy about it. They say they can't possibly have food and fuel and plenty of living space when all the while we Germans are homeless and starving."

"That's not what I've heard!" Ilse said, irritated. "Apparently, they look down on us as if we were the most primitive people and they are the only civilized ones."

"You're thinking of the officers' wives. They've stuck with the army's instructions not to fraternize with us and so on. But the ordinary soldiers' wives are all right. Patrick said they're even writing letters to their politicians at home to see that we're better looked after and they don't get so much for themselves."

Ilse still didn't believe me. "Why do the British get coal and we don't, then?" she asked. "In the Innocentiapark there's a huge pile of coal for the married quarters. If they're as noble as you say, your British wives, then they surely won't mind if we dip into that."

"Hmmm . . ." I gazed into space for a while. If the winter really turned out to be as hard as they were predicting, it would be stupid not to try everything possible to stay warm. And it was true what Ilse had said. If Patrick was telling the truth, the British women would be happy to share with us. "What are we waiting for?" I said at last.

Within minutes, we were in the Innocentiapark, having left Helmut to help my mother prepare dinner. We went to the fence encircling the army stores and walked directly toward two soldiers. "Hello!" we beamed, and they gave us a friendly greeting in return. We chatted, and they told us that that very night, a truck was coming to the Hochallee to deliver a load of coal. Ilse and I nudged each other, laughing with joy. We went home, waited for the load to be delivered, and spent the rest of the night shovelling coal.

Soon we were glad of the extra fuel we'd managed to get ahold of. It got colder and colder. From November 1946 to February 1947, we saw nothing but ice and snow. The Elbe was frozen solid for three months, something that hadn't happened before in my lifetime. It froze over so thickly that we were able to walk across it.

The electricity supply was restricted to once every three days. To cope with the overstretched demand, the British had divided Hamburg into three parts, each of which was given electricity in turn. Trains became increasingly unreliable as railway lines and engines fell victim to the frost; the trams ran only until 8 p.m. More and more factories had to close, and instead of working, the people of Hamburg streamed out of the city on the limited public transport to go in search of food. Those who had any possessions of any worth left took them to swap for whatever the farmers still had to offer. Potatoes and meat seemed to have ceased to exist; sugar and lard couldn't be found even on the black market.

At night, temperatures were as low as minus 26°C. When I left the house, I wrapped a scarf around my head, leaving just a slit for my eyes. My breath formed ice on the scarf, but if I took it off, the wind bit into my face. Children each had to take a piece of coal into school so that they could have a fire. Coal had become a necessity for survival, and we heard of thousands of convictions for coal theft. Nonetheless, everybody tried to get some from the trains or the army stores, as it was a matter of life or death.

The bitter winter of 1947 was followed by a catastrophic drought the likes of which had apparently not been known for 140 years. Food was the number-one topic of conversation, but the recipes we exchanged were for nettle soup, dandelion salad, horse chestnuts, and pine-needle tea. Patrick helped us where he could, and I shared what I had with my family and friends. We got to the point where we didn't believe it would ever get better, and then currency reforms were announced.

I joined the long lines in front of the banks. I was allowed to change 40 Reichsmark, for which I received 40 Deutsche Mark. Excited, I stepped out of the bank with my new money, strolling to the shops. I wasn't the only one. The streets were full of people, standing and looking into the shop windows as if they hadn't ever seen such displays before.

Wondering what was going on, I looked into the window of a hardware store. Strange, I murmured to myself, I could have sworn that half of that wasn't there the day before. Suddenly there were pans in several sizes, pretty decorated porcelain plates, collection cups, silver cutlery, and more. Amazed, I looked into the next window. There, too, there were things on display that yesterday I would have thought unobtainable. It was as if a miracle had happened overnight. From bicycles to hats, from curtains to soap, all of a sudden there were things to buy again. Would there be food as well? I raced to the butcher. Sausages! Where in the world had he got sausages from?

Prices were rising, however. Under Hitler's rule, prices had stayed constant. With the currency reform, this seemed to have ended. In September, I went to the bank again, but now I could change only 20 Reichsmark. I received a mere 6.50 Deutsche Mark for every 100 Reichsmark. My money-filled pillow turned out to be worth a great deal less than I'd expected.

"You should have bought shares," my mother scolded me. "Furniture, maybe, or paintings. You weren't thinking very far, putting all your money in your pillow and waiting until it was worthless!"

I shrugged my shoulders. "Money doesn't make you happy. At least we've still got our house. Just think: We weren't killed in the war. What more could you possibly want?"

I decided not to lose any sleep over it. We had more to eat now, and the people of Hamburg started to get back on their feet. My black-market connections melted away. Cigarettes were no longer an alternative currency; everyone was buying what they needed in the shops. I didn't shed any tears for the black market. The secrecy had been exciting while it lasted, but now my life was entering a new phase.

I went out a lot, sometimes with Ilse, mostly with Patrick. One day in early summer, he invited me to a very elegant restaurant.

"What are we celebrating?" I asked curiously, as a good-looking waitress filled our glasses.

"I've been relocated. In July, I'll be starting at Fallingbostel as a superintendent for the CCG, the Control Commission for Germany. I'm to organize supplies for the British families there. Do you want to come with me?"

Leave Hamburg? I hesitated for a moment. I'd been living here since I'd learned how to walk. But what would Hamburg be like without Patrick? I searched his eyes. Suddenly, I thought of Lutz on that day in Grömitz when he'd asked me to marry him. I'd looked for a sign of warmth in his eyes and hadn't found a hint of it. If I'd interpreted that correctly, I would have been spared a lot of suffering. When I looked into Patrick's eyes now, I saw the warmth that had been missing from Lutz's.

"I love you," he said tenderly.

"Of course I'll come with you. Will we live together?"

"We're to be given an apartment in the officers' mess. Apart from us, it'll just be the cook living there."

Patrick poured more wine into our glasses and we toasted our future together. It felt right, and Fallingbostel wasn't on the other side of the world, after all.

My mother reacted much more sympathetically than I'd antici-pated, although she still thought Patrick drank too much. "I think it's time you moved out anyway. Now that things are back to normal again, it's not quite right that you should still be living at your mother's. But I'll miss you. Visit me often!" I promised I would.

Sitting next to Patrick in the car as we set off from Hamburg, I was looking forward to the new place like a child going on holiday. Ilse had cried great tears and made me promise that I wouldn't lose touch. She'd helped me pack and given me a necklace as a memento, as if I would forget her otherwise. Clearing out my attic room, I'd felt as if I was closing one chapter in my life to open the next. I wouldn't be disappointed.

18

PATRICK

As we drove toward our new home, I watched the landscape flying by: wide fields of heather dotted with pine trees and birches, sandy paths through woods, juniper and broom, occasionally punctuated by small villages with age-old farmhouses ducking under huge oaks. Fallingbostel turned out to be a picturesque little town, full of British soldiers and their families.

We quickly settled in to our apartment in the officers' mess. Patrick gave me a job as a secretary, which enabled me to work as a translator, too. He loved his work, and all who dealt with him admired his capable, humorous manner. We made many friends and went to lots of parties. Time flew by. I didn't think a lot about the future, or the past; I was living day by day, until suddenly I started having spells of nausea. Worried about my health, I went to the doctor. When I was dressed again and stepped out from behind the curtain, he shook my hand and said cheerfully, "Congratulations!"

I stared at him. That couldn't be it. All those years when I had never taken any precautions, Lutz's desperate efforts . . . I needed an operation if I wanted to conceive—that's what they'd told me. Baffled, I went home and found Patrick waiting for me.

"Well?" he asked. "Are you all right?"

"I'm pregnant."

Patrick didn't say anything. I tried to look into his eyes, but he avoided my gaze. He went to the sideboard, poured himself a glass of whiskey, emptied it, and refilled it straightaway. As he swirled the golden liquid in the glass, he seemed to collect himself. "What are you planning to do?" he asked at last.

I had to sit down. "Me? What do you mean, what am *I* planning to do? If I remember my biology classes correctly, there are two people involved in making a baby."

He cleared his throat. "Listen, Gretel, I've been wanting to talk to you for quite a while now, but I didn't have the heart. Now I think it's time. They want to move me back. You know that the state of war with Germany is officially over. Well, more and more of our forces are being withdrawn. We're not needed anymore. It won't be long now until Germany is completely independent."

"You want to go back to England?" My voice must have sounded harsh and angry. He still wouldn't look at me.

"There's nothing for me to do here anymore. As I said—"

"Fine. I'll help you pack!"

I was doing a marvelous job of controlling my emotions; I was almost proud of myself. Don't think now, I told myself. Don't start asking questions or wonder "What if?" Don't plead, don't beg. Anything but that.

I was already on my way to the bedroom. "Gretel! Wait, Gretel!" called Patrick. Quickly, I slammed the big leather suitcase down on the bed, but then I started to pack my own things instead of his. "Gretel!" His voice took on an almost desperate tone. "We've had such a nice time together. Don't let us end it like this!"

For a moment, I paused and looked him in the eye. For the first time since I'd told him my news, he returned my gaze. "Have you actually taken in what I've told you?" I asked.

"Gretel, our life here has been wonderful. But you must have known right from the start that I'd have to go back one day."

"Don't worry, I won't run after you," I replied coolly, and carried on packing.

"And what do you . . . I mean . . . do you want to keep the . . . child?"

"You don't have to worry about that either. He wouldn't have a father. I might as well have an abortion."

Patrick looked uncomfortable. How long had he known that he was being sent back? Was that why I'd caught him looking so intently at me lately? I forbade myself to dwell on these thoughts before I got upset and my emotions broke loose. "A saint," I giggled. "A saint! The things you think sometimes . . ."

That same evening, I took the train to nearby Hanover to visit my uncle, whom I hadn't seen since the beginning of the war. Mother and I had not kept in touch with him very well, but I knew that he was still alive and quite wealthy. He had once mentioned in a letter that he'd be happy to help if we were ever stuck, and I thought that moment had come.

It took me a long time to find his house in Hanover, which had been almost completely destroyed during the war. It was late in the evening and already dark when I finally knocked on his door. Like us, he had been lucky enough to make it through the war with his house still standing, although the façade was badly damaged. No one came to the door, and I was afraid nobody was at home. Suddenly, I got cold feet about having come here. But then the heavy old oak door was unbolted by an elderly lady, my aunt. "Gretel!" she cried.

At least she recognized me straightaway. She led me into the kitchen and gave me something to eat. Uncle Hugo came and joined us, and soon I had told them my story.

"And now you need money to have it aborted?" my uncle asked when I was finished. I nodded. My aunt looked at her husband, appalled, but he ignored her. "I did say that I'd help you if you needed it. Now you've come to me and I will stand by my word. How much do you need?" He gave me 300 marks. It was a comparative fortune, but after Ilse's experience I was determined not to go to some backstreet abortionist but to a real doctor, which would be expensive.

I went back to Hamburg the next day and straight home to my mother. "Oh, Gretel, don't say it's over?" Only now did the tears come, and it was a long time before I pulled out of her embrace. "I'll make you up a bed. I rented out your little room ages ago. Tomorrow, we'll work out what to do." Unexpectedly, my mother turned out to be a great support. She accompanied me to a young, poor doctor whom she had heard about by word of mouth. I was far from the only unmarried woman who had fallen pregnant by an Allied soldier and decided not to have the baby. The doctor was understanding and seemed competent. He asked me if I was completely sure about my decision. I assured him that I knew what I was doing, and that I wouldn't have any regrets. But it wasn't as easy as I pretended it was.

The operation was short and without complications. I was given a general anesthetic. When I woke up, my mother was holding my hand and talking soothingly about going back to Sylt for a nice holiday. After a few hours, she took me home in a taxi, put me to bed, and let me sleep. The next morning, I was well enough to get up and sit in the kitchen.

I didn't allow myself to think about what would have happened had Patrick wanted our child, and how our lives might have turned out. At night, however, babies crawled into my dreams, and I saw distorted images of mothers in bomb shelters giving me reproachful looks. Once, I saw Lutz, saying, "Why else would I have married you?" I would wake up soaked in sweat and go downstairs to get myself a glass of water.

Gradually, the dreams stopped, and I decided to try to find work and an apartment to take my mind off things. By this time, there were more clothing shops around, and I walked thoughtfully through the streets looking for the best I could find. Eventually, I introduced myself at a grand-looking boutique at the Neuer Wall,

Jäger & Koch. The manager, Frau Vespermann, seemed very strict and fussy, but I didn't let that put me off.

"When were you thinking of starting?" she asked, looking me up and down.

"Immediately, if you like," I answered.

"We're moving soon, to Jungfernstieg on the corner of Colonnaden. That's where we're planning to introduce ladies' fashion, in which you specialize, as you say. Do come to our launch party. Then you can start straightaway."

I beamed all the way home. That had gone fantastically well! Finally, I was able to work in my real job, instead of spending my days at a desk or doing boring housework. The new shop was launched with an evening of champagne, music, and speeches, and it was simply stunning. Plate-glass windows looking out onto the canal, stylish furniture, plush carpets—you got the impression that this place was for high society only. But I wasn't afraid of the nobility, not after having sold black satin to the Prince of Prussia, I thought, grinning.

My enthusiasm infected Frau Vespermann, my colleagues, and, not least, the customers. Whoever asked for my advice was served thoroughly and honestly, whether she was looking for lingerie or an evening gown. Quite often, I managed to stop women from choosing unsuitable things, helping them instead to pick out something that would suit them in color and style. Frau Vespermann was more than happy with my work. My colleagues were not too keen on her because she was so strict, but I soon found that I could learn a lot from her. "Come over here, have a look," she might say. "This button shows that the dress must have been produced in Italy. Even without reading the label, you can clearly identify it as Italian." She pointed out many tricks of the trade, and I was truly interested and keen to learn from her.

What I enjoyed most was serving the soldiers who wanted to buy something for their lovers. Often, bizarre conversations developed, and I could hear my colleagues' suppressed giggles as they "happened" to be tidying the shelves nearby.

"What's her size?" I asked one customer. "I mean . . . is she . . . well built up here?" I would ask, gesturing around my breasts.

"Oh, I say!" he exclaimed, grinning. "Absolutely, darling! Yes, indeed, quite big!"

I exchanged a meaningful glance with my friend Rose, who had to press her hand over her mouth to stop herself from bursting out laughing, which in turn made her drop the pile of bras she had brought over to show the customer.

My English had come on well during my time with Patrick in Fallingbostel, so I served most of our British customers. It wasn't only the British who shopped there; I occasionally served Americans from the other zones of Hamburg, too. Not all the Americans were polite and respectful, though. One afternoon, I was called over by a desperate colleague. "Öle, please come over here. I really don't know what to do. Look! Can you think of something?" Elsa led me to the seating area, which was really meant for show, or for very special customers who had to sit down to discuss their particular requirements. An American soldier had spread himself out on the armchair, resting his legs on the coffee table, his cap pushed down over his face. He seemed to be having a catnap while his comrade strolled indecisively among the racks of ladies' lingerie.

"Hang on, I've got an idea!" I told Elsa. I fetched a tray, which I loaded with coffee things. Rattling, I marched over to the seating area. "Excuse me, please!" I thundered into the soldier's ear, before grabbing his uniformed legs and throwing them onto the floor. Before he could complain, I put the clattering tray on the table and looked at him defiantly. "Oh!" he exclaimed, surprised, looking from me to the coffee jug and back again. "How lovely!" Elsa sighed with relief.

That evening, Elsa urged me to go with her and some other women from the shop to the Kajüte, a pub under the arcades, and I was happy to accept. As soon as we stepped into the pub, I knew I would spend many an evening there. The atmosphere was fantastic. The place was packed with soldiers and young women; music played; there was talking, smoking, laughing, cards, food and drink. It was right up my alley. We managed to find a free table and pooled our money for a Strammer Max, the traditional Hamburg supper of rye bread with ham and egg, and a round of drinks. Before long, we were deep in conversation with soldiers who bought us one drink after another.

In the evenings, when I didn't go out with my colleagues, I roamed the streets looking for accommodation. Soon, I found what I was looking for, almost opposite my mother's house in the Hochallee. One of the houses had a "Room Vacant" sign pinned to the door, so I knocked to introduce myself.

A young woman opened the door. She was holding one child by the hand and kept turning around to check on another. "I'm here about the room," I told her. "We're sort of neighbors. I grew up just over there." I pointed to our house and studied her profile from the corner of my eye. She looked nice enough, but her face was tired and lined. Her hair looked lank and dull, and she was thin. The child in her arms, on the other hand, looked well fed, and his hair was shiny and neatly brushed. She obviously had her priorities right, looking after her children before herself, and I liked that.

She showed me the room. It was on the first floor and had a bed, a wardrobe, and a stove in the corner. "We've got to share the bathroom," she said, leading me through the house. The children shared a bedroom with their mother, who had rented out the other two bedrooms in the house as well. I wondered if she had lost her husband in the war. It was a typical villa, like all houses in the Hochallee. Maybe her husband had had a good position in the Party and was now imprisoned or even executed. I didn't like to ask.

"I'll take it if it's all right with you!" I said, and she shook my hand. An hour later, I had already started to move my things over the road. In the evening, Ilse came with a bottle of wine under her arm and we talked almost all night. It was the first chance we'd had to really talk since I'd come back to Hamburg. I told her about my job at Jäger & Koch, but the conversation kept coming back to Patrick. "I would never have thought he was capable of that," she repeated over and over again, shaking her head. "How wrong can you be about a man?"

"Well, I won't die of a broken heart," I replied, determined not to let my emotions show. "I know there aren't many men about at the moment, but if I want one, I'll have one, that's for sure!"

I refused to think of Patrick; whenever his image popped into my mind, I pushed it away again. Almost every evening, I went out to the Kajüte with Rose and Elsa. Sometimes we told ourselves strictly that we were definitely going straight home from work for an early night, but then one of us would rummage in her pockets until she found a bit of money, count it, and invite the other two to come along.

"Can't we go somewhere else for a change?" I asked one evening. "There's a new dance bar by the harbor. I've been wanting to check it out for ages. Go on, let's! I've got a date for tonight, but what about Saturday?"

It turned out to be a good idea. We weren't sitting alone at our table for long. Elsa had brought along her boyfriend, a Scotsman, and it was quite obvious that one gentleman was being shared between three ladies. Soon, we were joined by two men in their fifties who asked Rose and me for a dance.

"Claus Herzog," my dance partner introduced himself.

"Gretel Öhlgart. You really dance well!"

His face, which was deeply lined around the eyes and mouth, dissolved into a wide smile. "So do you!" he replied. "And why is it that an attractive young woman like yourself is without company? Did you lose your man in the war?"

"I am divorced." He seemed happy to leave it at that, and I was relieved that he didn't pry any further.

Claus and I danced the whole evening. Mindless chitchat gave way to deeper conversation; it was important for me to find out what his allegiances had been, whether I was having a good time with an ex-Nazi. "Were you a Party member?" I asked straight out.

To my disappointment, he nodded. "I couldn't avoid it. I am a printer. If I hadn't joined the Party, I would have lost my livelihood, for sure. In the end, I had to go to war anyway."

Uneasily, I imagined that Claus might have tried to shoot Patrick or Dixie. Of course, it was unlikely, but I minded the very thought of it. "Did you shoot at the British?" I asked.

Claus missed a step in the dance, then recovered quickly and laughed. "I was in France and Russia. I didn't shoot a gun at all. My task was simply to drive from here to there. Like a chauffeur, but usually I transported supplies rather than people."

I breathed out. If he had seen combat, I would have felt I had to walk away immediately. I still felt hypocritical. He had been on the side of the Nazis, effectively, and had helped their war effort. It was quite possible that he had driven senior Nazis at the front line, maintaining polite conversation with them, saying "Heil Hitler!" from dawn till dusk. But at least he hadn't fired a weapon himself, and I persuaded myself that this made a great deal of difference.

"Did you never think about joining the Resistance?"

Claus looked surprised. "What a question! Were you in the Resistance yourself?"

"Not really. I always wanted to be. But proper Resistance—no, me neither."

"What's that supposed to mean, anyway, 'proper Resistance'? For me, there was no choice. I had my wife and my child at home. If I'd deserted, they would have shot me. You don't think like that when you've got family."

"You say you have . . . had a wife and child?"

Claus's eyes dimmed. "I did. They died on the night of the firestorm."

I felt sorry for him. We were still dancing, but I didn't enjoy it anymore. Again, I suddenly thought of Lutz, who had been a Resistance fighter. Maybe it wasn't so simple to judge the character of a person according to whether they had worked for or against the government.

Claus took me home and promised to come back to visit. When I told Ilse about him, she just laughed. "Twenty years older! Oh, well. I knew you wouldn't stay on the shelf for long!"

The weeks passed. Summer turned to autumn; Christmas came and went. I spent my time in the Kajüte with Claus and Ilse. Often I looked in on my mother, who was glad I was close by. One Sunday morning, I was sitting with her at the kitchen table; the sun had fought its way through the clouds and it was starting to feel like spring. I had just promised Mother I would make the beds when I noticed that she was looking at me thoughtfully. She rummaged in the pocket of her apron and produced a letter. "That came the day before yesterday," she said simply. I took it and turned it over. It was marked "Airmail," with an English stamp. I recognized the handwriting at once.

Suddenly my hands were shaking. Should I tear it up unread? I didn't want to know any more about him. That would suit him, wouldn't it? I thought. Throwing my life into chaos again. No way. I was finished with him once and for all. I pushed the envelope into a pile of newspapers and left it there. I would decide what to do about it later. I threw myself into the housework, making beds, beating the rugs in the garden, offering to clean the windows.

When I returned to the kitchen, my mother said, "I thought we could bake a cake. It's Herr Mengel's birthday. I'm sure he'd love that. The oven's already lit. If you could get the eggs from the larder . . ."

All of a sudden, I felt very hot. My mother used newspapers to light the oven. Like a maniac, I searched desperately through the pile of papers. What would I do if she'd burned the letter?

"What in the world are you doing?" she asked.

I groaned. "The letter! Mother, the letter from this morning! I put it here among the papers. Please say you haven't burned it!"

Mother grinned. "Do you mean this letter?" she asked, producing it from her apron pocket.

I felt a weight fall from my chest; all thoughts of tearing it up banished. I cursed my stubbornness. With trembling fingers, I tore it open, pulling out a sheet of paper in Patrick's handwriting.

My dear Gretel! I'm sitting here in my room in Kent and don't know how to start. Every evening, I want to go out, but each time I leave the house I find myself at the beach, sitting in the sand. When I stare at the sea, all I can think of is how the same waves roll all the way to Hamburg and into the harbor, where you can see them. Then I look up at the sky and there are the stars, the same stars that you can see at night. When one of them blinks brighter than the others, I think that must be the one you are looking at at that moment.

Gretel, I miss you so much!

I am such an idiot. I should never have left you. My life is completely empty without you. Nothing is fun, no food is good, no theater is interesting, no music sounds beautiful when you are not with me.

Gretel, I cannot live without you. Do you want to come over to me? Please write back that you will. I'll wait for the postman every morning and won't go to work until I have a letter from you in which you tell me that you will come and spend the rest of your life with me.

I love you!
Forever yours,
Patrick

Mother was suspiciously busy in the kitchen, the crockery clattering so loudly it sounded as if she was about to smash it.

"Everything all right?" she called over her shoulder. "But you're crying! Is something wrong with Patrick?"

I sniffled and wiped my cheeks with the back of my hand. "No, no, everything's fine. Mother, what would you say if I were to move to England?"

EPILOGUE

Gretel's mother was not supported for long by Uncle Otto. He "went as quickly as he'd come, without so much as a phone call to say good-bye." She earned her living by letting rooms in her house and looking after her lodgers until her death from a blood clot at the age of seventy.

Ilse remained Gretel's best friend. Every year at Easter, Gretel joined her alone for a week in Hamburg, and at Christmas she would travel to Germany with her husband and son to celebrate with Ilse's family. As she grew older, Ilse developed dementia and had to give up her apartment and move into a home, where she died.

Lutz married Wilhelm's widow, Margot, who bore him a son. Gretel told me that Lutz took his own life after the war.

As their lives went in different directions, Gretel lost touch with **Hauptmann Kunert**, who later had a major role as a consultant to Hamburg Sport Verein, the famous football club.

Gretel never saw or heard from **Kuddel** again.

Georg Bram. The commemorative publication for the fiftieth anniversary of the Elisabethkirche records: "On March 13, 1965, Prälat Bram, the priest of the congregation, died unexpectedly after a short illness. The previous Sunday—the first during Lent—he had celebrated Mass with the congregation . . . Along with the Elisabethkirche, the whole Church of Hamburg mourned. Countless letters of condolence arrived at the parsonage . . . He was buried near Chapel 13 [in the cemetery of Ohlsdorf], near his spiritual brothers. Whoever visits his grave today will see that he is not forgotten."

Monsignor Bram's support of Jewish refugees during the war is not mentioned and may never have been publicly known.

Lydia and her family. The state archive of Hamburg found some information about the Seligmann family from tax records. These records provide some evidence that, contrary to the newspaper reports, Lydia's father survived the attack on the family's home. To Gretel's enormous joy, I read what I had found to her: "The family has probably emigrated together to the USA, as an existing restitution record by the manager of the finance department . . . states that Raphael Seligmann lived in . . . New York in 1952." The entry also listed Mr Seligmann's three daughters, Lucy, Lydia, and Helga.

Dr. Manes managed to join his son in Johannesburg, South Africa, where he lived until his death in old age.

Patrick died at the age of seventy-eight, only a week after his doctor diagnosed him with a brain tumor. He had a long and happy marriage to Gretel.

Gretel lived until her death in 2006 at the age of ninety-one with her family in various places in southeast England, where her son and three grandchildren still live. In her retirement, she took the bus to town or went for a beautiful walk every day, always open to meeting people and having conversations with them:

> I'm already curious about who I'm going to meet tomorrow. Usually, it's someone I've never seen before and won't see again unless by chance. We sit for hours on a park bench and talk about God and the world.
>
> I enjoy every day I've got, and I forget about my age. Only when the legs get tired after I've walked for miles do I sometimes think: "What's wrong with me?" And then I remember, "Of course! You're eighty-eight. That's completely normal. You've got to sit down for a moment!"

"But I want to carry on!"

"Well, you can't. So sit down now!"

That's how I talk to myself. So I sit down in a café and have a cup of coffee. Coffee is supposed to be bad for you, so I usually have a second one. Yesterday, I read in the papers that coffee is in fact good for something. The gall bladder—there you go.

My doctor told me to give up coffee, but that's when I rebelled. What else have I got left to enjoy? I hardly ever drink alcohol now; I gave up smoking when I was eighty-one; I can't have sex anymore because I'm too old. And now you want to deny me my coffee? No way!

AFTERWORD

I have spoken to many people who regret not having talked to their grandparents about their past. Often, we find out far too late what interesting lives they have led, and we wish we had asked questions when we still could.

When I met Gretel for the first time, she was seventy-eight years old and full of life. I had been listening to music at my friend's house, and Gretel, who was a neighbor, knocked at the door and stormed in, complaining about the noise. On hearing her German accent, I told her that I was German too, and we had a cup of coffee together. We agreed to meet again, which was the beginning of an unusual friendship.

If I had thought that retired people must be bored, she soon proved me wrong. Every day, she was out and about, going on huge walks on her own, taking the bus to nearby towns, visiting friends like me or chatting to anyone whom she wanted to talk to in cafés or on the street. She would frequently come to see me or ring me up to ask me to come around or to join her on a trip into town. Sometimes we drove through the country lanes, looking at the beautiful Sussex landscape and marveling at lovely houses.

Spending time with Gretel minimized my fears about growing old. If old age was like this, I would enjoy every day I had left, just like she did. Due to her age and my political interests, the question of her experiences during the Second World War came up. She told me that during the war she had lived in Hamburg, where she had grown up. Approaching the subject cautiously, I tried to find out what she had thought at the time about Hitler and the Nazis. She answered that she had hated the Nazi regime, her views probably influenced by her socialist grandfather, to whom she had been very close.

One question led to another, and soon I couldn't leave the subject alone. Had she worked during the war? Had she known any Jewish citizens? Had she been aware of what was happening to them under the Nazis? Had she ever tried to fight the system? Her answers stunned me. She had worked for the Wehrmacht, she told me, typing encoded messages. Was she referring to the Enigma machine? I wondered. Surely not. I went to the library to find pictures of the Enigma and showed them to her. Yes, she said, that was exactly the machine she had been trained to work with.

The more I asked, the more her story fascinated me. She had married a Resistance fighter but spoke of him with contempt. I asked her why, and she answered that he had been cruel and heartless.

It came to a point where I knew this was too much to keep to myself. "This is a book, Gretel," I said. "We have got to write this down!" Using a Dictaphone, I started recording our conversations. In the evenings after we'd met, I would type up what she'd told me about the past. Sometimes, she didn't feel like talking about it and just chatted about my children, her grandchildren, the weather, the garden, her latest trip to town.

As I accumulated more and more material, I realized I needed to organize it thematically. All the information about her youth, her upbringing, her mother, I collated under one heading. Anything to do with particular people she mentioned, like her Jewish friend Lydia, under other headings, and so on. Each time I saw her, I would ask her for more details about this or that. One day, she laughed and said that she had begun to go to sleep with a pen and paper on the bedside table, because she kept waking up in the middle of the night, suddenly remembering something else.

Gradually, I began to build up a full picture of Gretel's life during the war, but I still had questions that she couldn't answer.

That was when I started to write to German archives, museums, and libraries, doing my own research to confirm details and find out as much as I could about the historical background to her story. After about ten years working on the project, I had finished the story up to the point where she moved to England to marry and start a family with Patrick.

I used to think that had I lived in Germany under the Nazis, I would surely have been against Hitler and have fought heroically with the Resistance. How little I knew. I have the utmost respect for anyone who saw then what I know now with hindsight, and even more respect for those who dared to act, on however small a scale.

Claudia Strachan, 2009

ACKNOWLEDGMENTS

Special thanks to the following museums, archives, libraries, and individuals who helped me enormously with my research: The staff of Billingshurst Library; Mirella Cacace and Anne Reichert; Martina and Bernd; the library of the Altonaer Museum; the state archive, Hamburg; the Krügersche Haus, Geesthacht; Gemeindeleiter Klaus Alefelder, Elisabethkirche, Oberstraße, Hamburg; the Bundesarchiv/Militärarchiv, Freiburg; the Wehrbereichskommando I—Küste, Berlin; the Bundesarchiv, Berlin; the Militärgeschichtliche Forschungsamt, Potsdam; the Imperial War Museum, London, and the staff at their library; the KZ Gedenkstätte Neuengamme, Hamburg; the National Sound Archive, the British Library, London; the International Tracing Agency, Bad Arolsen; Herr Karl Gruber, Geesthacht; the British Library, London; the Zeitungsarchiv der Staats-und Universitätsbibliothek, Hamburg; Dr. Mark Baldwin and his lecture, "The Story of Enigma"; the staff at Bletchley Park; Frau Astrid Denzler, Jäger & Koch, Hamburg; Mr. Martin Klin; and everyone involved at Mainstream.

A huge thank-you to Sheila Haynes for all the corrections, and Robert Smith for his guidance and support, and the biggest thank-you of all to Claire Rose, for her fantastic work editing the manuscript.

BIBLIOGRAPHY

BOOKS

Absolon, Rudolf. *Wehrgesetz und Wehrdienst 1935–1945: Das Personalwesen in der Wehrmacht* (H. Boldt, Boppard am Rhein, 1960).

Brunswig, Hans. *Feuersturm über Hamburg* (Motorbuch Verlag, Stuttgart, 1983).

Calvocoressi, Peter. *Top Secret Ultra* (M&M Baldwin, Kidderminster, 2001).

Fest, Joachim. *Staatsstreich: Der lange Weg zum 20. Juli* (btb Verlag, Munich, 1997).

Goguel, Rudi. *Cap Arcona: Report über den Untergang der Häftlingsflotte in der Lübecker Bucht am 3 Mai 1945* (Roderberg Verlag, Frankfurt-am-Main, 1972).

Gruber, Karl. *Der Krümmel* (Flügge Printmedien, Geesthacht, 1999).

Hanke, C., and J. Paschen. *Hamburg im Bombenkrieg 1940–1945* (Medien-Verlag Schubert, Hamburg, 2001).

Hart-Davis, Duff. *Hitler's Games: The 1936 Olympics* (Century, London, 1986).

Hertz-Eichenrode, K. (ed.). *Ein KZ wird geräumt* (Edition Temmen, Bremen, 2000).

Jacobsen, Hans-Adolf (ed.). *Spiegelbild einer Verschwörung* (Seewald Verlag, Stuttgart, 1984).

Kaienburg, Hermann. *Das Konzentrationslager Neuengamme 1938–1945* (Dietz Verlag, Bonn, 1997).

Kirchner, Klaus (ed.). *Flugblattpropaganda im zweiten Weltkrieg: Europa*, Band 7, "Flugblätter aus England, aus den USA 1944–1945" (Verlag für zeitgeschichtliche Dokumente und Curiosa, Erlangen, 1980).

Mandell, Richard D. *The Nazi Olympics* (Souvenir Press, London, 1972).

Meehan, Patricia. *A Strange Enemy People: Germans under the British 1945–50* (Peter Owen Publishers, London and Chester Springs, 2001).

Rohde, Horst. *Das Deutsche Wehrmachtstransportwesen im Zweiten Weltkrieg: Entstehung, Organization, Aufgaben* (DVA, Stuttgart, 1971).

Rürup, Reinhard (ed.). *Topographie des Terrors* (Verlag Willmuth Arenhövel, Berlin, 1987).

Short, K. R. M. (ed.). *Film and Radio Propaganda in World War II* (Croom Helm, London and Canberra, 1983).

Williamson, D. G. *Germany from Defeat to Partition 1945–1963* (Pearson Education Ltd., Harlow, 2001).

JOURNALS / ARTICLES

KZ Gedenkstätte Neuengamme (ed.), *Kriegsende und Befreiung* (*Beiträge zur Geschichte der nationalsozialistischen Verfolgung in Norddeutschland*, Heft 2, Edition Temmen, Bremen, 1995).

Rademacher, C., "Hamburg: Eine Stadt lernt das Überleben im Chaos," *Hamburger Abendblatt*, March 8, 2003.

PRIMARY SOURCES

"Die Kirche sind wir alle," commemorative publication for the fiftieth anniversary of the Elisabethkirche, Hamburg, 1976.

Hamburger Anzeiger, July 21–25, 1944.

Heeres-Verordnungsblatt, Teil C, Dreiundzwanzigster Jahrgang 1941, Oberkommando des Heeres, Berlin, 1941.

"Reports on Neuengamme Concentration Camp and on German Atrocities," Appendices C and D to 12 Corps military government weekly newsletter for the week ending May 10, 1945.

The Times, August 4–15, 1936.

FILMS

Olympia: Fest der Völker and *Olympia: Fest der Schönheit*, Leni Riefenstahl (dir.), 1938.